LOGICAL THEORY AND SEMANTIC ANALYSIS

SYNTHESE LIBRARY

MONOGRAPHS ON EPISTEMOLOGY,

LOGIC, METHODOLOGY, PHILOSOPHY OF SCIENCE,

SOCIOLOGY OF SCIENCE AND OF KNOWLEDGE,

AND ON THE MATHEMATICAL METHODS OF

SOCIAL AND BEHAVIORAL SCIENCES

Editors:

VOLUME 63

STIG KANGER

LOGICAL THEORY
AND SEMANTIC ANALYSIS

Essays Dedicated to
STIG KANGER
on His Fiftieth Birthday

Edited by

SÖREN STENLUND
University of Uppsala

Co-editors

ANN-MARI HENSCHEN-DAHLQUIST, LARS LINDAHL,
LENNART NORDENFELT, and JAN ODELSTAD

University of Uppsala

D. REIDEL PUBLISHING COMPANY

DORDRECHT-HOLLAND / BOSTON-U.S.A.

Library of Congress Catalog Card Number 73–94456

ISBN 90 277 0438 4

Published by D. Reidel Publishing Company,
P.O. Box 17, Dordrecht, Holland

Sold and distributed in the U.S.A., Canada, and Mexico
by D. Reidel Publishing Company, Inc.
306 Dartmouth Street, Boston,
Mass. 02116, U.S.A.

TABLE OF CONTENTS

DAVID LEWIS

SEMANTIC ANALYSES FOR
DYADIC DEONTIC LOGIC*

I. INTRODUCTION

It ought not to be that you are robbed. *A fortiori*, it ought not to be that you are robbed and then helped. But you ought to be helped, given that you have been robbed. The robbing excludes the best possibilities that might otherwise have been actualized, and the helping is needed in order to actualize the best of those that remain. Among the possible worlds marred by the robbing, the best of a bad lot are some of those where the robbing is followed by helping.

In this paper, I am concerned with semantic analyses for dyadic deontic logic that embody the idea just sketched. Four such are known to me: the treatments in Bengt Hansson [4], Sections 10–15; in Dagfinn Føllesdal and Risto Hilpinen [2], Section 9; in Bas van Fraassen [9]; and in my own [8], Section 5.1.[1] My purpose here is to place these four treatments within a systematic array of alternatives, and thereby to facilitate comparison. There are superficial differences galore; there are also some serious differences.

My results here are mostly implicit in [8], and to some extent also in [7]. But those works are devoted primarily to the study of counterfactual conditionals. The results about dyadic deontic logic that can be extracted thence *via* an imperfect formal analogy between the two subjects are here isolated, consolidated, and restated in more customary terms.

II. LANGUAGE

The language of dyadic deontic logic is built up from the following vocabulary: (1) a fixed set of sentence letters; (2) the usual truth-functional connectives ⊤, ⊥, ~, &, ∨, ⊃, and ≡ (the first two being zero-adic 'connectives'); and (3) the two dyadic deontic operators $O(-/-)$ and $P(-/-)$, which we may read as '*It ought to be that…, given that…*' and '*It is permissible that…, given that…*', respectively. They are meant to be

S. Stenlund (ed.), Logical Theory and Semantic Analysis, 1–14. All Rights Reserved.
Copyright © 1974 by D. Reidel Publishing Company, Dordrecht-Holland.

interdefinable as follows: either $P(A/B) =^{df} \sim O(\sim A/B)$ or else $O(A/B) = {} = ^{df} \sim P(\sim A/B)$. Any sentence in which $O(-/-)$ or $P(-/-)$ occurs is a *deontic sentence*; a sentence is *iterative* iff it has a subsentence of the form $O(A/B)$ or $P(A/B)$ where A or B is already a deontic sentence. (We regard a sentence as one of its own subsentences.) In metalinguistic discourse, as exemplified above, vocabulary items are used to name themselves; the letters early in the alphabet, perhaps subscripted, are used as variables over sentences; and concatenation is represented by concatenation.

III. INTERPRETATIONS

$[\![\ ]\!]$ is an *interpretation* of this language *over* a set I iff (1) $[\![\ ]\!]$ is a function that assigns to each sentence A a subset $[\![A]\!]$ of I, and (2) $[\![\ ]\!]$ obeys the following conditions of standardness:

(2.1) $[\![\top]\!] = I$,
(2.2) $[\![\bot]\!] = \emptyset$,
(2.3) $[\![\sim A]\!] = I - [\![A]\!]$,
(2.4) $[\![A \,\&\, B]\!] = [\![A]\!] \cap [\![B]\!]$,
(2.5) $[\![A \vee B]\!] = [\![A]\!] \cup [\![B]\!]$,
(2.6) $[\![A \supset B]\!] = [\![\sim A \vee B]\!]$,
(2.7) $[\![A \equiv B]\!] = [\![(A \supset B) \,\&\, (B \supset A)]\!]$,
(2.8) $[\![P(A/B)]\!] = [\![\sim O(\sim A/B)]\!]$.

We call $[\![A]\!]$ the *truth set* of a sentence A, and we say that A is *true* or *false at* a member i of I (*under* the interpretation $[\![\ ]\!]$) according as i does or does not belong to the truth set $[\![A]\!]$.

We have foremost in mind the case that I is the set of all possible worlds (and we shall take the liberty of calling the members of I *worlds* whether they are or not). Then we can think of $[\![A]\!]$ also as the proposition expressed by the sentence A (under $[\![\ ]\!]$): an interpretation pairs sentences with propositions, a proposition is identified with the set of worlds where it is true, and a sentence is true or false according as it expresses a true or false proposition.

The sentences of the language are built up from the sentence letters by means of the truth-functional connectives and the deontic operators. Likewise an interpretation is determined stepwise from the truth sets of the sentence letters by means of the truth conditions for those connectives and operators. (2.1–7) impose the standard truth conditions for the former. (2.8) transforms truth conditions for $O(-/-)$ into truth conditions for $P(-/-)$, making the two interdefinable as we intended. The truth conditions for $O(-/-)$ have so far been left entirely unconstrained.

IV. VALUE STRUCTURES

Our intended truth conditions for $O(-/-)$ are to depend on a posited structure of evaluations of possible worlds. We seek generality, wherefore we say nothing in particular about the nature, source, or justifiability of these evaluations. Rather, our concern is with their structure. A mere division of worlds into the ideal and the less-than-ideal will not meet our needs. We must use more complicated value structures that somehow bear information about comparisons or gradations of value.

An interpretation is *based, at* a particular world, *on* a value structure iff the truth or falsity of every sentence of the form $O(A/B)$, at that world and under that interpretation, depends in the proper way on the evaluations represented by the value structure.

Let $[\![\ ]\!]$ be an interpretation over a set I, and let i be some particular world in I. In the case we have foremost in mind, I really is the set of all possible worlds; and i is our actual world, so that truth at i is actual truth, or truth *simpliciter*. We consider value structures of four kinds.

First, a *choice function f over I* is a function that assigns to each subset X of I a subset fX of X, subject to two conditions: (1) if X is a subset of Y and fY is nonempty, then fY also is nonempty; and (2) if X is a subset of Y and X overlaps fY, then $fX = X \cap fY$. $[\![\ ]\!]$ is *based, at i, on* a choice function f over I iff any sentence of the form $O(A/B)$ is true at i under $[\![\ ]\!]$ iff $f[\![B]\!]$ is a nonempty subset of $[\![A]\!]$. Motivation: fX is to be the set of the best worlds in X. Then $O(A/B)$ is true iff, non-vacuously, A holds throughout the B-worlds chosen as best.

Second, a *ranking* $\langle K, R \rangle$ *over I* is a pair such that (1) K is a subset of I; and (2) R is a weak ordering of K. R is a *weak ordering*, also called a *total preordering*, of a set K iff (1) R is a dyadic relation among members of K; (2) R is transitive; and (3) for any j and k in K, either jRk or kRj – that is, R is *strongly connected* on K. $[\![\ ]\!]$ is *based, at i, on* a ranking $\langle K, R \rangle$ over I iff any sentence of the form $O(A/B)$ is true at i under $[\![\ ]\!]$ iff, for some j in $[\![A \& B]\!] \cap K$, there is no k in $[\![\sim A \& B]\!] \cap K$ such that kRj.

DAVID LEWIS

Motivation: K is to be the set of worlds that can be evaluated – perhaps some cannot be – and kRj is to mean that k is at least as good as j. Then $O(A/B)$ is true iff some B-world where A holds is ranked above all B-worlds where A does not hold.

Third, a *nesting* $\mathcal{S}$ *over* I is a set of subsets of I such that, whenever S and T both belong to $\mathcal{S}$, either S is a subset of T or T is a subset of S. $[\![\ ]\!]$ is *based, at i, on* a nesting $\mathcal{S}$ over I iff any sentence of the form $O(A/B)$ is true at i under $[\![\ ]\!]$ iff, for some S in $\mathcal{S}$, $S \cap [\![B]\!]$ is a nonempty subset of $[\![A]\!]$. Motivation: each S in $\mathcal{S}$ is to represent one permissible way to divide the worlds into the ideal ones (those in S) and the non-ideal ones. Different members of $\mathcal{S}$ represent more or less stringent ways to draw the line. Then $O(A/B)$ is true iff there is some permissible way to divide the worlds on which, non-vacuously, A holds at all ideal B-worlds.

Fourth, an *indirect ranking* $\langle V, R, \mathfrak{f} \rangle$ *over* I is a triple such that (1) V is a set; (2) R is a weak ordering of V (defined as before); and (3) $\mathfrak{f}$ is a function that assigns to each j in I a subset $\mathfrak{f}(j)$ of V. $[\![\ ]\!]$ is *based, at i, on* an indirect ranking $\langle V, R, \mathfrak{f} \rangle$ iff any sentence of the form $O(A/B)$ is true at i under $[\![\ ]\!]$ iff, for some v in some $\mathfrak{f}(j)$ such that j belongs to $[\![A \,\&\, B]\!]$, there is no w, in any $\mathfrak{f}(k)$ such that k belongs to $[\![\sim A \,\&\, B]\!]$, such that wRv. Motivation (first version): V is to be a set of 'values' realizable at worlds; wRv is to mean that w is at least as good as v; and $\mathfrak{f}(j)$ is to be the set of values realized at the world j. Then $O(A/B)$ is true iff some value realized at some B-world where A holds is ranked higher than any value realized at any B-world where A does not hold. Motivation (second version): we want a ranking of worlds in which a single world can recur at more than one position – much as Grover Cleveland has two positions in the list of American presidents, being the 22nd and also the 24th. Such a 'multipositional' ranking cannot be a genuine ordering in the usual mathematical sense, but we can represent it by taking a genuine ordering R of an arbitrarily chosen set V of 'positions' and providing a function $\mathfrak{f}$ to assign a set of positions – one, many, or none – to each of the objects being ranked. Then $O(A/B)$ is true iff some B-world where A holds, in some one of its positions, is ranked above all B-worlds where A does not hold, in all of their positions.

The *value structures over* I comprise all four kinds: all choice functions, rankings, nestings, and indirect rankings over I. Note that (unless I is empty) nothing is a value structure of two different kinds over I.

An arbitrary element in our truth conditions must be noted. A value structure may ignore certain *inevaluable* worlds: for a choice function f, the worlds that belong to no fX; for a ranking $\langle K, R \rangle$, the worlds left out of K; for a nesting $\mathcal{S}$, the worlds that belong to no S in $\mathcal{S}$; and for an indirect ranking $\langle V, R, \mathfrak{f} \rangle$, the worlds j such that $\mathfrak{f}(j)$ is empty. Suppose now that B is true only at some of these inevaluable worlds, or that B is impossible and true at no worlds at all. Then $O(-/B)$ and $P(-/B)$ are *vacuous*. We have chosen always to make $O(A/B)$ false and $P(A/B)$ true in case of vacuity, but we could just as well have made $O(A/B)$ true and $P(A/B)$ false. Which is right? Given that $0 = 1$, ought nothing or everything to be the case? Is everything or nothing permissible? The mind boggles. As for formal elegance, either choice makes complications that the other avoids. As for precedent, van Fraassen has gone our way but Hansson and Føllesdal and Hilpinen have gone the other way. In any case, the choice is not irrevocable either way. Let $O'(-/-)$ and $P'(-/-)$ be just like our pair $O(-/-)$ and $P(-/-)$ except that they take the opposite truth values in case of vacuity. The pairs are interdefinable: either let $O'(A/B) =^{\mathrm{df}} =^{\mathrm{df}} O(\top/B) \supset O(A/B)$ or else let $O(A/B) =^{\mathrm{df}} \sim O'(\bot/B)$ & $O'(A/B)$.

V. TRIVIAL, NORMAL, AND UNIVERSAL VALUE STRUCTURES

There exist *trivial* value structures, of all four kinds, in which every world is inevaluable. We might wish to ignore these, and use only the remaining non-trivial, or *normal*, value structures. Or we might go further and use only the *universal* value structures with no inevaluable worlds at all. It is easily shown that a value structure is normal iff, under any interpretation based on it at any world i, some sentence of the form $O(\top/B)$ is true at i. (And if so, then in particular $O(\top/\top)$ is true at i.) Likewise, a value structure is universal iff, under any interpretation based on it at any world i, any $O(\top/B)$ is true at i except when B is false at all worlds.

VI. LIMITED AND SEPARATIVE VALUE STRUCTURES

The *limited* value structures are, informally, those with no infinitely ascending sequences of better and better and better worlds. More precisely, they are: (1) all choice functions; (2) all rankings $\langle K, R \rangle$ such that every nonempty subset X of K has at least one R-*maximal element*, that being a world j in X such that jRk for any k in X; (3) all nestings $\mathcal{S}$ such that, for any nonempty subset $\mathbf{S}$ of $\mathcal{S}$, the intersection $\bigcap \mathbf{S}$ of all sets in $\mathbf{S}$ is itself a member – the smallest one – of $\mathbf{S}$; and (4) all indirect rankings $\langle V, R, \mathfrak{f} \rangle$ such that, if we define the *supersphere* of any v in V as the set of all worlds j such that wRv for some w in $\mathfrak{f}(j)$, then for any nonempty set $\mathbf{S}$ of superspheres, the intersection $\bigcap \mathbf{S}$ of all sets in $\mathbf{S}$ is itself a member of $\mathbf{S}$. Clearly some but not all rankings, some but not all nestings, and some but not all indirect rankings are limited. Value structures of any kind over finite sets, however, are always limited.

Semantically, a limited value structure is one that guarantees (except in case of vacuity) that the full story of how things ought to be, given some circumstance, is a possible story. That is not always so. For instance, let the value structure be a ranking that provides an infinite sequence $j_1, j_2, \ldots$ of better and better worlds. Let B be true at all these worlds and no others; let A_1 be true at all but j_1, A_2 at all but j_1 and j_2, and so on. Then $O(\text{-}/B)$ is not vacuous and all of $O(B/B)$, $O(A_1/B)$, $O(A_2/B), \ldots$ are true; yet at no world are all of B, A_1, $A_2, \ldots$ true together, so even this much of the story of how things ought to be, given that B, is impossible. A limited ranking would preclude such a case, of course, since the set $\{j_1, \ldots\}$ has no maximal element. In general, a value structure is limited iff, under any interpretation based on it at any world i, whenever $O(\text{-}/B)$ is non-vacuous and $\mathbf{A}$ is the set of all sentences A for which $O(A/B)$ is true at i, there is a world where all the sentences in $\mathbf{A}$ are true together.

The *separative* value structures are, informally, those in which any world that surpasses various of its rivals taken separately also surpasses all of them taken together. More precisely, they are: (1) all choice functions; (2) all rankings; (3) all nestings $\mathcal{S}$ such that, for any nonempty subset $\mathbf{S}$ of $\mathcal{S}$, the intersection $\bigcap \mathbf{S}$ is the union $\bigcup \mathbf{T}$ of some subset $\mathbf{T}$ of $\mathcal{S}$; and (4) all indirect rankings such that, for any nonempty set $\mathbf{S}$ of superspheres, the intersection $\bigcap \mathbf{S}$ is the union $\bigcup \mathbf{T}$ of some set $\mathbf{T}$ of superspheres. All limited value structures are separative, but not conversely. Some but not all non-limited nestings are separative, as are some but not all non-limited indirect rankings. Semantically, a value structure is separative iff, under any interpretation based on it at any world i, if (1) A is true at just one world, (2) $O(A/B)$ is true at i for every B in a set $\mathbf{B}$, and (3) C is true at just those worlds where at least one B in $\mathbf{B}$ is true, then $O(A/C)$ is true at i.

VII. CLOSED AND LINEAR VALUE STRUCTURES

A nesting $\mathcal{S}$ is *closed* iff, for any subset S of $\mathcal{S}$, the union $\bigcup$ S of all sets in S belongs to $\mathcal{S}$. Closure has no semantic effect, as we shall see, but we must mention it in order to make contact with my results in [8]. Note that a closed nesting $\mathcal{S}$ is separative iff, for any nonempty subset S of $\mathcal{S}$, $\bigcap$ S belongs to $\mathcal{S}$.

An indirect ranking $\langle V, R, \mathfrak{f} \rangle$ is *linear* iff there are no two distinct members v and w of V such that both vRw and wRv. We shall see that linearity also has no semantic effect.

VIII. EQUIVALENCE

We call two value structures *equivalent* iff any interpretation that is based, at a world, on either one is also based, at that world, on the other. Equivalence is rightly so called: it is a reflexive, symmetric, transitive relation among value structures, and consequently it partitions them into equivalence classes. If two value structures are equivalent, they must be value structures over the same set; and if one is trivial, normal, universal, limited, or separative, then so is the other.

If f is any choice function over I, an equivalent ranking $\langle K, R \rangle$ over I may be derived thus: let K be the set of all i in I such that i is in $f\{i\}$, and let iRj (for i and j in K) iff i is in $f\{i, j\}$.

If $\langle K, R \rangle$ is any limited ranking over I, an equivalent choice function f over I may be derived thus: for any subset X of I, let fX be the set of all R-maximal elements of $X \cap K$ (and empty if $X \cap K$ is empty). Note that if the given ranking had not been limited, the derived f would not have been a genuine choice function.

If $\langle K, R \rangle$ is any ranking over I, an equivalent nesting $\mathcal{S}$ over I may be derived thus: let $\mathcal{S}$ contain just those subsets of K such that for no j in the subset and i outside it does iRj hold.

If $\mathcal{S}$ is any separative nesting over I, an equivalent ranking $\langle K, R \rangle$ over I may be derived thus: let K be the union $\bigcup \mathcal{S}$ of all sets in $\mathcal{S}$, and let iRj (for i and j in K) iff there is no set in $\mathcal{S}$ that contains j but not i. Note that if the given nesting had not been separative, the derived ranking would not have been equivalent to the nesting.

If $\mathcal{S}$ is any nesting over I, an equivalent indirect ranking $\langle V, R, \mathfrak{f} \rangle$

over I may be derived thus: let V be $\mathcal{S}$, let vRw (for v and w in V) iff v is included in w, and let $\mathfrak{f}(i)$, for any i in I, be the set of all members of V that contain i.

If $\langle V, R, \mathfrak{f} \rangle$ is any indirect ranking over I, an equivalent nesting $\mathcal{S}$ may be derived thus: let $\mathcal{S}$ be the set of all superspheres of members of V.

If $\mathcal{S}$ is any nesting over I, an equivalent closed nesting $\mathcal{S}'$ may be derived thus: let $\mathcal{S}'$ be the set of all unions $\bigcup S$ of subsets S of $\mathcal{S}$.

Finally, if $\langle V, R, \mathfrak{f} \rangle$ is any indirect ranking over I, an equivalent linear indirect ranking $\langle V', R', \mathfrak{f}' \rangle$ over I may be derived thus: let V' be a subset of V such that, for any v in V, there is exactly one w in V' such that vRw and wRv; let R' be the restriction of R to V'; and let $\mathfrak{f}'(i)$, for any i in I, be $\mathfrak{f}(i) \cap V'$.

We can sum up our equivalence results as follows. Say that one class of value structures is *reducible to* another iff every value structure in the first class is equivalent to one in the second class. Say that two classes are *equivalent* iff they are reducible to each other.

(1) The following classes are equivalent:

> all nestings,
> all indirect rankings.

(2) The following classes are equivalent; and they are reducible to the classes listed under (1), but not conversely:

> all rankings,
> all separative nestings,
> all separative indirect rankings.

(3) The following classes are equivalent; and they are reducible to the classes listed under (2) and (1), but not conversely:

> all choice functions,
> all limited rankings,
> all limited nestings,
> all limited indirect rankings.

(4) Parts (1)–(3) still hold if we put 'closed nesting' throughout in place of 'nesting', or if we put 'linear indirect ranking' throughout in place of 'indirect ranking', or both.

(5) Parts (1)–(4) still hold if we restrict ourselves to the normal value

structures of each kind, or to the universal value structures of each kind.

So the fundamental decision to be taken is not between our four kinds of value structures *per se*. Rather, it is between three levels of generality: limited, separative, and unrestricted. Once we have decided on the appropriate level of generality, we must use some class of value structures versatile enough to cover the chosen level; but it is a matter of taste which of the equivalent classes we use.

IX. FRAMES

Suppose that an interpretation is to be based, at our actual world, on a given value structure of some kind. Suppose that the truth sets of the sentence letters also are given. To what extent is the interpretation thereby determined? First, we have the truth sets of all non-deontic sentences – that is, of all truth-functional compounds of sentence letters. Second, we have the actual truth values of all non-iterative deontic sentences – that is, of all truth-functional compounds of sentences of the forms $O(A/B)$ and $P(A/B)$, where A and B are non-deontic, together perhaps with non-deontic sentences. But there we stop, for we know nothing about the truth conditions of $O(-/-)$ and $P(-/-)$ at non-actual worlds. Hence we do not have the full truth sets of the non-iterative deontic sentences. Then we do not have even the actual truth values of iterative deontic sentences. (Apart from some easy cases, as when a deontic sentence happens to be a truth-functional tautology.)

To go on, we could stipulate that the interpretation is to be based at *all* worlds on the given value structure. But that would be too rigid. Might not some ways of evaluating worlds depend on matters of fact, so that the value structure changes from one world to another? What we need, in general, is a family of value structures – one for each world. Call this a *frame*. A frame might indeed assign the same value structure to all worlds – then we call it *absolute* – but that is only a special case, suited perhaps to some but not all applications of dyadic deontic logic.

We have four kinds of frames. A *choice function frame* $\langle f_i \rangle_{i \in I}$ *over* a set I assigns a choice function f_i to each i in I. A *ranking frame* $\langle K_i, R_i \rangle_{i \in I}$ *over* I assigns a ranking $\langle K_i, R_i \rangle$ to each i in I. A *nesting frame* $\langle \$_i \rangle_{i \in I}$ *over* I assigns a nesting $\$_i$ to each i in I. An *indirect ranking frame* $\langle V_i, R_i, \mathfrak{f}_i \rangle_{i \in I}$ *over* I assigns an indirect ranking $\langle V_i, R_i, \mathfrak{f}_i \rangle$ to each i in I.

(I ignore *mixed frames*, which would assign value structures of more than one kind.) A frame is *trivial, normal, universal, limited, separative, closed,* or *linear* iff every value structure that it assigns is so. An interpretation over *I* is *based on* a frame over *I* iff, for each world *i* in *I*, the interpretation is based at *i* on the value structure assigned to *i* by the frame. Given that an interpretation is to be based on a certain frame, and given the truth sets of the sentence letters, the interpretation is determined in full.

Two frames are *equivalent* iff any interpretation based on either one is based also on the other, and that is so iff both are frames over the same set *I* and assign equivalent value structures to every *i* in *I*. One class of frames is *reducible to* another iff every frame in the first class is equivalent to one in the second. Two classes of frames are *equivalent* iff they are reducible to each other. Then we have reducibility and equivalence results for frames that are just like the parallel results for single value structures.

X. VALIDITY

A sentence is *valid under* a particular interpretation over a set *I* iff it is true at every world in *I*; *valid in* a frame iff it is valid under every interpretation based on that frame; and *valid in* a class of frames iff it is valid in all frames in that class. Let us consider six sets of sentences, defined semantically in terms of validity in classes of frames. The sentences in each set are just those that we would want as theorems of dyadic deontic logic if we decided to restrict ourselves to the frames in the corresponding class, so we may call each set the *logic determined by* the corresponding class of frames.

> **CO**:　the sentences valid in all frames.
> **CD**:　the sentences valid in all normal frames.
> **CU**:　the sentences valid in all universal frames.
> **CA**:　the sentences valid in all absolute frames.
> **CDA**: the sentences valid in all absolute normal frames.
> **CUA**: the sentences valid in all absolute universal frames.

The six logics differ: by restricting ourselves to the normal, universal, or absolute frames we validate sentences that are not valid in broader classes. But the logics do not change if, holding those restrictions fixed, we also restrict ourselves to the separative frames, the limited frames, or the frames over finite sets; or to the indirect ranking frames, linear indirect ranking frames, nesting frames, closed nesting frames, ranking frames, or choice function frames. By these latter restrictions we validate no new sentences.

For instance, take any sentence A that does not belong to the logic **CO**, not being valid in all frames. Then in particular, by our equivalence results, it is invalid under some interpretation $[\![\ ]\!]$ based on a nesting frame $\langle \mathscr{S}_i \rangle_{i \in I}$. Now define $\langle \mathscr{S}_i^* \rangle_{i \in I^*}$ and $[\![\ ]\!]^*$ as follows: (1) for each i in I, let D_i be a conjunction of all the subsentences or negated subsentences of A that are true (under $[\![\ ]\!]$) at i; (2) let I^* be a subset of I that contains exactly one world from each nonempty $[\![D_i]\!]$; (3) for any subset S of I, Let $*S$ be the set of all i in I^* such that $[\![D_i]\!]$ overlaps S; (4) for each i in I^*, let $\mathscr{S}_i^*$ be the set of the $*S$'s for all S in $\mathscr{S}_i$; and (5) let $[\![\ ]\!]^*$ be an interpretation based on $\langle \mathscr{S}_i^* \rangle_{i \in I^*}$, which is a nesting frame, such that whenever B is a sentence letter, $[\![B]\!]^*$ is $[\![B]\!] \cap I^*$. It may then be shown (see [8], Section 6.2, for details) that whenever C is a subsentence of A, $[\![C]\!]^*$ is $[\![C]\!] \cap I^*$. Since that is so for A itself, A is invalid under $[\![\ ]\!]^*$. Further, I^* is finite: it contains at most 2^n worlds, where n is the number of subsentences of A. So we do not validate A by restricting ourselves to the class of nesting frames over finite sets, the broader class of limited nesting frames, the still broader class of separative nesting frames, or any other class equivalent to one of these. Exactly the same proof works for the other five logics; we need only note that if $\langle \mathscr{S}_i \rangle_{i \in I}$ is normal, universal, or absolute, then so is $\langle \mathscr{S}_i^* \rangle_{i \in I^*}$.

As a corollary, we find that our six logics are decidable. The question whether a sentence A belongs to one of them reduces, as we have seen, to the question whether A is valid in the appropriately restricted class of nesting frames over sets with at most 2^n worlds, n being the number of subsentences of **A**; and that is certainly a decidable question.

XI. AXIOMATICS

We may axiomatize our six logics as follows. For **CO** take the rules R1–R4 and the axiom schemata A1–A8.[2] For **CD** add axiom A9; for **CU** add A10 and A11; for **CA** add A12 and A13; for **CDA** add A9, A12, and A13; and for **CUA** add A10, A12, and A13.

R1.   All truth-functional tautologies are theorems.

R2.   If A and $A \supset B$ are theorems, so is B.

R3.   If $A \equiv B$ is a theorem, so is $O(A/C) \equiv O(B/C)$.

R4.   If $B \equiv C$ is a theorem, so is $O(A/B) \equiv O(A/C)$.

A1. $P(A/C) \equiv {\sim} O({\sim} A/C)..$

A2. $O(A \,\&\, B/C) \equiv . \, O(A/C) \,\&\, O(B/C)$.

A3. $O(A/C) \supset P(A/C)$.

A4. $O(\top/C) \supset O(C/C)$.

A5. $O(\top/C) \supset \, O(\top/B \vee C)$.

A6. $O(A/B) \,\&\, O(A/C). \supset O(A/B \vee C)$.

A7. $P(\bot/C) \,\&\, O(A/B \vee C). \supset O(A/B)$.

A8. $P(B/B \vee C) \,\&\, O(A/B \vee C). \supset O(A/B)$.

A9. $O(\top/\top)$.

A10. $A \supset O(\top/A)$.

A11. $O(\top/A) \supset P(\bot/P(\bot/A))$.

A12. $O(A/B) \supset P(\bot/{\sim} O(A/B))$.

A13. $P(A/B) \supset P(\bot/{\sim} P(A/B))$.

These axiom systems for **CO**, **CD**, **CU**, **CA**, **CDA**, and **CUA** have been designed to use as many as possible of the previously proposed axioms discussed in [2], [4], and [9]. To establish soundness and completeness, we need only check that our axiom systems are equipollent to those given in [8], Section 6.1, for the 'V-logics' **V**, **VN**, **VTU**, **VA**, **VNA**, and **VTA**, respectively; for those logics, in a definitional extension of our present language, are known to be determined by the appropriately restricted classes of separative closed nesting frames (there called *systems of spheres*). Our **CO** and **CD** are equipollent also to their namesakes in [7] and [9], respectively.

XII. COMPARISONS AND CONTRASTS

It is an easy task now to compare the four previous treatments listed at the beginning. I include also my treatment of **CO** in [7], although **CO** is presented there only as a minimal logic for counterfactuals, without mention of its deontic reinterpretation.

A. *Hansson* [4]. (We take only the final system **DSDL3**.) Language: operators with the truth conditions of our $O'(\text{-}/\text{-})$ and $P'(\text{-}/\text{-})$; iteration prohibited; truth-functional compounding of deontic and non-deontic sentences also prohibited. Semantic apparatus: universal limited rankings. (The relation of these to choice functions is studied in Hansson [3].)

B. *Føllesdal and Hilpinen* [2]. Language: operators with the truth conditions of our $O'(-/-)$ and $P'(-/-)$: iteration not discussed. Semantic apparatus: semiformal; essentially our universal choice functions. It is suggested that the best worlds where a circumstance holds are those that most resemble perfect worlds. That improves the analogy, otherwise merely formal, with counterfactuals construed as true (as in my [7] and [8]) iff the consequent holds at the antecedent-worlds that most resemble our actual world. But I feel some doubt. Lilies that fester may smell worse than weeds, but are they also less similar to perfect lilies?

C. *Van Fraassen* [9]. Language: $O(-/-)$ and $P(-/-)$; iteration permitted. Semantic apparatus: normal linear indirect ranking frames. These are motivated in the first of our two ways: values realized at worlds are ranked, not whole worlds with all their values lumped together. The idea may be that values are too diverse to be lumped together; but if so, are they not also too diverse to be ranked? (Van Fraassen may agree, for in [10] he has since developed a pluralistic brand of deontic logic meant to cope with clashes of incomparable values.) The need for non-separative indirect rankings does not seem to me to have been convincingly shown.

D. *Lewis* [8]. Language: operators with the truth conditions of all four of ours; iteration permitted. Semantic apparatus: separative closed nesting frames, with normality, universality, and absoluteness considered as options; ranking frames also are mentioned by way of motivation. It is argued that more than limited frames are needed, since infinite sequences of better and better worlds are a serious possibility.

E. *Lewis* [7]. Language: one operator, with the truth conditions of our $O'(-/-)$; iteration permitted. Semantic apparatus (three versions): (α) partial choice function frames; (β) nesting frames; and (γ) ranking frames.

Princeton University

NOTES

* This research was supported by a fellowship from the American Council of Learned Societies.
[1] Some other treatments of dyadic deontic logic fall outside the scope of this paper because they seem, on examination, to be based on ideas quite unlike the one I wish to consider. In particular, see the discussions in [4], [2], and [9] of several systems proposed by von Wright and by Rescher.
[2] For any fixed C, we can regard $O(-/C)$ and $P(-/C)$ as a pair of monadic deontic operators. R1–R3 and A1–A3, in which the fixed C figures only as an inert index, constitute an axiom system for Lemmon's weak deontic logic **D2** (see [5], [6]) for each such pair. **D2** falls short of the more standard deontic logic **D** for the pair by lacking the theorem $O(T/C)$; nor should that be a theorem since it is false in case of vacuity and some instances of $O(-/C)$ are vacuous. Had we used $O'(-/-)$ and $P'(-/-)$ we would still fall short of **D**: in case of vacuity we would then have $O'(T/C)$, but we would lose the instances of A3. Rather we would have the logic **K** for each pair, as in the basic conditional logic of Chellas [1].

BIBLIOGRAPHY

[1] Brian F. Chellas, 'Basic Conditional Logic', dittographed 1970, University of Pennsylvania.
[2] Dagfinn Føllesdal and Risto Hilpinen, 'Deontic Logic: an Introduction', in Risto Hilpinen (ed.), *Deontic Logic: Introductory and Systematic Readings*, Reidel, 1971.
[3] Bengt Hansson, 'Choice Structures and Preference Relations', *Synthese* **18** (1968), 443–458.
[4] Bengt Hansson, 'An Analysis of Some Deontic Logics', *Noûs* **4** (1970), 373–398; reprinted in Hilpinen (ed.), *Deontic Logic*.
[5] E. J. Lemmon, 'New Foundations for Lewis Modal Systems', *Journal of Symbolic Logic* **22** (1957), 176–218.
[6] E. J. Lemmon, 'Algebraic Semantics for Modal Logic, I & II', *Journal of Symbolic Logic* **31** (1966), 46–65 and 191–218.
[7] David Lewis, 'Completeness and Decidability of Three Logics of Counterfactual Conditionals', *Theoria* **37** (1971), 74–85.
[8] David Lewis, *Counterfactuals*, Blackwell, 1973.
[9] Bas van Fraassen, 'The Logic of Conditional Obligation', *Journal of Philosophical Logic* **1** (1972), 417–438.
[10] Bas van Fraassen, 'Values and the Heart's Command', *Journal of Philosophy* **70** (1973), 5–19.

ARTO SALOMAA

SOME REMARKS CONCERNING MANY-VALUED
PROPOSITIONAL LOGICS

I. INTRODUCTION

The purpose of this paper is to discuss some special properties of n-valued propositional logics. As a general introduction to the field, the reader is referred to Rescher [2]. Our definitions below are very much in the spirit of the classical work of Rosser and Turquette [3].

Consider the set $N = \{1, ..., n\}$, $n \geq 2$, whose elements are referred to as *truth-values*. A function mapping the Cartesian power N^m, $m \geq 1$, into N is said to be an *m-place* *truth-function* in n values. Two sets of primitive (undefined) signs are now introduced: one denumerable set of signs $\{p, q, r, ...\}$ called *propositional variables* and another finite set of signs

$$\{F_1^{a_1}, F_2^{a_2}, ..., F_k^{a_k}\}$$

called *connectives*. In particular, $F_i^{a_i}$ is said to be a connective with a_i argument places. A finite sequence of primitive signs is said to be a *well-formed formula (wff)* iff it either consists of a sole propositional variable or equals $F_i^{a_i} \alpha_1 \alpha_2 ... \alpha_{a_i}$ where each α_j is a well-formed formula. The set of all well-formed formulas is denoted by *WFF*. (In what follows, we often use ordinary punctuation instead of the Polish notation and write connectives between the arguments. Also the upper index a_i will be omitted.)

Let *VA* and *NVA* be two subsets of *WFF* which are closed under alphabetical variance of variables. Iff the intersection of *VA* and *NVA* is empty and their union equals *WFF* then the ordered triple $L = \langle WFF, VA, NVA \rangle$ is said to be a *propositional logic*. L is said to be an *n-valued* $(n \geq 2)$ propositional logic iff the following conditions are satisfied:

(i)   To each distinct variable of L there is correlated a distinct numerical variable.

(ii)   To each primitive connective $F_i^{a_i}$ of L there is correlated an a_i-place truth-function in n values.

S. Stenlund (ed.), Logical Theory and Semantic Analysis, 15–21. All Rights Reserved.
Copyright © 1974 by D. Reidel Publishing Company, Dordrecht-Holland.

(iii)   To each wff there is correlated a truth-function in n values such that the following condition is satisfied. For any wffs α, β and γ where α is the result of substituting β for a variable p uniformly in γ, the correlate of α is the result of substituting the correlate of β for the correlate of p uniformly in the correlate of γ.

(iv)   There is a natural number d such that $1 \leq d \leq n-1$ and VA is exactly the set of those wffs whose correlates assume a value $\leq d$, for any assignment of values for the variables.

The integers $1, \ldots, d$ are referred to as *designated* truth-values. L is said to be a *many-valued* propositional logic iff there is an integer n such that L is an n-valued propositional logic.

Let AX be a subset of WFF which is closed under alphabetical variance of variables and let OP be a set of closure operations on WFF. Then the ordered triple $AS = \langle WFF, AX, OP \rangle$ is called an *axiom system*. The closure PR of AX under the members of OP forms the set of *provable formulas* under AS. AS is said to be *inconsistent* iff $PR = WFF$. A consistent axiom system AS is said to be *complete* iff, for any wff α which does not belong to PR, the closure of $AX \cup \{\alpha\}$ under the members of OP equals WFF.

An axiom system $AS = \langle WFF, AX, OP \rangle$ is said to be an *axiomatization* of a propositional logic $L = \langle WFF, VA, NVA \rangle$ iff $PR = VA$. L is *non-trivially axiomatizable* iff it possesses an axiomatization where the set AX is finite. Iff AS is an axiomatization of L then L is said to be a *model* for AS. AS possesses a *finite* model iff there is a many-valued propositional logic L which is a model for AS.

II. FINITE MODELS

Two main tasks in the study of many-valued propositional logics are to find a finite model for a given axiom system and to find a non-trivial axiomatization for a given many-valued propositional logic. As regards the latter of these problems, Slupecki [5] has shown that an n-valued propositional logic L possesses a complete non-trivial axiomatization if every truth-function in n values can be expressed as a finite composition of the truth-functions corresponding to the primitive connectives of L.

This implies that if L is a many-valued propositional logic with a single primitive connective whose corresponding truth-function is a Sheffer function then L possesses a complete non-trivial axiomatization.

In the following theorem, which is an extension of the result of Gödel [1], we use the expression 'the set PR is closed under a two-place connective G' to mean that if $\alpha \in PR$ and $\beta \in WFF$ then $\alpha G\beta \in PR$ and $\beta G\alpha \in PR$.

THEOREM 1. *Let* $AS = \langle WFF, AX, OP \rangle$ *be an axiom system where WFF contains two two-place connectives F and G such that pFp belongs to the set PR and PR is closed under G. Define recursively wffs α_t as follows:*

$$\alpha_2 = p_1 Fp_2,$$
$$\alpha_{i+1} = \beta^i_{i+1} G\alpha_i \quad (i \geq 2)$$

where

$$\beta^1_k = p_1 Fp_k, \quad \text{for any } k$$

and

$$\beta^{j+1}_k = (p_{j+1} Fp_k) G\beta^j_k.$$

If α_t does not belong to PR and an n-valued propositional logic L_n is a model of AS then $n \geq t$. In particular, if α_t does not belong to PR, for any t, then AS possesses no finite model.

Proof. Suppose α_t does not belong to PR and L_n is a model of AS where $n < t$. Since PR is closed under G, the truth-function $g(x, y)$ correlated to G satisfies the following condition: if x is designated then $g(x, y)$ and $g(y, x)$ are both designated, for any y. α_t contains, by definition, all wffs of the form $p_i Fp_j$ $(1 \leq i < j \leq t)$ connected by G's. Since there are only n truth-values, any assignment will assign two of the variables in α_t the same value. Let these variables be $p_{i'}$ and $p_{j'}$ where $i' < j'$. Then $p_{i'} Fp_{j'}$ will get a designated value, for the assignment in question. By an obvious inductive argument it is seen that α_t gets a designated value, for this assignment, because $g(x, y)$ has the property mentioned above. But since we are dealing with an arbitrary assignment we conclude that α_t assumes always a designated value. Hence α_t belongs to VA of L_n and, therefore, to PR. But this is a contradiction, and the proof has been completed.

Theorem 1 is readily generalized to the case where there are u connectives $F_1, \ldots, F_u$ and v connectives $G_1, \ldots, G_v$ which satisfy the conditions imposed on F and G above. In this case, corresponding to α_t we have a set of wffs obtained from α_t by replacing F by some (one or more) of the F_i's and G by some (one or more) of the G_i's.

Consider the n-valued truth-function $\delta(x, y)$ defined as follows:

$$\delta(x, y) = n \quad \text{for} \quad x \leq n-1, \qquad \delta(n, y) = y+1,$$

where addition is carried out modulo n. It is shown in [4] that $\delta(x, y)$ is a Sheffer function. This gives rise to the following theorem.

THEOREM 2. *For any n and d such that $n \geq 2$ and $1 \leq d \leq n-1$, there is an n-valued propositional logic $L_{n,d}$ with d designated values and with a single primitive connective C such that $L_{n,d}$ possesses a complete nontrivial axiomatization where modus ponens with respect to C is one of the rules of inference.*

Proof. Let n and d be fixed. Choose C to be a 2-place connective whose truth-function is the function $\delta(x, y)$. Then n, d and C determine an n-valued propositional logic

$$L_{n,d} = \langle WFF, VA, NVA \rangle$$

with d designated values. Since $\delta(x, y)$ is a Sheffer function, $L_{n,d}$ satisfies the hypothesis of Slupecki's theorem and, therefore, possesses a complete non-trivial axiomatization

$$AS = \langle WFF, AX, OP \rangle.$$

In addition to the operations in OP, modus ponens with respect to C can be taken as one of the rules of inference since, although this is done, the set PR remains unaltered. This is true because x and $\delta(x, y)$ can never both assume a designated value, i.e., in modus ponens the premisses α and $C(\alpha, \beta)$ are incompatible. This completes the proof.

III. COMMUTING

In this section we discuss a property of wffs α involving a 2-place connective F. For simplicity, we assume that α does not contain other connectives. In every occurrence of F in α, interchange the two arguments.

The resulting wff β is said to be obtained from α by *commuting* with respect to F, in symbols,

$$\beta = CO(\alpha).$$

For instance, if α is the wff

$$pFq.Fq:F.pFr$$

then β is the wff

$$rFp.F:qF.qFp.$$

Obviously if β results from α by commuting with respect to F then also α results from β by commuting with respect to F, i.e.,

$$CO^2(\alpha) = \alpha.$$

In what follows we discuss the question of how the values assumed by the truth-functions of α and $CO(\alpha)$ – or, shortly, the truth-values of α and $CO(\alpha)$ – are interrelated. The answer is clear if the truth-function corresponding to F is symmetric. Then α and $CO(\alpha)$ assume the same truth-value, for any assignment of values for the variables. This might be the case also when the truth-function corresponding to F is not symmetric. For instance, let $n=2$, F be the material implication and α the wff

$$qF.pFq:F:qF.pFq.$$

Then both α and $CO(\alpha)$ assume always the truth-value 1.

Let i and j be two distinct truth-values. We say that a 2-place connective F possesses *property* $Q(i, j)$ iff the following two conditions are satisfied:

(1)   There is a wff α involving F as the only connective and assuming always the truth-value i.

(2)   Whenever α is a wff involving no other connective than F and assuming always the truth-value i then $CO(\alpha)$ assumes always the truth-value j, and vice versa.

Clearly, a connective F possesses property $Q(i, j)$ iff its truth-function

$f(x, y)$ satisfies the following two conditions:

(1) $f(x, y)$ generates the function $g(x)$ which assumes always the value i.

(2) $$f_{tr}(x, y) = f_P(x, y)$$
where P is the transposition (ij). (Here $f_P(x, y)$ is the conjugate of $f(x, y)$ under the permutation P, and $f_{tr}(x, y)$ is the transpose of $f(x, y)$: $f_{tr}(x, y) = f(y, x)$, for all x and y.)

We are now going to investigate under what conditions connectives F possessing property $Q(i, j)$ exist. Property $Q(i, j)$ could be generalized by taking instead of i and j two mutually disjoint sets of truth-values. We do not discuss this generalization.

Suppose first $n=2$, i.e., suppose we are dealing with a 2-valued propositional logic. If a connective F possesses property $Q(1, 2)$ then commuting with respect to F changes tautologies into contradictions, and vice versa. However, it is easily verified that the Equation (2) is in this case satisfied by no function $f(x, y)$.

If $n=3$ it is possible to find functions $f(x, y)$ such that (2) is satisfied. An example is the function

$$\begin{vmatrix} 1 & 2 & 2 \\ 3 & 2 & 1 \\ 3 & 1 & 3 \end{vmatrix}$$

which satisfies (2) with $P=(23)$. Hence, if F is the connective whose truth-function is this function then in any wffs α and $CO(\alpha)$ involving F as the only connective the truth-values 2 and 3 are permuted: $CO(\alpha)$ assumes the value 2 as many times as α assumes the value 3, and vice versa. However, F does not possess property $Q(2, 3)$ since condition (1) is not satisfied. In fact, it can be shown that (in the case $n=3$) whenever condition (2) is satisfied then condition (1) is not satisfied.

In the case $n=4$ there is, for any i and j, a connective possessing property $Q(i, j)$. For instance, let F be a connective whose truth-function $f(x, y)$ is defined by the following matrix:

$$\begin{vmatrix} 2 & 2 & 2 & 2 \\ 3 & 3 & 4 & 2 \\ 2 & 1 & 2 & 2 \\ 2 & 3 & 2 & 2 \end{vmatrix}.$$

Then F possesses property $Q(1, 4)$. Condition (2) is clearly satisfied. An example of a wff α assuming always the truth-value 1 is the following

$$\beta F.\beta F\beta:F:\beta F.\beta F\beta.:F.:\beta F.\beta F\beta:F:\beta F.\beta F\beta::F.:$$
$$\beta F.\beta F\beta:F:\beta F.\beta F\beta$$

where

$$\beta = pFq.F.pFq.$$

Hence commuting with respect to F changes wffs assuming always the truth-value 1 to wffs assuming always the truth-value 4, and vice versa. Moreover, $f(x, y)$ is a Sheffer function and, therefore, any connective can be expressed in terms of F.

In general, if $n \geq 4$ then there is, for any i and j, a connective F which possesses property $Q(i, j)$ and, in addition, 'generates' all connectives. We have shown this for the case $i = 3$ and $j = 4$ in [4]. But it is easy to see that using a similar method we get required functions for any i and j. To sum up, we have the following

THEOREM 3. *In a 2- or 3-valued propositional logic there is no connective possessing property $Q(i, j)$. For any $n \geq 4$, i and j, there is an n-valued propositional logic with a single primitive connective which possesses property $Q(i, j)$ and generates all connectives.*

Theorem 3 shows one feature in which a 4-valued propositional logic can be richer than any 3-valued one.

University of Turku

BIBLIOGRAPHY

[1] Gödel, Kurt, 'Zum intuitionistischen Aussagenkalkül', *Ergebnisse eines mathematischen Kolloquiums* (Karl Menger herausg.) **4** (1933), 40.
[2] Rescher, N., *Many-Valued Logic*, McGraw-Hill, 1969.
[3] Rosser, J. and Turquette, A., *Many-Valued Logics*, North-Holland Publ. Co., 1952.
[4] Salomaa, A., 'On the Composition of Functions of Several Variables Ranging over a Finite Set', *Ann. Univ. Turku, Ser. AI* **41** (1960).
[5] Slupecki, J., 'Dowód aksjomatyzowalności wielowartościowyck systemów logici zdań', *Comptes Rendus des Séances de la Société des Sciences et des Lettres de Varsovie*, Classe III, XXXII Année (1939), 110–128.

BRIAN F. CHELLAS

CONDITIONAL OBLIGATION*

Let us rehearse what may be termed the standard account of the meaning of the monadic deontic operator $\bigcirc$. Relative to each possible world, including our own, there is a non-empty class of possible worlds that are deontic alternatives to the given world. A sentence of the form $\bigcirc A$ is adjudged true at a possible world just in case A itself holds true at each of the world's deontic alternatives. The picture is of a non-empty class of worlds functioning collectively as a moral standard: What is true at all such worlds is what ought to be true. Let us call the logic of $\bigcirc$ that arises from this account *standard monadic deontic logic*, or **D***. On the basis of ordinary propositional logic, it is given by the rule of inference

ROM. $\quad \dfrac{A \rightarrow B}{\bigcirc A \rightarrow \bigcirc B},$

together with the axioms

OD. $\quad \neg \bigcirc \bot,$
ON. $\quad \bigcirc \top,$

and

OK. $\quad (\bigcirc A \wedge \bigcirc B) \rightarrow \bigcirc (A \wedge B).$

According to ROM, obligations are closed under implication – which is to say that a proposition is obligatory if it is implied by an obligatory proposition. OD, which states that nothing impossible is obligatory, is the fundamental deontic axiom. It is a version of the *sollen-können* principle, the dictum that *ought* implies *can*. OD is secured as an axiom by the provision that the moral standards of possible worlds not be null. The presence of the axiom ON is equivalent to the thesis that obligations exist at every possible world, for if $\bigcirc A$ holds at every world, for some A or other, then by ROM so does $\bigcirc \top$. The axiom OK states in effect that obligations are closed under consequence – that a proposition is

S. Stenlund (ed.), Logical Theory and Semantic Analysis, 23–33. All Rights Reserved.
Copyright © 1974 *by D. Reidel Publishing Company, Dordrecht-Holland.*

obligatory if it is a consequence of obligatory propositions. It is this axiom that licenses the view that the obligations that obtain at a world are determined by a single class of deontic alternatives.

It may be questioned whether the axioms ON and OK properly belong among the principles of a basic deontic logic. Regarding ON, it is not obvious that there are obligations, however trivial, at every possible world; and there may be ethical theories that affirm $\bigcirc A$ for no A at all. The axiom OK is more seriously controversial. On the basis of ROM and OK the axiom OD is equivalent to

OD*. $\neg(\bigcirc A \wedge \bigcirc \neg A)$.

The import of OD* as an axiom is that conflicts of obligation are impossible – a proposition arguably different from that expressed by OD. But it is not obvious that no ethical theory can accept the possibility of genuine conflicts of obligation. There may even be ethical theories that provide a plurality of competing grounds of obligation.

If ON is rejected, the standard account of the meaning of $\bigcirc$ must be modified so that not every possible world need be possessed of a moral standard. If OK is rejected, the assumption of the uniqueness of a world's moral standard falls away. In order that the standpoint adopted here be minimal, we shall reject both ON and OK (and so, too, OD*). Thus our account of the meaning of $\bigcirc$ is that a sentence of the form $\bigcirc A$ is true at a possible world just in case the world has a non-empty class of deontic alternatives throughout which A is true. The picture is one of possibly empty collections of non-empty classes of worlds functioning as moral standards: What ought to be true is what is entailed by one of these moral standards. The logic of $\bigcirc$ determined by this account is given, on the basis of propositional logic, by the rule ROM and the axiom OD. It is *minimal monadic deontic logic*, or **D**.

Now let us consider conditional obligation. Suppose that both $\bigcirc \neg A$ and A are true, so that an obligation to the effect that A be false is unfulfilled. This gives rise to new obligations – obligations conditional on A. For example, you ought not to cough during the concert, but you do. Given the transgression, what then is obligatory? Formally, the question is what sentences B ought to be true on the condition given by A, and it bears emphasis that this question can be raised regardless of the truth value of either $\bigcirc \neg A$ or A.

Most proposals for understanding conditional obligation seek an analysis in terms of a primitive dyadic operator $\bigcirc(\ /\ )$, based on an analogy with the monadic operator $\bigcirc$. For each A, the dyadic operator should yield a monadic operator $\bigcirc(\ /A)$ which behaves exactly like $\bigcirc$. From a purely formal point of view, the dyadic counterpart of the minimal monadic deontic logic **D** is gotten simply by conditionalizing the occurrences of $\bigcirc$ in the rule ROM and the axiom OD. The result is the rule of inference

$$\text{RCOM.}\quad \frac{B \to B'}{\bigcirc(B/A) \to \bigcirc(B'/A)}$$

and the axiom

$$\text{COD}^+.\quad \neg\bigcirc(\bot/A).$$

According to RCOM, conditional obligations are closed under implication, in the sense that a proposition is obligatory on a condition if it is implied by a proposition itself obligatory on that condition. The content of COD^+ is that the impossible is obligatory under no condition.

The attendant account of the meaning of $\bigcirc(\ /\ )$ is that $\bigcirc(B/A)$ is true at a possible world if and only if the condition given by A at the world determines some non-empty class of deontic alternatives at each of which B is true. So to speak, the antecedent determines a collection of grounds of obligation with respect to each world.

If the conditions of conditional obligations are propositions and not merely sentences, another rule of inference appears:

$$\text{RCOEA.}\quad \frac{A \leftrightarrow A'}{\bigcirc(B/A) \leftrightarrow \bigcirc(B/A')}.$$

That is, when A and A' express the same proposition the operators $\bigcirc(\ /A)$ and $\bigcirc(\ /A')$ are essentially the same.

The axiom COD^+ does not appear in many logics of conditional obligation, and perhaps with good reason – it may not be the proper analogue of OD. The analysis at hand rules out even impossible propositions as conditions of impossible obligations: $\neg\bigcirc(\bot/\bot)$ is a theorem. But it may be more reasonable to require only that the impossible never be obligatory under any *possible* condition. This weakening of COD^+

can be expressed by

COD. $\diamond A \rightarrow \neg \bigcirc (\perp / A)$,

where $\diamond A$ means that A is true at some possible world. In order that COD$^+$ be discounted in favor of COD, the account of the meaning of $\bigcirc (\; / \;)$ requires the additional stipulation that a class of deontic alternatives determined by a condition at a world is never null if the condition is not.

We shall accept this as the preferred account, and consider *minimal dyadic deontic logic* – **CD** – to be characterized on the basis of propositional logic by the rules RCOM and RCOEA and the axiom COD.

Not unexpectedly, we reject the dyadic counterparts of the principles ON and OK:

CON. $\bigcirc (\top / A)$;
COK. $(\bigcirc (B/A) \wedge \bigcirc (B'/A)) \rightarrow \bigcirc (B \wedge B'/A)$.

With both CON and COK added to the minimal system **CD** the account of the meaning of $\bigcirc (\; / \;)$ becomes like that of $\bigcirc$ in the so-called standard sense. Associated with each possible world and condition there is a single class of deontic alternatives, empty only if the condition is null; and $\bigcirc (B/A)$ is true at a possible world if and only if B is true at all the worlds in the class determined by the condition given by A at the world. Here as in the monadic case CON means that relative to every possible world and condition there is at least one obligation; and the presence of COK reflects the uniqueness of the ground of obligation relative to any condition. This strong system – *standard dyadic deontic logic*, or **CD*** – furnishes a dyadic analogue of the law that conflicts of obligation are impossible,

COD*. $\diamond A \rightarrow \neg (\bigcirc (B/A) \wedge \bigcirc (\neg B/A))$

– absent from **CD**. And if COD is strengthened to COD$^+$, in **CD***, the antecedent of COD* also disappears, to give

COD*$^+$. $\neg (\bigcirc (B/A) \wedge \bigcirc (\neg B/A))$.

We shall consider other extensions of the system **CD** presently, but at this juncture it is worth while to register some critical remarks.

Analyses of conditional obligation which utilize a primitive dyadic operator fuse the notions of obligation and conditionality, with the result that their connections with other notions are made opaque. In particular, the connection between the notion of obligation involved in $\bigcirc(\ /\ )$ and that expressed in non-conditional contexts is not evident – although $\bigcirc$ may be definable in terms of $\bigcirc(\ /\ )$, for example, as $\bigcirc(\ /\top)$. More important, the connection between the notion of conditionality involved in $\bigcirc(\ /\ )$ and that expressed in non-deontic conditionals is not perspicuous. Yet it is unlikely that they are unrelated, or related only, as it were, through meaning postulates.

Another problem with the unanalyzed deontic conditional operator concerns conditional permission, typically taken to be expressed by sentences of the form $\neg\bigcirc(\neg B/A)$, by analogy with the rendering $\neg\bigcirc\neg A$ for unconditional permission. It is not clear that this is a faithful representation of conditional permission; $\neg\bigcirc(\neg B/A)$ appears to be more the denial of a conditional prohibition than the conditional affirmation of a permission.

By all odds, it is more natural to expect that the fusion of obligation and conditionality found in expressions of conditional obligation should be the result of a fusion of distinct idioms, one for each of the notions involved. A better approach to understanding conditional obligation divorces questions of obligation and conditionality. Obligation on this view is represented as usual, by $\bigcirc$. Conditionality, as a separate, non-deontic idiom, is represented by a dyadic operator $\Rightarrow$. Conditional obligation is expressed by sentences of the form $A \Rightarrow \bigcirc B$. We have already settled on a minimal account of the meaning of $\bigcirc$, so it remains to articulate an account of the meaning of $\Rightarrow$.

Without any deontic complications, it seems appropriate to say that a sentence of the form $A \Rightarrow B$ is true at a possible world just in case B is true at each of the possible worlds in a (unique) class determined by the condition given by A at the world. If there are no constraints on the determination of the class of possible worlds by a condition at a world the logic of the operator $\Rightarrow$ is given, on the basis of propositional logic, by the rules of inference

RCK. $$\frac{(B_1 \wedge \ldots \wedge B_n) \to B}{((A \Rightarrow B_1) \wedge \ldots \wedge (A \Rightarrow B_n)) \to (A \Rightarrow B)}$$

and

    RCEA. $\dfrac{A \leftrightarrow A'}{(A \Rightarrow B) \leftrightarrow (A' \Rightarrow B)}$

(When $n = 0$ in RCK the conditional $\rightarrow$ is identified with its consequent.) This logic of $\Rightarrow$ is called **CK**.

With $\Rightarrow$ so construed and $\bigcirc(B/A)$ defined as $A \Rightarrow \bigcirc B$, the logic of conditional obligation turns out to be quite meager: only the rules RCOM and RCOEA hold; COD and the rest do not. So there is nothing especially deontic about $\bigcirc(\ /\ )$. In order that further principles should appear further assumptions must be made about the meanings of $\bigcirc$ or $\Rightarrow$.

A most plausible initial assumption about the meaning of $\Rightarrow$ is that the class of possible worlds determined by a condition at a world is empty only if the condition is. Then there emerges the axiom

    CD. $\Diamond A \rightarrow \neg(A \Rightarrow \bot).$

In this extension – **CKD** – of **CK** the deontic axiom COD becomes valid, and so minimal dyadic deontic logic, **CD**, is attained. Indeed, on the basis of **D** + **CK**, CD and COD are equivalent; so CD is the least addition to **CK** to yield **CD**. It should be noted that CD is also equivalent on the basis of **CK** to

    CD*. $\Diamond A \rightarrow \neg((A \Rightarrow B) \wedge (A \Rightarrow \neg B)).$

But the presence of CD* does not implicate that of the stronger dyadic deontic axiom COD*. The most that comes from CD* is the instance $\Diamond A \rightarrow \neg((A \Rightarrow \bigcirc B) \wedge (A \Rightarrow \neg \bigcirc B)).$

Neither CON nor COK holds in **D** + **CKD**. But if the logic of $\bigcirc$ includes ON the logic of $\bigcirc(\ /\ )$ includes CON; and if the logic of $\bigcirc$ includes OK the logic of $\bigcirc(\ /\ )$ includes COK – and consequently COD*. In short, **D*** + **CKD** yields **CD***. Of course COD$^+$ fails to appear as a theorem, unless it be insisted that the classes of possible worlds determined by conditions at worlds are never under any circumstance empty – an unlikely thought. And COD*$^+$ appears only when both COK and COD$^+$ are present.

Let us turn now to a formalization of the matters so far contemplated. We consider a language with sentences formed out of a denumerable stock of atomic sentences, $\mathbb{P}_0$, $\mathbb{P}_1$, $\mathbb{P}_2$, ..., by means of the truth-functional operators $\bot$ and $\rightarrow$, a necessity operator $\Box$, $\bigcirc$, and $\Rightarrow$. $\bot$ and $\rightarrow$ are falsity and truth-functional conditionality; other truth-functional operators may be regarded as defined in some usual way. Possibility, $\diamondsuit$, is defined $\neg \Box \neg$. The deontic conditional $\bigcirc$ (/) is defined by $\bigcirc(B/A) = A \Rightarrow \bigcirc B$.

By a *model* for the language we mean a structure $\langle W, R, f, P \rangle$ in which: (i) W is a non-empty set; (ii) R is a relation in $W \times \mathscr{P}(W)$ such that $R(\alpha, \emptyset)$ for no $\alpha \in W$; (iii) f is a function from $W \times \mathscr{P}(W)$ into $\mathscr{P}(W)$ such that for all $\alpha \in W$ and $X \subseteq W$, $f(\alpha, X) = \emptyset$ only if $X = \emptyset$; and (iv) P is a mapping from the set of natural numbers $\{0, 1, 2, ...\}$ into $\mathscr{P}(W)$. Intuitively: (i) W is a set of possible worlds; (ii) R associates possible worlds with moral standards (sets of deontic alternatives); (iii) f picks out a set of possible worlds for each world and condition (set of possible worlds); and (iv) for each natural number n, P_n is the set of possible worlds at which the corresponding atomic sentence $\mathbb{P}_n$ holds.

We write $\models^M_\alpha A$ to mean that A is *true at the world α in the model* $M = \langle W, R, f, P \rangle$, and write $\| A \|_M$ for the *truth set of A in* M, that is, $\{ \alpha \in W : \models^M_\alpha A \}$. The definition of truth is as follows:

(i) $\models^M_\alpha \mathbb{P}_n$ iff $\alpha \in P_n$,   for $n = 0, 1, 2, ...$;

(ii)   not $\models^M_\alpha \bot$;

(iii) $\models^M_\alpha A \rightarrow B$ iff if $\models^M_\alpha A$ then $\models^M_\alpha B$;

(iv) $\models^M_\alpha \Box A$ iff for every $\beta \in W$, $\models^M_\beta A$;

(v) $\models^M_\alpha \bigcirc A$ iff for some $X \subseteq W$ such that $R(\alpha, X)$, $X \subseteq \| A \|_M$;

(vi) $\models^M_\alpha A \Rightarrow B$ iff $f(\alpha, \| A \|_M) \subseteq \| B \|_M$.

When A is true at every world in every member of a class of models we say that A is *valid in* the class; and when A is valid in a class of models satisfying a certain condition we say that the condition *validates* A. A is simply *valid* when A is valid in the class of all models. The valid sentences include the theorems of propositional logic, the system S5 for $\Box$, the system **D** for $\bigcirc$, and the system **CKD** for $\Rightarrow$. The logic of the deontic conditional $\bigcirc$ (/) is **CD**.

There are many possible additions to the corpus of laws for obligation, conditionality, and conditional obligation. We shall survey just a few of the more salient. Consider the following conditions on a model $M =$

$\langle W, R, f, P \rangle$, for every $\alpha \in W$ and $X, Y \subseteq W$:

(on) $R(\alpha, W)$;
(ok)   if $R(\alpha, X)$ and $R(\alpha, Y)$ then $R(\alpha, X \cap Y)$;
(def) $f(\alpha, W) = \{\alpha\}$;
(mp)   if $\alpha \in X$ then $\alpha \in f(\alpha, X)$;
(dil) $f(\alpha, X \cup Y) \subseteq f(\alpha, X) \cup f(\alpha, Y)$;
(aug) $f(\alpha, X) \subseteq f(\alpha, X \cup Y)$;
(id) $f(\alpha, X) \subseteq X$.

The axiom ON, and hence CON, is validated by the condition (on); and OK, hence COK, is validated by (ok). When both ON and OK are present, so that the logic of $\bigcirc$ is **D***, another sort of model can be described for $\bigcirc$ – a structure $\langle W, R^*, f, P \rangle$ in which W, f, and P are as before and R^* is a relation in $W \times W$ satisfying the condition that for every $\alpha \in W$ there is a $\beta \in W$ such that $R^*(\alpha, \beta)$. For such a model M* the truth conditions for $\bigcirc$ are given by:

(v*) $\models_\alpha^{M^*} \bigcirc A$ iff for every $\beta \in W$ such that
$$R^*(\alpha, \beta), \models_\beta^{M^*} A.$$

These are the standard models for deontic logic, in which a single moral standard exists for each possible world. Note, however, that single moral standards do not always exist in models of the original variety satisfying (on) and (ok).

The condition (def) (in which the identity may be weakened to an inclusion) validates

DEF. $A \leftrightarrow (\top \Rightarrow A)$,

which has the virtue of providing as an instance

ODEF. $\bigcirc A \leftrightarrow \bigcirc(A/\top)$.

If $\bigcirc(\ /\ )$ were the primitive operator $\bigcirc$ would likely be defined in this way; and if both $\bigcirc$ and $\bigcirc(\ /\ )$ were primitive one would expect something like ODEF as an axiom.

The condition (mp) validates a principle of modus ponens for $\Rightarrow$,

MP. $(A \Rightarrow B) \rightarrow (A \rightarrow B)$,

and so also a parallel principle for obligation,

OMP. $\bigcirc(B/A)\rightarrow(A\rightarrow\bigcirc B)$.

Notice that halves of DEF and ODEF, $(\top\Rightarrow A)\rightarrow A$ and $\bigcirc(A/\top)\rightarrow\bigcirc A$, follow from MP and OMP.

The condition (dil) validates principles of dilemma for $\Rightarrow$ and $\bigcirc(\ /\ )$:

DIL. $((A\Rightarrow B)\wedge(A'\Rightarrow B))\rightarrow((A\vee A')\Rightarrow B)$;

ODIL. $(\bigcirc(B/A)\wedge\bigcirc(B/A'))\rightarrow\bigcirc(B/A\vee A')$.

These are reasonable additions to the logic of $\Rightarrow$ and $\bigcirc(\ /\ )$, but their converses are not – being equivalent, respectively, to the following principles of augmentation:

AUG. $(A\Rightarrow B)\rightarrow((A\wedge A')\Rightarrow B)$;

OAUG. $\bigcirc(B/A)\rightarrow\bigcirc(B/A\wedge A')$.

OAUG is clearly unacceptable: The point of conditional obligation is that obligations can differ under different conditions. Hence AUG, which implies OAUG, cannot hold; and the condition (aug), which validates AUG, must be rejected.

A principle of identity may well hold for $\Rightarrow$:

ID. $A\Rightarrow A$.

Validated by the condition (id), ID implies $\bigcirc(\perp/\perp)$. It is the possibility of ID as a theorem for $\Rightarrow$ that leads us to adopt COD rather than COD$^+$ as the basic axiom of dyadic deontic logic.

It should be observed that ID does not imply its deontic counterpart,

OID. $\bigcirc(A/A)$.

ID reflects the view that in order to determine what ought to be the case under a given condition one inspects certain possible worlds at which the condition actually obtains, to see what is obligatory there. But OID affirms that one examines such worlds to see what (else) is true there; that is, deontic alternatives to the possible worlds constituting a condition are thought to be among those worlds. This is to see obligation and conditionality as linked more intimately than seems sensible. Either a condition determines a class of worlds independent of deontic considerations – in which case there is no good reason to think that such worlds are deontic alternatives – or it determines a class of deontic alternatives – in which case there is no good reason to think that the condition holds at all of them.

Acceptance of OID must also be weighed against acceptance of OMP. For if both are valid so is $A \rightarrow \bigcirc A$, which is to say that whatever is the case ought to be – a wholly unacceptable consequence.

These considerations against OID tell as well against the weaker principle

OID⁻. $\bigcirc (B/A) \rightarrow \bigcirc (A/A)$.

This reflects an attenuated version of the idea that in order to determine what ought to be the case under a given condition one inspects deontic alternatives at which the condition holds. According to OID⁻, one inspects such worlds for that purpose in case they exist at all. Moreover, in the presence of OMP this principle produces the theorem $\bigcirc (B/A) \rightarrow (A \rightarrow \bigcirc A)$ – hardly more palatable than the shorter form.

University of Pennsylvania

NOTE

* I wish to thank Audrey McKinney for valuable advice and assistance in preparing this paper.

SELECTED BIBLIOGRAPHY

Chellas, Brian F., 'Basic Conditional Logic', Dittographed, University of Pennsylvania, 1970.
Føllesdal, Dagfinn, and Hilpinen, Risto, 'Deontic Logic: An Introduction', in *Deontic Logic: Introductory and Systematic Readings* (ed. by Risto Hilpinen), D. Reidel Publishing Company, Dordrecht, 1971, pp. 1–35.
Gabbay, Dov M., 'A General Theory of the Conditional in Terms of a Ternary Operator', *Theoria* **38** (1972), 97–104.
Hansson, Bengt, 'An Analysis of Some Deontic Logics', *Noûs* **3** (1969), 373–398. Reprinted in *Deontic Logic: Introductory and Systematic Readings* (ed. by Risto Hilpinen), D. Reidel Publishing Company, Dordrecht, 1971, pp. 121–147.
Lewis, David K., 'Completeness and Decidability of Three Logics of Counterfactual Conditionals', *Theoria* **37** (1971), 74–85.
Lewis, David K., *Counterfactuals*, Basil Blackwell, Oxford, 1973.
Lewis, David K., 'Semantic Analyses for Dyadic Deontic Logic', this volume, p. 1.
Rescher, Nicholas, 'An Axiom System for Deontic Logic', *Philosophical Studies* **9** (1958), 24–30, 64.

Rescher, Nicholas, 'Conditional Permission in Deontic Logic', *Philosophical Studies* **13** (1962), 1–6.
Rescher, Nicholas, *The Logic of Commands*, Dover Publications, Inc., New York, 1966.
Rescher, Nicholas, 'Semantic Foundations for Conditional Permission', *Philosophical Studies* **18** (1967), 56–61.
Rescher, Nicholas, 'Deontic Logic', in *Topics in Philosophical Logic*, D. Reidel Publishing Company, Dordrecht, 1968, pp. 321–331.
Segerberg, Krister, 'Some Logics of Commitment and Obligation', in *Deontic Logic: Introductory and Systematic Readings* (ed. by Risto Hilpinen), D. Reidel Publishing Company, Dordrecht, 1971, pp. 148–158.
Stalnaker, Robert C., 'A Theory of Conditionals', in *Studies in Logical Theory (American Philosophical Quarterly Supplementary Monograph Series)* (ed. by Nicholas Rescher), Basil Blackwell, Oxford, 1968, pp. 98–112.
Stalnaker, Robert C. and Thomason, Richmond H., 'A Semantic Analysis of Conditional Logic', *Theoria* **36** (1970), 23–42.
van Fraassen, Bas C., 'The Logic of Conditional Obligation', *Journal of Philosophical Logic* **1** (1972), 417–438. Also in *Exact philosophy: Problems, Tools, and Goals* (ed. by Mario Bunge), D. Reidel Publishing Company, Dordrecht, 1973, pp. 151–172.
van Fraassen, Bas C., 'Values and the Heart's Command', *The Journal of Philosophy* **70** (1973), 5–19.
von Wright, Georg Henrik, 'A Note on Deontic Logic and Derived Obligation', *Mind* **65** (1956), 507–509. Reprinted in *Contemporary Readings in Logical Theory* (ed. by Irving M. Copi and James A. Gould), The Macmillan Company, New York, 1967, pp. 316–318.
von Wright, Georg Henrik, 'A New System of Deontic Logic', *Danish Yearbook of Philosophy* **1** (1964), 173–182. Reprinted in *Deontic Logic: Introductory and Systematic Readings* (ed. by Risto Hilpinen), D. Reidel Publishing Company, Dordrecht, 1971, pp. 105–120.
von Wright, Georg Henrik, 'A Correction to a New System of Deontic Logic', *Danish Yearbook of Philosophy* **2** (1965), 103–107. Sections 2–5 reprinted in 'A New System of Deontic Logic', in *Deontic Logic: Introductory and Systematic Readings* (ed. by Risto Hilpinen), D. Reidel Publishing Company, Dordrecht, 1971, pp. 105–120.
von Wright, Georg Henrik, 'Deontic Logics', *American Philosophical Quarterly* **4** (1967), 136–143.
Åqvist, Lennart, 'Revised Foundations for Imperative-Epistemic and Interrogative Logic', *Theoria* **37** (1971), 33–73.
Åqvist, Lennart, 'Modal Logic with Subjunctive Conditionals and Dispositional Predicates', *Journal of Philosophical Logic* **2** (1973), 1–76.

RICHARD C. JEFFREY

REMARKS ON INTERPERSONAL
UTILITY THEORY

It seems doubly appropriate that I use this occasion to discourse theoretically on a topic in practical philosophy – or, perhaps more accurately:
to discuss a theoretical problem which is important to the extent that it
bears upon practice. The first reason is that Stig Kanger's own work has
often and interestingly straddled that boundary; the second is that the
ideas reported here were the topic of a seminar which I gave at Uppsala
some years ago, at Stig's invitation, and they bear marks of his partici-
pation.

I had intended to write a book on political utilitarianism in the light
of contemporary understanding of the notions of preference and utility,
but have not been able to overcome a suspicion of futility: I think I see
that interpersonal comparison of utilities *is* possible, but I am plagued
by a strong suspicion that political utilitarianism, which is therefore a
perfectly intellegible doctrine, is nevertheless unacceptable on moral and
political grounds. Then the interesting question seems to concern that
unacceptability; and that is a question which I remain unclear about.

Still, there is some interest in interpersonal utility theory itself, and I
have written on that topic in *The Journal of Philosophy* **68** (1971), 647–656,
confining myself to rather technical considerations for lack of space.
Here I shall try to put those technicalities into perspective with the aid
of a homely example, and try to respond to some criticisms as well.

I. AN EXAMPLE OF INTERPERSONAL COMPARISON OF
PREFERENCE INTENSITIES

Problem: Shall we open the can of New England Clam Chowder or the
can of Tomato Soup, for the children's lunch? Adam prefers the chowder;
his sister Eve prefers the other. Their preferences conflict. But it is ac-
knowledged between them that Adam finds tomatoes really repulsive,
and loves clams, whereas Eve can take clam chowder or leave it alone,
but is moderately fond of tomato soup. They agree to have the chowder.

S. Stenlund (ed.), Logical Theory and Semantic Analysis, 35–44. *All Rights Reserved.*
Copyright © 1974 *by D. Reidel Publishing Company, Dordrecht-Holland.*

The children are convinced that Adam's preference for clam over tomato exceeds Eve's preference for tomato over clam. Are they right? I think so. I also think that you are not in a position to have an opinion, not having been present at the interaction, and not knowing the children. But I can tell you what makes me think that they have accurately compared the intensities of their preferences; and I expect that when you have heard my reasons, you will go along with my conclusion.

One thing you don't know is whether or not Adam is simply being contrary: whether Adam's expressed loathing for tomatoes and his expressed love for clams are expressions not of his taste in food but of his wish to frustrate his sister. You don't know, but I do, and so does his mother, and his sister. We can assure you that Adam is a genuine clam fan, and that he is genuinely disgusted by tomatoes. (Not as much, I would say, as *I* am disgusted by boiled tripe, but that's not at issue.) We have seen Adam in restaurants unhesitatingly choosing clams, when available, and anxiously inquiring into the tomato content of unfamiliar dishes when the choice is among them. And eschewing New York-style clam chowder, which contains tomatoes. We have also seen Eve choose clam chowder sometimes, and tomato soup more frequently. We also know that Eve can be as vehement as Adam, in her attitudes toward other foods; and that her general style is more vivid than Adam's. It is unlike her, in general, to dissimulate her feelings and (given everybody's mood at this lunch) very difficult to imagine that the present issue is an exception. Nor does one of them generally manage to dominate the other. In particular, their agreement that Adam shall have his way at this lunch seems to none of us the expression of Eve's (nonexistent) submissiveness to her big brother.

It seems to me – and I think it should seem to you, now that you have heard the story – that Adam and Eve correctly agreed that the fair thing to do would be for them to have the chowder. Mind you, some of us, if pressed, might have expressed some reservations about the *quality* of Adam's loathing for tomatoes. Perhaps it's not the taste, and not some threatening subconscious idea about tomatoes in particular that puts him off them. Perhaps tomatoes are simply an item about which he successfully dug his heels in, on some forgotten occasion years ago when he was in a contrary mood and tomatoes were what we were trying to get him to eat. Perhaps he cherishes that victory, and even now uses tomatoes to reaffirm his autonomy, and test our acceptance of it. That's as may be. But to deny that his attitude toward tomatoes is radically gastronomical is not to deny its strength.

I have gone into so much detail in order to remind you of the complexity and variety of considerations which we bring to bear, in forming judgements about comparative intensities of preferences. Note well, that some of the relevant data are extrapreferential, and that the theory of preference is not the only relevant theory. Thus, it is relevant in my example that Eve's style is generally more vivid than Adam's. That was a factual claim, couched in the language of a commonplace theory (or prototheory) in which people (anyway, some people) are said to have styles which are describable and comparable in various ways, e.g. in terms of vividness. Of course, this talk of comparative vividness implicates interpersonal comparisons of preferences: to a first approximation, the claim that Eve's style is generally more vivid than Adam's involves a claim that when their preferences are equally intense, Eve can be expected to use stronger language and more urgent gesture than Adam, to express them.

Have I then *smuggled in* an assumption about interpersonal comparability of preferences, in comparing different people's styles? Well, if it was smuggling, I've just confessed it, and unabashedly. It seems to me that preferences belong to a large family of attitudes and states which we impute to ourselves and others in ways which make it apt to compare intensities interpersonally as well as intrapersonally. Examples are *needs*, e.g. for food, which we share with plants and other animals; *pleasure* in activities like feeding and generating, which we share with other animals; and various distinctively human states and attitudes, e.g. Left Hegelianism, and the desire for a job in the East. These states and attitudes can implicate one another, in familiar if hazy ways.

II. BUT PREFERENCE IS A TECHNICAL CONCEPT

This is all very well (you may say), but preference is a technical concept which, I have suggested, lives and moves and has its being in theories like those of Ramsey, and von Neumann and Morgenstern. In those theories the concept of preference is implicated, not with needs and pleasures and desires for jobs, but with the technical concept of judgemental probability and the more homely concept of choice or voluntary action. It is through this latter concept that preference (and through it, personal utility) is thought to acquire its character of observability or testability: its operationalistic legitimacy. But matters are not so simple, I think. Offered A or B as he will, the subject chooses A. This voluntary action evidences his preference for A over B or, more accurately, his nonpreference for B over A. But to function as evidence in this way, the event in question must genuinely be an act; must be voluntary; and must be deliberate: considered, not rash, not perverse. The choice, in other words, must have been a preferential choice. The question, whether a response was a preferential choice, may arise when we try to understand a sequence of events which seem to imply intransitivity of the subject's preferences. Sometimes, we use data about someone's preferences in order to determine the status of an event: whether or not it was a preferential choice of A over B. (We may conclude that he misspoke himself, or that he was confused about which was which, or that he was trying to mislead us about his true preferences.) I am far from subscribing to the neopositivistic view which is adopted as a matter of course by many economists, psychologists and others. I take it that in applying theories like those of Ramsey and von Neumann and Morgenstern we rightly connect such technical terms as preference and judgemental probability with homelier talk of hunger, doubt, and so on.

Still, I think it important to cite fairly clear theoretical contexts in which interpersonal comparison of preferences are important – if only because such intercomparisons have become a watchword among economists: a paradigm of hocus-pocus. To that end, I centered my paper in the *Journal of Philosophy* around work of the economists Fleming and Harsanyi – work which demonstrates that utilitarianism has great *prima facie* plausibility as a norm for social decision-making, and which, turned wrong way round, provides an interpersonal analogue of the Ramsey-von Neumann-Morgenstern account of in*tra*personal comparison of preference intensities. It turns out that if social preferences, like personal preferences, are to satisfy the von Neumann-Morgenstern axioms, and if the social preferences are related to those of the individuals in two very plausible ways, then it is always possible to view the social preferences as having been obtained from those of the individuals in a straightforwardly utilitarian manner: there will be a utility function which repre-

sents the social preferences, and utility functions for the various individual preferences which yield the social utility function by straightforward
Benthamite summation. Furthermore, all of these utility functions will
be determined by the various preference rankings as uniquely as need
be, for purposes of interpersonal comparison of preference intensities!
The two plausible conditions are *functionality* and *positivity*, on p. 653
of the *Journal*.

I take this to be a way of connecting the notion of interpersonal comparison of preferences with the notion of evenhanded compromise between individuals, e.g. Adam and Eve in my example. I take it that we
can sometimes determine, not only the preferences of the individuals,
but also the social preferences which they have arrived at, *and can also
determine the fact that they regard those social preferences as representing
an evenhanded compromise between their conflicting personal preferences.*
In such cases, the Fleming-Harsanyi-Domotor results allow us to find
commensurate unit intervals for the personal utility scales which are involved, i.e., we can perform interpersonal comparisons of preferences.

Let me reiterate that I do not therefore subscribe to utilitarianism as
a general norm for social decision-making. But I do think that there are
special circumstances where it is appropriate – fairly common circumstances.

III. COLLATION OF PREFERENCES

In case 'society' consists of just two individuals – Adam and Eve, say –
Harsanyi's results can be stated as at the top of p. 655 of my *Journal*
article: the intensity of Adam's preference for X over Y is greater than
or less than or the same as the intensity of Eve's preference for V over
W accordingly as 'society' prefers a 50-50 gamble between X and W to
a 50-50 gamble between Y and V, or has the opposite preference, or is
indifferent between the two gambles. In our example, where $X = W =$
$=$ clam and $Y = V =$ tomato, this scheme simplifies down to: Adam's
preference for clam over tomato exceeds Eve's preference for tomato
over clam because society prefers clam to tomato, i.e., prefers a 50-50
gamble between clam and clam to a 50-50 gamble between tomato and
tomato. Then this is a particularly vivid illustration of how direction of
social preference can reveal comparative intensity of individual preferences, when social and individual preferences have the characteristics

which Harsanyi demonstrated to be necessary and sufficient for social decision-making to be viewable in a neoBenthamite light.

But use of this criterion requires prior success in the project of forming a social preference ranking which represents an even-handed compromise between the conflicting personal preference rankings. Where such a social preference ranking is not available, however, other methods may be used, with the aid of which an even-handed social compromise can be identified, in favorable circumstances. Our example is a case in point, for I take it that the children compared the intensities of their preferences by *collating* the relevant parts of their personal preference rankings, as follows:

	Adam's	*Eve's*
	Preferences	*Preferences*
	Clam	
		Tomato
		Clam
	Tomato	

Thus, they agree that *Adam likes clam more than Eve likes tomato*, and that *Eve likes clam more than Adam likes tomato*:

$$u_{Adam}(\text{Clam}) > u_{Eve}(\text{Tomato})$$
$$u_{Eve}(\text{Clam}) > u_{Adam}(\text{Tomato})$$

Note that these are absolute intercomparisons of utilities. Coupling them with the unproblematical claim that Eve prefers tomato to clam,

$$u_{Eve}(\text{Tomato}) > u_{Eve}(\text{Clam}),$$

we have the result that Adam's preference for clam over tomato is more intense than Eve's preference for tomato over clam:

$$u_{Adam}(\text{Clam}) - u_{Adam}(\text{Tomato}) > u_{Eve}(\text{Tomato}) - u_{Eve}(\text{Clam}).$$

Thus we have our interval intercomparison of utilities, from which it follows that utilitarian society ought to prefer clam to tomato: transposing, we have

$$u_{Adam}(\text{Clam}) + u_{Eve}(\text{Clam}) > u_{Adam}(\text{Tomato}) + u_{Eve}(\text{Tomato}).$$

The absolute intercomparisons of utilities which led to this interval intercomparison and neoBenthamite compromise have their theoretical home in the scheme for social decision-making which I noticed briefly at the top of p. 651 of my *Journal* article. To apply that scheme one needs something more than the interval comparability of utility scales which suffices for the neoBenthamite scheme. The idea behind the new scheme is that different individuals' likes and dislikes among social prospects should sometimes be weighted differently, in forming the social sum. If I know more about farming than you, my attitudes about agricultural policy may deserve more weight than yours, in forming society's attitude. If you use libraries more than I do, your attitude about hours when the libraries shall be open may deserve more weight than mine. And if you represent a group whose interests have been systematically ignored in the past when questions of schooling and public housing were at issue, your attitudes on such matters may deserve more weight than mine.

IV. FACTUAL JUDGEMENT OR MORAL IMPUTATION?

Schick [1] holds that the question, 'What are Adam's personal preferences', like the corresponding question about Eve, is a factual one: but that it is pointless or perhaps meaningless to ask whether one of Adam's preferences is more intense than one of Eve's. Instead, he proposes a Procrustean solution: adopt identical upper limits for their two utility scales, and common lower limits, and justify this imputation on moral grounds, viz., that in that way we are treating them alike. Having imposed absolute commensurability in this way, we obtain an *assimilation of* their utility scales which he declines to describe as a comparison.

Schick says,

Some people are said to be capable of greater intensities of feeling than others. The meaning of this is in doubt, and so of course also its truth. But however the claim is understood, I do not see why it should concern us. Adam values his *summum bonum* as highly as he values anything, and his *summum malum* is for him the worst of all possibilities. The same is true for Eve. Why then should Adam's voice on his *extrema* be given any weight different from that given Eve's voice on hers?... why should a fanatic count for more than a person with tired blood? I see no reason why he should, and so have equalized the limits of the utility ranges. (665-5)

As you will have suspected, I find this unconvincing. First, interpersonal comparison of preference intensities is not a matter of interpersonal comparison of intensities of *feeling*, any more than intrapersonal comparisons are. To speak of feelings here is to invite specious questions: 'How can I feel your pains?' and the like. But Eve's judgement about Adam's preference for clam over tomato is no pretense to interlocking of nervous systems, or sharing of sense data. It is based on empathy, if you like, but that empathy is no occult intuition. Rather, it is an *attitude* with which she observes and recalls his behavior at table, in our kitchen and in restaurants. That attitude is the one we normally adopt in observing and interpreting the behavior of other people. It is a matter of viewing them and treating them *as people*. What constitutes treating someone as a person may vary significantly from culture to culture and from era to era within a developing culture; and at various stages of various cultures it may be thought right to treat cows or dogs or other animals as people, and to decline to treat certain humans as people. Then the scope and perquisites of the status, *person*, are time- and culture-relative; to hold that the status belongs to every human is to make a moral commitment; and to judge that Adam's preference for clam over tomato exceeds Eve's preference for tomato over clam is to go beyond bare facts (if bare facts there be).

I suppose that Schick may go along with this; but he goes further. He suggests that, implicit in the commitment to treat humans as people is a commitment to treat everybody's highest goods on a par, and similarly for the *infima mala* at the bottoms of their preference rankings. But I see no reason to believe that; indeed, I think we need not go far to fetch cases in which adoption of the attitude that Adam and Eve are people implies (given the facts of the particular cases) that their preferential *extrema* should not be treated on a par. Surely the argument is not advanced by the tautologous observations that Adam values his *summum bonum* as highly as he values anything, that his *infimum malum* is for him the worst of all possibilities, and that the same is true for Eve. Surely the question remains, whether Adam's *summum bonum* merits the same weight and the same utility as Eve's, when it is time to make a social decision. What would we say in a case where an older Adam's *summum bonum* is identical with Eve's *infimim malum*, viz., Eve's imminent death, whereupon Adam will set up house with Lillith?

Why should a fanatic count for more than a person with tired blood? Surely there is no *general* reason why he should, but as surely there are cases where he should, e.g. *some* cases where the 'fanatic' is an Eve in the strength of youth, with her life before her; where the person with 'tired blood' is an Adam dying of leukemia, with a week to live; and where the consequences of their social decision will be faced next year by Eve, but not by Adam.

These two examples need further study (which I shall not undertake here), perhaps in the light of the nonegalitarian aggregation schemes (6) and (7) of my *Journal* article. There are threads in these examples which ought to be separated, but they are the same threads which, I think, need separation in Schick's argument for his assimilation scheme, viz., assumptions about aggregation and assumptions about intercomparison or assimilation.

Let me conclude by returning to the issue of clam vs. tomato. I grant the *prima facie* attractiveness of hypothesis that Adam values his *summum bonum* precisely as much as Eve values hers, and similarly for their *infima mala*; and I note that clam is not Adam's *summum bonum*, nor is tomato Eve's. (Rather, those items are *extrema* in tiny fragments of their overall preference rankings.) But there is another hypothesis which has its own strong attractions in the light of the facts about Adam and Eve as I have recounted them; and this second hypothesis may well conflict with Schick's in the light of global characteristics of the two personal preference rankings, outside the small fragments we have been discussing. To repeat: Schick's hypothesis (or, his method of assimilation) determines a definite collation of Adam's and Eve's total preference rankings, and that collation may conflict with the collation arrived at above, of the clam and tomato fragments. In effect, Schick proposes that any such conflict be resolved in favor of the collation which follows from his assimilation scheme. But what if we consider a variety of small fragments of the two personal rankings, corresponding to various social decision problems, and find plausible collations in each case which, viewed globally, prove to be consistent with each other but not with Schick's uniform collation? I suggest that in such a case one would abandon Schick's hypothesis, despite its abstract, *prima facie* attractions.

But let me not overemphasize my differences with Schick on the matter of intercomparison. (His general treatment of dependencies, which I find very attractive, is compatible with other modes of assimilation.) I may be wrong; and it would be no bad thing if Schick were right, and the interpersonal comparisons (or assimilations) of preferences obtained by mapping everybody's preferences onto the unit interval can be relied upon to agree with substantial bodies of local collations and weaker local intercomparisons of preference intervals. Nor, I suspect, do we differ much about what constitutes being right, here: we agree that the question is (at least in large part) a moral one, and we agree that standardization on the unit interval has strong attractions as a moral principle, viz., simplicity and universality. My contention is that there are cases fairly close to home in which Schick's principle looks not simple but simplistic, and in which its generality looks like Procrustean indifference to the facts and to the moral perquisites of the status, *person*. In support of this contention I have cited three cases (*lunch*, *Lillith*, and *leukemia*) and two methods (interval intercomparison after Harsanyi *et al.* and absolute intercomparison *via* collation) which, where applicable, can yield interpersonal comparisons or assimilations in which the utility differences between the *extrema* of different people's preference rankings cannot be equal.

University of Pennsylvania

NOTE

[1] 'Beyond Utilitarianism', *J. Phil.* **68** (1971), 657–666.

JAAKKO HINTIKKA

ON THE PROPER TREATMENT OF
QUANTIFIERS IN MONTAGUE SEMANTICS

The grammatical and semantical theories of the late Richard Montague present us with a most interesting treatment, perhaps the most interesting existing treatment, of certain aspects of the syntax and semantics of natural languages.[1] These theories are not satisfactory in their present form, however, not even if we restrict our attention to those linguistic phenomena that Montague himself primarily wanted to cover, together with certain closely related phenomena. The most central of these seems to be the variety of ways in which quantification is represented in natural languages. This concern is highlighted by the title of Montague's last published paper, 'The Proper Treatment of Quantification in Ordinary English'. In my own paper, I shall concentrate on the nature of natural-language quantifiers for the same reasons as Montague. In view of the importance of the problem of treating natural-language quantifiers, it is in order to point out and to discuss a number of shortcomings of Montague semantics in this department. It is of course the very precision and force of Montague's treatment that lends a special interest to these shortcomings. Just because Montague was so successful in carrying out certain general strategic ideas in the formal theory of language, the shortcomings of his treatment point to general morals in the theory and methodology of linguistics and of the logical analysis of natural language.

Of the general ideas underlying Montague's theories, the following three may perhaps be singled out here:

(i) The analysis of meaning entities as functions from possible worlds (more generally, points of reference) to extensions.[2]

(ii) The idea that semantical objects are correlated with each meaningful expression by rules which correspond one-to-one with the formation rules (syntactic rules) by means of which the expression is built up.[3] The meaning of a well-formed expression is in other words derived stage by stage in step with the operations through which it is put together syntactically. (The rules of semantics work their way from inside out.)

(iii) The idea that such *quantifier phrases* as 'every man' and 'a girl'

S. Stenlund (ed.), Logical Theory and Semantic Analysis, 45–60. All Rights Reserved.
Copyright © 1974 by D. Reidel Publishing Company, Dordrecht-Holland.

behave semantically like other singular terms.[4] Of course, this is in some rough sense obviously rather close to the *syntax* of English. Montague's highly interesting idea was to devise a *semantics* in which the same holds, that is, in which the sentences 'John is happy' and 'every man is happy' are on a par.[5]

Of these principles, (i) is the main principle underlying possible-worlds semantics. It can be considered an outgrowth and generalization of Carnap's ideas of the semantics of modal logic.[6] (ii) is a form of a principle often attributed to Frege. (iii) is perhaps the principle most original with Montague, but even it had been partly anticipated by Bertrand Russell in the *Principles of Mathematics*.[7]

The general idea (i) will here come into the play only partially, through the treatment of individuals in the different possible worlds. This aspect of Montague's theories can in fact be described very simply: Montague assumed a constant domain of individuals as the range of those functions which are the senses of singular terms.[8]

Although my several objections to Montague semantics and Montague syntax in its present form are not unrelated, they can be collected into two different groups, one dealing mainly with difficulties arising in connection with the idea (i) and the other with problems related to the strategy (iii). The latter leads us to cast some doubts also on the assumption (ii).

In what follows, I shall mainly keep in mind Montague's formulations in his paper, 'The Proper Treatment of Quantifiers in Ordinary English', in short PTQ. I shall assume that my readers are familiar with the main features of Montague's theories.

One limitation of Montague's treatment is the absence of any analysis of subordinate questions in epistemic contexts – that is to say, of constructions like 'knowing who', 'remembering where', 'seeing what', etc. This is a philosophical limitation because of Montague's avowed interest in clarifying the nature of such philosophical entities as the objects of propositional attitudes.[9] The limitation seems to me important also linguistically and logically. Elsewhere, I have shown that for a large class of cases – possibly all of them – English wh-phrases (indirect questions) are nothing more and nothing less than quantifier phrases.[10] Hence any proper treatment of quantification in ordinary English presumably ought to cover them.

Now there is a natural way of accommodating a large class of subordinate questions in a possible-worlds semantics. It is the treatment I suggested more than ten years ago.[11] It is illustrated by the paraphrase of

(1)   John knows who the prime minister of Norway is

in terms of the that-construction as

(2) $(\exists x)$ John knows that (the prime minister of Norway $= x$).

(The values of variables here are of course assumed to be persons.) The naturalness of this paraphrase need not be advertised. What else can we mean by knowing who a is than knowing of some particular individual that *he* is a? I have shown earlier how this translation can be carried out more systematically.[12] It is not unproblematic, however, until the precise assumptions concerning the individuals over which 'x' ranges are spelled out and defended. That will be my main aim in the next few paragraphs.

Of course we have by any token to distinguish here between *de dicto* and *de re* readings of (1).[13] The former is (2), and the latter will be representable as something like

(3) $(\exists x)$ $(x =$ the prime minister of Norway &
        $(\exists y)$ John knows that $(x = y))$.

Here it is said that John knows of the individual who in fact is the prime minister of Norway who that individual is, without presupposing that John can identify him as the prime minister. Clearly, (3) does not entail (2).

It goes without saying that we also have to analyse knowledge here in terms of a special kind of alternativeness relation which for any world W and any person b picks out the set of all worlds compatible with everything b knows in W as epistemic b-alternatives to W.

Yet such translations do not work in the framework of Montague semantics. I suspect that Montague may have perceived some of the difficulties himself and may have been deterred by them from trying to treat the highly important problem of subordinate questions in his semantics.

Symptoms of trouble are easily found. They are nicely illustrated by the fact that in the very natural extension of Montague semantics we are here envisaging, the following sentences are valid:

(4) (x) $((\exists y)$ $(x = y) \supset (\exists y)$ $(y = x$ & $(\exists z)$ John knows that $(y = z)))$

(5) $(x) ((\exists y)$ John knows that $(x = y))$
           $\supset (\exists y) (y = x \,\&\, (\exists z)$ Bill knows that $(y = z))$

Quantifiers must here be given a suitable semantics. What it is will soon be explained informally. Given this reading, what (4) says is that John knows of each actually existing individual who that individual is (in the *de re* sense). What (5) says is that Bill knows of each individual whose identity is known to John who that individual is, again in the *de re* sense. Both (4) and (5) are in most cases blatantly false, and therefore should not be considered valid.

To be more careful, this conclusion is unproblematic as long as we do not have to care about the possible nonexistence of individuals in epistemically possible worlds. I shall soon argue that such nonexistence does not alter the picture, however.

It is easy to see what the source of the trouble is. Montague assumes that there is a fixed set of individuals (possible denotations of name phrases) which serves as the range of the functions that constitute meanings of name phrases (cf. assumption (i)).[14] Barring only the possible non-existence of some of these individuals in some worlds (which Montague does *not* allow anyway in PTQ[15]), any member of any world is therefore tied by a Kaplanesque TWA or 'trans world heir line' to some individual in any other world. In this sense, any individual is well defined in *all* these worlds. This is what forces us to say that (4) and (5) are valid in the kind of extension of Montague semantics we are envisaging here. Hence we must allow more freedom in our treatment of trans world heir lines. For one thing, we must not assume that they can be continued *ad libidum*, for that turns out to be *ad absurdum*.

Now in Montague's own formulations of intensional logic, we do not have to worry about possible nonexistence, for one and the same individuals are available to us as possible denotations of name phrases in each possible world. Hence the criticism just presented applies to Montague's own semantics.

However, it is more interesting to ask whether Montague semantics can be modified in a natural way so as to accommodate the facts of the situation. What if we allow for the possible nonexistence of individuals in some worlds?[16]

It turns out that my objection is still applicable. The point can be put

as follows. In order for John to know who Homer was it is not necessary
that his knowledge excludes all worlds in which Homer fails to exist. It is
for this reason that I said that in quantifying into a knowledge-context
like '$(\exists x)$ John knows that $F(x)$' we need not presuppose that a world line
exists connecting an existing individual from each of John's epistemically
possible worlds. What is required is merely that we can tell of the individual in question whether or not it exists in each given world. This is precisely
the case with John's knowledge of Homer when he knows who Homer
was. His knowledge must merely exclude worlds of which one cannot
tell whether Homer existed there or not. They are precisely the worlds
in which the candidates for Homer's identity are not narrowed down to at
most one person. (Thus we see that the question concerning the continuation of world lines in the sense just indicated is really quite different from
the question concerning the possible failure of individuals to exist.) It
thus turns out that what I have said of (4) and (5) remains valid also in the
teeth of the possible nonexistence of individuals because we have to presuppose a semantics in which an existential sentence involving quantifying into an epistemic context, for instance,

(6) $(\exists x)$ John knows that $F(x)$

can be true even when no world line picks out an existing individual x
from each of John's epistemically possible worlds satisfying $F(x)$, as long
as the question whether or not that individual exists there makes sense
in each such world.[17] (What is being ruled out is merely a situation in
which it is in principle impossible to tell whether or not the individual in
question exists in one of these worlds.)

    In still other words, when we are trying to extend a world line of an
individual i to a new world W, we have to distinguish between two different kinds of failure:

    (a) We can tell what the case would have to be in W for i to exist there,
but we can in principle ascertain that it does not. (Uniqueness holds, but
not existence.)

    (b) It makes no sense to ask whether i exists in W or not. (The candi-
dates for the role of i are not narrowed down to one at most, or are not
well defined at all.) The fundamental reason for this second kind of failure
is (I have argued) that the 'trans world heir lines' can only be drawn on
the basis of comparisons between the different worlds in question. These

comparisons utilize certain regularities (for instance, spatiotemporal continuity) obtaining in each of them. If these regularities fail in a world W, there just is no way of trying to find 'counterparts' for a given individual in W.

In order for (6) to be true, there will have to be at least one world line connecting all of John's knowledge-worlds which does not exhibit any failures of the second type (b). It may exhibit failures of type (a). The naturalness of this requirement was already argued for, and will also be illustrated below.

The details of this type of semantics is spelled out a little more fully in my earlier papers.

If we merely allow failures of the first kind (a), the awkward sentences (4)–(5) will still be valid in our semantics. Hence we must recognize the possibility that world lines break down in the more sweeping fashion (b) and not only in the relatively innocuous way (a). This marks an important further step away from Montague's oversimplified assumption of a constant domain of individuals, independent of the different possible worlds we are considering.

Now the semantics just presented is not chosen at random. It seems to me to be precisely the one which is needed to enable us to interpret (2)–(5) in the intended way as translations of certain wh-sentences of English.[18] Hence it represents the best hope there is to straighten out Montague semantics so as to be able to handle wh-phrases. The situation may be illustrated further by considering sentences of the form

(7)   John knows that Homer did not exist.

Here we are saying that in each of John's epistemically possible worlds Homer fails to be around. That implies that in each of them it makes sense to ask whether Homer existed there or not, in other words, it implies that we can in principle specify what it would mean for Homer to exist there. Hence we have to distinguish here especially sharply between the *uniqueness* of an individual in each alternative (in the sense that it makes sense to ask whether this individual exists there or not) and its *existence* in each of them. Homer's epistemically possible nonexistence does not make his identity unknown to John. On the contrary, in order for John to know that Homer does *not* exist, he may have to know who Homer (that very individual) is.

What all this adds up to is that there is no way in which an unmodified Montague semantics can cope with wh-phrases (subordinate questions). Barring a radical reformulation, the only means of accommodating failures of world lines to be continued *ad libidum* in Montague semantics is to allow for the individual in question to fail to exist in some possible worlds. What we have seen means, however, that this kind of failure is not at all what is needed here. In order to handle the very question of the epistemic possibility of nonexistence of particular individuals, we have to allow for a more radical kind of failure of a world line. In some cases, such a world line cannot be continued to a new world in the sense that there is no way of telling whether the individual in question exists there or not. And in the current Montague semantics there just is no way of allowing for this.

This does not invalidate the general principle (i), but it puts it into a new perspective. Meaning entities are still functions from possible worlds (contexts of usage) to extensions, but this set of extensions is not a constant one nor even a variable subset of some fixed given superset. We just have to allow much less well-behaved world lines than Montague was prepared to countenance.

This problem comes up in the course of his discussion in PTQ. There he is led to maintain (on p. 240) that the only viable reading of sentences like

(11)   John is seeking a unicorn and Mary is seeking it, too

is one which entails that there in fact are unicorns. It is true that on the only natural reading of (11) the quantifier implicit in it is the one on which 'a unicorn' has wider scope than 'is seeking'. However, examples like (11) illustrate vividly the fact that such a reading should not commit us to the existence of unicorns. For obviously two people can look for the same individual even when it does not exist.[19] Such examples as (11) therefore serve to point to the same difficulty with Montague semantics as I have been calling your attention to.

This particular problem involved in (11) can of course be corrected merely by allowing well-defined individuals not to exist in some possible worlds, which involves only a relatively modest change. However, the natural reading of slightly more complicated sentences brings in all the difficulties we have discussed. The following is perhaps a case in point:

John does not know whether any unicorns exist, but he is
nevertheless seeking a unicorn because Mary is seeking it, too.

Here John must be able to recognize one particular unicorn (for otherwise it would not be true that he is seeking *it*) in spite of countenancing
its possible nonexistence.

Plenty of other specific problems are easily forthcoming which illustrate
the same general fact, viz., the impossibility of extending Montague
semantics so as to cover wh-constructions without revising substantially
the assumptions concerning the treatment of individuals in this semantics.
By and large, the requisite changes amount to allowing for the possibility
of sufficiently ill-behaved world lines.

If we make the precise assumptions Montague makes in PTQ, sentences
of the following form are all valid:

(8)   John knows that $(\exists x)\,(x=a) \supset (\exists x)$ John knows that $(x=a)$

where a is a proper name. However, on the proposal we are considering
(8) says that John knows who is referred to by a proper name as soon as
he knows that it is not empty. This is of course often false. Thus world
lines cannot run together with the lines connecting the individuals referred
to by a given name.

Similar points can be made about common nouns. They just cannot
pick out the same individuals in all the worlds we want to consider,
contrary to what Montague assumes. Otherwise, we could not analyse
sentences like

(9)   It seems to John that this bush is a bear

along the lines here envisaged into the language of possible-worlds semantics. (No other half-way reasonable analysis has been proposed.)

Other problems arise when the same treatment is extended to perceptual concepts.[20] (This will have to be done if all wh-constructions are to
be discussed, for perceptual verbs sport such constructions rather
prominently.) For instance, all the sentences of the following form will
be contradictory in the proposed extension of Montague semantics:

(10) $(\exists x)\,(\exists y)\,(x=y$ & it appears visually to John that x is to the
            right of $y)$.

Yet on one reasonable interpretation of (10) it describes a perfectly possible and in fact not especially recondite situation, viz., one in which John sees one object as two.

What the trouble here is, is that world lines may sometimes split (when we move from a world to its alternatives). Yet in the present-day formulations of Montague semantics this simply cannot happen. For it is the same set of individuals – or possibly a subset of it – that crops up in each possible world as its domain. Hence no splitting or merging is ever possible. Yet there is no general reason to rule out such a behavior of world lines completely.[21]

A striking way for the world lines to 'misbehave' is for them to split into two entirely different sets of world lines, connecting the same set of worlds but proceeding in different ways. I have shown earlier that two different warps of world lines are needed in order to spell out the semantics of the direct-object contradiction with such verbs as 'sees', 'perceives', 'remembers', and 'knows'.[22] It follows that the treatment of individuals (world lines) in Montague semantics will have to be loosened in this respect, too.

I am not saying that Montague semantics cannot be modified so as to correct these defects. This has after all been done already in somewhat different versions of possible-worlds semantics.[23] The interesting point is not even that this involves a fairly radical reformulation of the semantics underlying Montague's intensional logic. It seems to me that an interesting general point here is that there is a great deal of tension in this very matter of the treatment of individuals in one's possible-worlds semantics between on the one hand pragmatic and linguistic realism and on the other hand mathematical elegance. Only this elegance looks to me a little too much like the spurious elegance which according to Georg Cantor should be a concern of tailors and shoemakers rather than of logicians.

Those shortcomings of Montague-type semantics that we have noted are also interesting in that they point to the direction into which any satisfactory possible-worlds semantics will have to be developed.

There is another class of problems with quantifiers in Montague semantics. They are more of the nature of problems that so far have been left untreated in Montague semantics than difficulties about what it already contains. It is nevertheless highly interesting to see what perhaps can be done about them along the lines Montague indicated.

By and large, Montague grammar and Montague semantics show how many quantificational ambiguities come about as a result of the possibility of building up the ambiguous expressions in more than one way. This applies both to purely quantificational ambiguities like

(12)   a woman loves every man

(if it is an ambiguity) and ambiguities involving the interplay of quanti-fiers and intensional notions, for instance,

(13)   John is seeking a dog.

However, the account we obtain from Montague grammar and Montague semantics is unsatisfactory as it stands, even in its overall features. What it explains is why certain expressions *can be* ambiguous, not which ex-pressions *in fact* are ambiguous. Taken at its face value, it predicts far too many ambiguities.[24] In other words, it does not give any account of the grammatical principles by means of which natural language often resolves ambiguities involving quantifiers. These principles are among the most important aspects of natural-language quantification, and should therefore be covered by any proper treatment of quantifiers in ordinary English.

One class of disambiguating principles deal with the logical order (scope) of different semantical elements in an expression. How indispen-sable such ordering principles may be is shown by the fact that disregard-ing them can even lead one's syntax astray. For instance, as soon as a Montague-type grammar allows for the formation of conditionals, it will also allow (unless modified) the step from

(14)   if he contributes, he will be happy

to

(15)   if every man contributes, he will be happy

which is not grammatical (except in a context which provides an anteced-ent for 'he'). This step simply uses Rule S 14 of PTQ with $n=0$. The underlying reason for the difficulty is clearly the fact that in English 'if' has the right of way with respect to 'every', so that the 'every man' in (15) cannot pronominalize 'he'.[25]

Additional principles are thus needed in Montague grammars to regulate the order in which the different syntactical and semantical rules may be applied. They are of interest because they would represent an entirely new type of ingredient in Montague's theories. It is not clear, however, that some of them could not simply be built into the syntactical rules. For instance, by any token the first principles needed here include something like George Lakoff's global constraints on the derivation of quantified expressions.[26] They say in effect that a quantifier in a higher sentence has a wider scope than a quantifier in a subordinate one and that the left-right order serves as a tiebreaker for quantifiers in the same clause. These can presumably be built into Montague-type formation rules, at least partly.

However, they do not hold without exceptions. Hence the whole situation needs more scrutiny before we can be happy with any of the existing treatments.

Moreover, certain special quantifiers in English involve systematic violations of Lakoff's constraints. Their meaning can in other words be described only in terms of certain special ordering principle (scope conventions). The most important of these quantifiers in English is 'any'. I have recently developed what looks like a promising analysis of its semantical behavior in English. Can it be accounted for in a suitable extension of Montague semantics?

Let us take some examples. Let us consider the following sentence:

(16)   John does not believe that Mary likes any boy.

This has (besides the colloquial sense of 'believing not') only one non-deviant meaning in English, viz. the one which can be represented as follows

(17) $\sim$ John believes that $(\exists x)$ (x is a boy & Mary likes x)

Now how could (16) be built up in a suitable extension of Montague grammar? In order to obtain the right reading, some expressions of the sort indicated in (18) (next page) must be constructed in the course of the process of building up (16).

The details do not matter greatly here. The point is that somewhere along the line in constructing the that-clause we must deal with the expression 'any boy'. Now the semantical object correlated with it must be

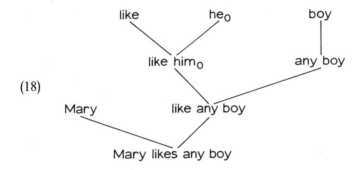

(18)

the same as that correlated by Montague with 'a boy'. Otherwise we just cannot get in the existential quantifier which (17) shows we need.

This is a disaster, however, for other examples show that the semantical object that must be correlated with 'any boy' is the same as is correlated with 'every boy'. In fact, this is the case in

(19)   Mary likes any boy

occuring alone.[27]

Hence the way in which a semantical object is correlated with 'any x' must depend on the context in which this expression occurs. This is apparently a serious violation of the Fregean principle (ii).

Now the plausible-looking ways out of this difficulty are not very satisfactory. (Of course it is primarily a difficulty only for someone who believes in (ii)–(iii).)

The way out closest at hand is probably to try to generate (16) in a way which involves the insertion of 'any boy' for a variable only at some later stage of the formational history of (16), perhaps so as to obtain it from 'any boy' and

(20)   John does not believe that Mary likes him_0.

However, the resulting reading of (16) is not tenable. And even if it were, it would not catch the intended one, viz. (17). For (16) says that it is compatible with what John believes that Mary should fail to like any boy, whereas the reading obtainable through (20) says that of each boy it holds that John fails to believe that Mary likes him. The latter is, e.g., compatible with John's mistakenly believing in the existence of other boys liked by Mary and hence compatible with the falsity of (17).

Another way out is not much better. It is to say that 'any' is ambiguous, that there are essentially different uses of 'any'. Although this seems to be the current consensus among linguists,[28] it is not a very satisfactory view intuitively, and constitutes an instant black mark against the kind of approach I am criticizing as soon as an alternative theory is developed which makes 'any' unequivocal. Such a theory seems to be in the offing, as a matter of fact.[29]

What is worse, this attempted way out does not offer us any real diagnosis of the semantical behavior of 'any' in ordinary English. I shall not attempt such a diagnosis here, although I believe that one can be given. Suffice it to say that it is the peculiar way in which the negation enters into (16) that makes the difference in this particular case.[30]

What we have seen is nevertheless enough to illustrate the main features of the situation. What we need is a way of telling how the interpretation of 'any x' depends on the context – e.g., a way of going back to 'any man' in (16) when we come to the negation. There are perhaps ways of trying to do so while preserving some elements of Montague semantics. All of them nevertheless involve violations of the Fregean principle (ii) in spirit, if not in the letter. They all mean that we cannot build the semantical objects connected with a complex expression step by step in a natural fashion. At some point we have to go back to the earlier stages of the derivation and revise them in the light of later stages. Instructions to do so may perhaps be coded in different ways in the notational aspects formation rules. However, this will only mean that they do not realize faithfully the spirit of the Fregean idea (ii).

Here we are in fact dealing with a general methodological point. Chomsky has repeatedly emphasized that there is in principle no difference between a 'generative' and an 'analytical' point of view in transformational grammar.[31] The very same rules which enable us to assemble a sentence automatically yield a way of as it were disassembling it. However, this remark is not applicable without qualifications. In semantics, one may want to abide by a principle which is not symmetrical with respect of building and of analysing sentences. The prime example is just the Fregean principle (ii).[32] If our semantical rules operate from the outside in, we can afford to let this principle be violated, for we can always look from the outside into the depths of a sentence to make the semantical role of an inside constituent depend on its context. This is not always feasible if the Fregean principle (ii) is strictly adhered to. Thus, in semantics the direction of our rules may make a great deal of difference, and I believe that the same holds for the syntax of 'any', too. It is for this reason that examples like (16) above are so interesting. They suggest that instead of trying to stick to the Fregean principle (ii) we should perhaps start thinking in terms of rules of semantical interpretation which operate from the outside in, unlike the semantical rules of Montague semantics.

Of course the situation is not a cut-and-dried one. There are tricks of coding information into suitable grammatical devices which can surreptitiously transmit it from one part of one's expression into another so as to create an illusion that the Fregean principle (ii) is adhered to when in reality it is not.

Independently of any particular problem, however interesting it may be in itself, it seems to me that the general question of whether one can stick to the Fregean principle (ii) in a natural Montague-type semantics probably has to be answered in the negative. I cannot discuss here problems connected with the third major idea of Montague's mentioned earlier, viz. (iii), at length. I can nevertheless register my belief that the most natural way of carrying out the principle (iii) leads us away from the principle (ii).[33] In other words, meaning entities are not to be constructed step by step from simpler ones in tandem with syntactical operations. Rather, they should be thought of, in some cases at least, as rules of semantical analysis. In brief, the proper treatment of quantifiers in ordinary English will differ from Montague's in this important respect, too.

Academy of Finland

NOTES

[1] See the following papers by Montague: 'Pragmatics', in *Contemporary Philosophy: A Survey* (ed. by Raymond Klibansky), La Nuova Italia Editrice, Florence, 1968, pp. 102–122; 'On the Nature of Certain Philosophical Entities', *The Monist* **53** (1969), 159–194; 'English as a Formal Language', in *Linguaggi nella societa e nella tecnica* (ed. by Bruno Visentini *et al.*), Milan, 1970, pp. 189–223; 'Universal Grammar', *Theoria* **36** (1970), 373–398; 'Pragmatics and Intensional Logic', in *Semantics of Natural Language* (ed. by Donald Davidson and Gilbert Harman), D. Reidel, Dordrecht, 1972, pp. 142–168; 'The Proper Treatment of Quantification in Ordinary English', in *Approaches to Natural Language* (ed. by Jaakko Hintikka, Julius M. E. Moravcsik, and Patrick Suppes), D. Reidel, Dordrecht and Boston, 1973, pp. 221–242.

Cf. also Richard Montague's shorter papers and notes on related topics, including 'Comments on Moravcsik's Paper' in *Approaches to Natural Language*, pp. 289–294; (together with Donald Kalish) 'That', *Philosophical Studies* **10** (1959), 54–61; 'Logical Necessity, Physical Necessity, Ethics, and Quantifiers', *Inquiry* **4** (1960), 259–269.

The development of Montague's views on the foundations of logic and linguistics was not without sharp turns, however. At one point he rejected altogether intensional logic as a viable tool of logical, philosophical, and grammatical analysis. This rejection was not recorded in print, however. (Cf. nevertheless his paper, 'Syntactical Treatments of Modality', *Acta Philosophica Fennica* **16** (1963), 153–167.)

[2] Cf., e.g., 'Pragmatics and Intentional Logic' on the specification of intensions.

[3] Cf., e.g., 'English as a Formal Language', pp. 202–203.

[4] Cf., e.g., PTQ, pp. 233–234 and *passim*.

[5] As seen from PTQ, p. 233, rule T2, Montague in effect proposed to use as the semantical object correlated with 'every man' the class of all predicates all men have, and as the semantical object correlated with 'John' the class of all the predicates John has. The desired parallellism then becomes obvious. However, the naturalness or unnaturalness of this procedure (especially in connection with the semantical objects correlated with such phrases as 'the wife of every man' or 'the brother of some woman') has not been discussed satisfactorily in the literature.

[6] See my paper, 'Carnap's Semantics in Retrospect', *Synthese* **25** (1972–73), 372–397.

[7] See Chapter 5, entitled 'Denoting', in *The Principles of Mathematics*, Allen and Unwin, London, 1903, pp. 53–65.

Peter Geach finds further anticipations in the medieval literature; see *Logic Matters*, Blackwell, Oxford, 1972, pp. 6, 8.

[8] Cf., e.g., 'English as a Formal Language', p. 193, and PTQ, p. 231.

[9] Cf. 'On the Nature of Certain Philosophical Entities'.

[10] In a forthcoming study of natural-language quantification. Cf. also next few references.

[11] *Knowledge and Belief*, Cornell University Press, Ithaca, N.Y. 1962, Ch. 6; 'The Modes of Modality', reprinted in my *Models for Modalities*, D. Reidel, Dordrecht, 1969, Ch. 5.

[12] See the papers collected in *Models for Modalities*.

[13] This important distinction has not yet received the systematic modern treatment it amply deserves. See nevertheless my *Models for Modalities*, pp. 120–121.

[14] See PTQ, p. 230.

[15] See PTQ, p. 231, clause (7).

[16] This was in fact allowed in Montague's earlier formulations. Cf., e.g., 'Pragmatics and Intensional Logic', p. 146.

[17] This shows up in the treatment outlined in my paper 'Existential Presuppositions and Uniqueness Presuppositions' (*Models for Modalities*, Ch. 7) in the form of the independence of '$(\exists x)(x=a)$' and '$(\exists x)b$ knows that $(x=a)$'.

[18] Other reasons were given (however sketchily) for this kind of treatment in my paper 'The Semantics of Modal Notions and the Indeterminacy of Ontology', in *Semantics of Natural Language* (ed. by Donald Davidson and Gilbert Harman), D. Reidel, Dordrecht and Boston, 1972, pp. 398–414.

[19] This is the starting-point of Peter Geach's problem of 'intentional identity', cf. *Logic Matters*, Blackwell Oxford, 1972, Ch. 4.4.

[20] Cf. my 'On the Logic of Perception' in *Models for Modalities* (note 11).

[21] Cf. my 'Existential Presuppositions and Uniqueness Presuppositions' (note 17).

[22] See 'On the Logic of Perception' (note 20).

[23] Cf. 'Existential Presuppositions and Uniqueness Presuppositions' (note 17).

[24] In 'English as a Formal Language', p. 217, Montague mentions that "English has...
certain... devices for reducing ambiguity." He lists several, including the peculiar behavior
of 'any'. Unfortunately neither Montague's diagnosis of the reasons for the peculiar behavior of 'any' (it is alleged to have the maximal scope) nor the cure he prescribes (changing
the syntactical rules for other quantifiers) are correct, it seems to me.
[25] Notice that this problem is not solved by the procedure Montague advocates in 'English
as a Formal Language', p. 217 (see the preceding footnote).
[26] See George Lakoff, 'On Generative Semantics', in *Semantics: An Interdisciplinary
Reader* (ed. by Danny D. Steinberg and Leon A. Jakobovits), Cambridge University Press,
Cambridge, 1971, pp. 232–296, especially pp. 240–246. Notice that their effects on the scopes
of quantifiers can always be gathered from the surface structure, however.
[27] If you do not find this plausible, feel free to change the original example (16) into 'John
does not believe that Mary can seduce any boy', which clearly contains an existential
quantifier, not a universal one, in the description of what John fails to believe.
[28] Cf. Edward S. Klima, 'Negation in English', in *The Structure of Language* (ed. by Jerry
A. Fodor and Jerrold J. Katz), Prentice-Hall, Englewood Cliffs, N.J., 1964, pp. 246–323,
especially pp. 276–280.
[29] I am in the process of trying to develop one, based on what I call the game-theoretical
semantics for natural-language quantifiers. Cf. 'Quantifiers vs. Quantification Theory',
Linguistic Inquiry (forthcoming).
[30] Klima's theory (note 28) correctly predicts that 'any' has existential force in (16). It fails
for other reasons, however, and hence does not offer an acceptable way out here. Montague
was right, it seemed to me, in holding that 'any' has only the force of a universal quantifier,
Klima notwithstanding.
[31] See, e.g., Noam Chomsky, 'Deep Structure, Surface Structure, and Semantic Interpretation', in *Semantics* (note 26), pp. 183–216, especially pp. 187–188.
[32] Of course, I am assuming here that transformations do not always preserve meaning.
The alleged meaning preservation of transformations seems to me a lost cause, however,
by any reasonable standards.
[33] See note 29.

BRIAN H. MAYOH

EXTRACTING INFORMATION FROM LOGICAL PROOFS

Logicians have long realized that the language of first order logic has great expressive power. In the early days of computers they tried to program the art of theorem-proving in the hope that the machine would then provide a steady stream of new and interesting results. Even although these hopes have faded more and more people are writing theorem proving programs. Why? Because the computer can extract information from the proofs of even simple theorems, that it can use for some other purpose. The techniques for doing this have been developed for theorem-provers that use local methods like resolution. Here we shall describe a technique for extraction of information from global theorem-provers of the kind developed by Prawitz, Kanger and others.

I. THE KIND OF INFORMATION TO BE EXTRACTED

First a few examples that show how the proof of a theorem can give useful information. The basic idea is to write the theorem to be proved in the form

$$\exists x_1 \exists x_2 \dots \exists x_n \quad Q(x_1, \dots, x_n)$$

and, from the substitutions for the variables $x_1 \dots x_n$ within the proof, to disentangle the required information.

EXAMPLE 1 (Question-Answering). For many years linguists in Aarhus have been collecting extensive data on the local dialects of Danish. Now two students, Inger Lytje and Ulla Christensen, are designing a scheme for burying this information in the memory of a computer in such a way that a linguist can sit at a terminal and converse in natural language with the machine, until it understands his question and can provide an answer. Such projects for keeping information in a computer memory for later retrieval are becoming more and more common. We can illustrate some of the problems by

Stored facts	Socrates is a man.
	All men are mortal.
Corresponding axioms	Man (Socrates)
	$\forall x[\text{Man}(x) \supset \text{Mortal}(x)]$
Question	Is anyone mortal?
Corresponding theorem	$\exists y \, \text{Mortal}(y)$
Substitution in proof	Socrates for y
Answer	Socrates is mortal.

More information on question-answering can be found in [7, 22]. The difficult and crucial problem of formalizing natural language is discussed in [20, 21].

EXAMPLE 2 (Problem solving). Since the days of Turing many computer scientists have been fascinated by the possibility of 'machine intelligence' [23]. As a simple illustration let us see how a robot might solve a variation of the traditional monkey-banana problem. In Figure 1 we see the robot about to attempt the problem: 'Switch on the light'. It knows that it can only reach the light if it climbs on a box under the switch.

Stored facts

Initially the robot is at a, the box at b, the switch at c.
The robot can run around the room.

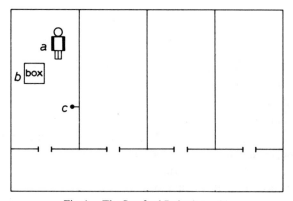

Fig. 1.   The Stanford Robot's world.

If the robot is at the box, it can push the box.
If the robot is at the box, it can climb on top.
If the box is under the switch with the robot on top, then the
robot can put on the light.

Corresponding axioms

Down (a, b, c, start)

$\forall x \forall y \forall z \forall t \forall x' [\text{Down}(x, y, z, t) \supset$

$\supset \text{Down}(x', y, z, \text{run}(x, x', t))]$

$\forall y \forall z \forall t \forall x' [\text{Down}(y, y, z, t) \supset$

$\supset \text{Down}(x', x', z, \text{push}(y, x', t))]$

$\forall y \forall z \forall t [\text{Down}(y, y, z, t) \supset \text{Up}(y, y, z, \text{climb}(t))]$

$\forall z \forall t [\text{Up}(z, z, z, t) \supset \text{Light}(\text{turn on}(t))]$

Problem

Switch on light.

Corresponding theorem

$\exists t [\text{Light}(t)]$

Substitution in proof

t replaced by turn on $(\text{climb}(\text{push}(b, c, \text{run}(a, b, \text{start})))))$

Solution

Run to box; push to switch; climb, turn on light.

For another approach to this particular problem see [15], for a more detailed discussion of the area, see [4, 5]. It is not clear that first order logic
is the most appropriate for problem solving, and the case for other logics
is given in [3, 8, 9, 16].

EXAMPLE 3 (Quandaries). To illustrate the fact that the information
extracted from a proof may be frustrating, let us imagine a computer
program such that:

if there is an odd perfect number *exists*,
then the computer prints it;
if there is a planar map that cannot be four-coloured,

then the computer draws it;
if neither if the above is true,
then the computer draws the moon.

Now consider the question: What will the program do? Careless formalization gives:

Axioms:

$\forall n [\text{Odd perfect }(n) \supset \text{Draw }(n)]$
$\forall n [\text{Map sensation }(n) \supset \text{Draw }(n)]$
$\neg \exists n [\text{Odd perfect }(n) \vee \text{Map sensation }(n)] \supset \text{Draw (Moon)}$

Theorem:

$\exists n \, \text{Draw }(n)$

Substitution in proof:

n is replaced by an odd perfect number *or* a sensational map *or* the Moon.

As a counterweight to such a frivolous example, our next two examples will illustrate applications of theorem-proving to problems of great practical importance.

EXAMPLE 4 (Program Analysis). How can one verify that a computer does what it is supposed to do? As a simple example of the way theorem-proving can help, consider the program in Figure 2.

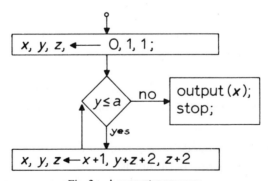

Fig. 2.   A computer program.

Suppose we introduce the predicates:

$Q(a, b, c, d)$: the computation from a passes through the diamond with $x=b$, $y=c$, $z=d$;

$S(a, t)$:   the computation from a stops with the output t.

The semantics of the programming language gives:

(Axiom 1) $Q(a, 0, 1, 1)$
(Axiom 2) $\forall x \forall y \forall z [Q(a, x, y, z) \ \& \ y \leqslant a \supset Q(a, x+1, y+z+2, z+2)]$
(Axiom 3) $\forall x \forall y \forall z [Q(a, x, y, z) \ \& \ y > a \supset S(a, x)]$

The programmer, knowing what his program is supposed to compute, may guess and prove

(Axiom 4) Axiom 1 & Axiom 2 $\supset \exists x [Q(a, x, (x+1)^2, 2x+1) \ \&$
$$\& \ x^2 \leqslant a < (x+1)^2]$$

Now he can prove $\exists t S(a, t)$ by using modus ponens to get the conclusion of Axiom 4, and then substituting:

the integral part of the square root of a

for the variable t. It follows that this particular number is the output of the program.

An excellent survey of the area can be found in [11]. Our example is one of those discussed in [13].

EXAMPLE 5 (Program Synthesis). To show how a computer might invent its own programs, let us adapt an example from [14]. Suppose the computer knows that: if it can prove

(Theorem 1) $\exists y' \exists z' [y' = g(0) \ \& \ z' = f(0)]$
(Theorem 2) $\forall x \forall y \forall z \exists y' \exists z' [[y = g(x) \ \& \ z = f(x)] \supset$
$$\supset [y' = g(x+1) \ \& \ z' = f(x+1)]]$$

then the program in Figure 3 will compute the function $f(n)$, where the constants a, b and the functions k, l are given by the substitutions for y', z' in the proof of Theorems 1 and 2 respectively.
Suppose the computer is told to compute the nth Fibonacci number and is given:

Axioms:

$$f(0)=1$$
$$f(1)=1$$
$$\forall n[f(n+2)=f(n+1)+f(n)]$$
$$\forall n[g(n)=f(n+1)]$$

To prove Theorem 1 the computer establishes

$$1=g(0) \ \& \ 1=f(0)$$

and extracts $1=a$ and $1=b$. To prove Theorem 2 it establishes

$$y=g(x) \ \& \ z=f(x) \supset [y+z=g(x+1) \ \& \ y=f(x+1)]$$

and extracts $k(x, y, z)=y+z$ and $l(x, y, z)=y$.

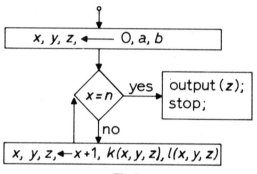

Fig. 3.

While one should not get the impression from this example that computers are going to invent large, useful programs in the immediate future, Floyd's example in [6] shows that this approach may provide a valuable assistant for a human programmer.

II. THE WAY OF EXTRACTING INFORMATION

Our next task is to describe a global theorem-prover. Because several examples will be given and there are excellent textbooks [2, 17], the description can be concise. Suppose

$$T, A_1, A_2, ..., A_n$$

are formulae in first order logic. To prove T from the axioms $A_1, A_2, ..., A_n$

one can show that the following set of formulae is unsatisfiable

$$\neg T, A_1, A_2, ..., A_n.$$

One way of showing this is:

(Step 1) Put each of the formulae in the set in Skolem standard form. For $\neg T$ this puts the theorem in the form
$\exists x_1, ..., \exists x_n Q(x_1 ... x_n)$

(Step 2) Omit the quantifiers and write the matrices in conjunctive normal form. The conjuncts are called *clauses*, and each of them is a disjunct of *literals* (atomic formulae and their negations).

(Step 3) Choose one or more copies of some of these clauses, and make alphabetic changes of variables so that no two clauses share a variable.

(Step 4) Find a new set of substitution equations that make the conjunction of the clauses into a propositional contradiction. If there is no such set, return to step 3 and make a new choice.

(Step 5) If the set of substitution equations is consistent, then stop; otherwise return to step 4.

As indicated by Prawitz [18], there are only finitely many possible sets of substitution equations to be found in step 4 and there is an algorithm that lists them all. The only reason why the technique does not give a decision procedure for first order logic is that there is no bound on the choice in step 3. The technique can easily be programmed for a computer, but before doing so, one should consult [1, 19].

How do we extract information from our theorem prover? Let us define a *critical clause* to be one that stems from the theorem to be proved. In the simplest case there is only one critical clause and our proof is 'constructive'. The set of substitution equations, on which the theorem-prover stops, will include the required information – the terms to be substituted for the existentially quantified variables of the theorem.

EXAMPLE 1 ctd. The clauses chosen at step 3 could be

Man (Socrates)
$\neg$ Man $(x) \vee$ Mortal (x)
$\neg$ Mortal (y)

Substitution equations: $x = $ Socrates, $x = y$
Information: $y = $ Socrates.

EXAMPLE 2 ctd. The clauses chosen at step 3 could be

$$\text{Down}(a, b, c, \text{Start})$$
$$\neg\text{Down}(x_1, y_1, z_1, t_1) \vee \text{Down}(x_1', y_1, z_1, \text{run}(x_1, x_1', t_1))$$
$$\neg\text{Down}(y_2, y_2, z_2, t_2) \vee \text{Down}(x_2', x_2', z_2, \text{push}(x_2, x_2', t_2))$$
$$\neg\text{Down}(y_3, y_3, z_3, t_3) \vee \text{Up}(y_3, y_3, y_3, z_3, \text{climb}(t_3))$$
$$\neg \quad \text{Up}(z_4, z_4, z_4, t_4) \vee \text{Light}(\text{turn on}(t_4))$$
$$\neg\text{Light}(t_5)$$

Substitution equations: $x_1 = a,\ y_1 = b,\ z_1 = c,\ t_1 = \text{Start},\ x_1' = b$
$$y_2 = b,\ z_2 = c,\ t_2 = \text{run}(a, b, t_1),\ x_2' = c$$
$$y_3 = c,\ z_3 = c,\ t_3 = \text{push}(b, c, t_2)$$
$$z_4 = c,\ t_4 = \text{climb}(t_3)$$
$$t_5 = \text{turn on}(t_4)$$

Information: $t_5 = $ turn on (climb (push $(b,\ c,\ \text{run}\ (a, b, \text{Start}))))$.

In the general case when the proof of a theorem uses several critical clauses, it is a little more difficult to extract information. Each critical clause gives an *alternative* and we want to know when to take which alternative. The procedure is: to substitute for the variables not in the critical clauses, to use the propositional calculus to simplify as much as possible, and then to substitute for the variables in the critical clauses. Often (but not always) the resulting set of clauses has the form

$$P_1 \vee R_1 \text{ (alternative 1)}$$
$$P_2 \vee R_2 \text{ (alternative 2)}$$
$$\vdots$$
$$P_m \vee R_m \text{ (alternative } m)$$
$$\neg R_1 \text{ (alternative 1)}$$
$$\neg R_2 \text{ (alternative 2)}$$
$$\vdots$$
$$\neg R_m \text{ (alternative } m)$$

and the required information will be:

if $\neg P_1$ *then* alternative 1 *else if* $\neg P_2 \ldots$ *else* alternative m.

EXAMPLE 6

Axioms: $P \supset Q(a, c)$
            $\neg P \supset Q(b, d)$
Theorem: $\exists x \exists y Q(x, y)$
Clauses: $\neg P \vee Q(a, c)$
            $P \vee Q(b, d)$
            $\neg Q(x_1, y_1)$
            $\neg Q(x_2, y_2)$
Substitution equations: $x_1 = a, y_1 = c$
                        $x_2 = b, y_2 = d$
Information: *if P then a else b* for x
              if P then c else d for y

Our next three examples illustrate the parameter-interpretation problem
[7, 12]. Eliminating existential (universal) quantifiers from axioms (theorems) causes Skolem functions to appear in clauses. These Skolem
functions may occur in the set of simultaneous equations that proves
the theorem and even in the information extracted from the proof.
However, if we remember where the various Skolem functions were
created, their interpretation is not difficult.

EXAMPLE 3 ctd. The clauses chosen at step 3 could be

$\neg$Odd perfect $(n_1) \vee$ Draw (n_1)
$\neg$Map sensation $(n_2) \vee$ Draw (n_2)
Odd perfect $(n_0) \vee$ Map sensation $(n_0) \vee$ Draw (Moon)
$\neg$Draw (m_1)
$\neg$Draw (m_2)

Substitution equations: $n_1 = n_0$ $n_2 = n_0$
                         $m_1 = n_0$ $m_2 = $ Moon
Information: *if* Odd perfect $(n_0) \vee$ Map sensation (n_0) *then* n_0 *else* Moon

EXAMPLE 4 ctd. The clauses chosen in step 3 could be

$Q(a, 0, 1, 1)$
$\neg Q(a, x_1, y_1, z_1) \vee y_1 > a \vee Q(a_1 x_1 + 1, y_1 + z_1 + 2, z_1 + 2)$
$\neg Q(a, x_2, y_2, z_2) \vee y_2 \leqslant a \vee S(a, x_2)$
$\neg S(a, x')$

together with the six clauses given by:

$$\neg Q(a, 0, 1, 1)$$
$$\vee [Q(a, x_1, y_1, z_1) \& y_1 \leqslant a \& \neg Q(a, x_1+1, y_1+z_1+2, z_1+2)]$$
$$\vee [Q(a, x, (x+1)^2, 2x+1) \& x \leqslant a < (x+1)^2]$$

Substitution equations: $x_1 = x_1, y_1 = y_1, z_1 = z_1$
$$x_2 = x, \quad y_2 = y_2 = (x+1)^2, z_2 = 2x+1$$
$$x' = x$$

Information: x' is x, the Skolem function introduced for

$$\exists x [Q(a, x, (x+1)^2, 2x+1) \& x^2 \leqslant a < (x+1)^2]$$

EXAMPLE 5 ctd. In proving Theorem 1 the chosen clauses could be:

$$f(0) = 1$$
$$f(1) = 1$$
$$g(n) = f(n+1)$$
$$y' \neq g(0) \vee z' \neq f(0)$$

Substitution equations: $n = 0, y' = 1, z' = 1$.
In proving Theorem 2 the chosen clauses could be:

$$f(n+2) = f(n+1) + f(n)$$
$$g(m) \quad = f(m+1)$$
$$g(m') \quad = f(m'+1)$$
$$y \quad = g(x)$$
$$z \quad = f(x)$$
$$y' \quad = g(x+1) \vee z' = f(x+1)$$

Substitution equations: $n = x, \quad m = x, \quad m' = x+1$
$$y' = y + z, \quad z' = y$$

All that remains is to check the viability of the method when we have several critical clauses. Remember that we do in fact have the proof of a theorem. From this it follows that substituting for variables and simplifying puts the non-critical clauses in the form

$$\mathscr{A}_1 \vee \mathscr{B}_1$$
$$\mathscr{A}_2 \vee \mathscr{B}_2$$
$$\vdots$$
$$\mathscr{A}_m \vee \mathscr{B}_m$$

where $\mathscr{A}_1$ & $\mathscr{A}_2$ & ... & $\mathscr{A}_m$ is a contradiction and $\mathscr{B}_1\mathscr{B}_2 ... \mathscr{B}_m$ are non-empty disjunctions of the negations of critical clauses. We have already described the information extraction algorithm for the case when each $\neg\mathscr{B}_1$ is a single critical clause. The following example indicates the modification for the general case.

EXAMPLE 7

Axioms: $\forall x \forall y[\neg P(x, y) \supset Q(x) \vee Q(b)]$
$\forall x \forall y[\ P(x, y) \supset Q(y) \vee Q(a)]$
Theorem: $\exists x\, Q(x)$
Clauses: $P(x, y) \vee Q(x) \vee Q(b)$
$\neg P(x', y') \vee Q(y') \vee Q(a)$
$\neg Q(w)$
$\neg Q(w')$
Substitution equations: $x = x' = w = a$ $\quad y = y' = w = b$
Information: x is *if* $P(a, b)$ *then* one of a or b *else* one of a or b.

This example is cunningly chosen to show how more information can be extracted from a cleverer proof.

EXAMPLE 7 ctd. With different substitution equations

$$x = x' = w = b \qquad y = y' = w' = a$$

we can simplify the non-critical clause set to

$$P(b, a) \vee Q(b)$$
$$\neg P(b, a) \vee Q(a)$$

and the information extracted is more precise,

$$x \text{ is } if \ P(b, a) \ then \ a \ else \ b.$$

One may well ask: What happens if the axioms are inconsistent? In this case there are no critical clauses, substituting for the variables, and simplifying eliminates *all* clauses, and no information whatsoever can be extracted. Since anything can be proved from an inconsistent set of axioms, we cannot expect useful information from such a proof.

University of Aarhus

72   BRIAN H. MAYOH

BIBLIOGRAPHY

MI – refers to the book series *Machine Intelligence*, Edinburgh Univ. Press;
AI – refers to the journal *Artificial Intelligence*, North-Holland Publ. Co., Amsterdam.

[1] R. S. Boyer and J. S. Moore, 'The Sharing of Structure in Theorem Proving Programs', MI 7 (1972), pp. 101–116.

[2] C. L. Chang and R. C. T. Lee, *Symbolic Logic and Mechanical Theorem Proving*, Academic Press, 1973.

[3] J. L. Darlington, 'Deductive Plan Formulation in Higher Order Logic', MI 7 (1972), pp. 129–137.

[4] R. E. Fikes, 'REF-ARF, A System for Solving Problems Stated as Procedures', AI 1 (1970), pp. 27–120.

[5] R. E. Fikes and N. J. Nilsson, 'STRIPS, A New Approach to the Application of Theorem Proving to Problem Solving', AI 2 (1971), pp. 189–208.

[6] R. W. Floyd, *Toward Interactive Design of Correct Programs*, Proc. IFIP Congress (1971) N. Holland Publ. Co., Amsterdam, pp. 1–4.

[7] C. Cordell Green, 'Theorem Proving by Resolution as a Basis for Question Answering Systems', MI 4 (1969), pp. 183–208.

[8] P. J. Hayes, 'Robotologic', MI 5 (1970), pp. 533–554.

[9] P. J. Hayes, 'A Logic of Actions', MI 6 (1971), pp. 495–520.

[10] S. Kanger: *A Simplified Proof Method for Elementary Logic, Computer Programming and Formal Systems* (ed. by P. Braffort and D. Hirschberg), N. Holland Publ. Co., Amsterdam, 1963.

[11] T. A. Linden, *A Summary of Programs Toward Proving Program Correctness*, AFIPS Proc. Fall Joint Comp. Conf. (1972), N. Holland Publ. Co., Amsterdam, pp. 201–211.

[12] D. Luckham and N. J. Nilsson, 'Extracting Information from Resolution Proof Trees', AI 2 (1971), pp. 27–54.

[13] Z. Manna, S. Ness, and J. Vuillemin, 'Fixpoint Approach to Theory of Computation', *Comm. Ass. Comp. Mach.* 15 (1972), 528–536.

[14] Z. Manna and R. J. Waldinger, 'Towards Automatic Program Synthesis', *Comm. Ass. Comp. Mach.* 14 (1971), 151–165.

[15] B. H. Mayoh, *Sprog, logik og tænkende maskiner, Sprog og Virkelighed* (ed. by M. Jacobsen), Gyldendal, 1973.

[16] J. McCarthy and P. J. Hayes, 'Some Philosophical Problems from the Standpoint of Artificial Intelligence', MI 4 (1969), pp. 463–502.

[17] N. J. Nilsson, *Problem Solving Methods in Artificial Intelligence*, McGraw-Hill, 1971.

[18] D. Prawitz, 'Advances and Problems in Mechanical Proof Procedures', MI 4 (1969), pp. 59–72.

[19] J. A. Robinson, 'Computational Logic, the Unification Computation', MI 6 (1971), pp. 63–72.

[20] E. Sandewall: 'Representing Natural Language Information in Predicate Calculus', MI 6 (1971), 255–280.

[21] E. Sandewall, 'Formal Methods in the Design of Question-Answering Systems', AI 2 (1971), pp. 129–146.

[22] R. F. Simmons, 'Natural Language Question-Answering Systems', *Comm. Ass. Comp. Mach.* 13 (1970), 15–30.

[23] A. M. Turing, 'Computing Machinery and Intelligence', *Mind* 59 (1950); reprinted in *Mind and Machine* (ed. by A. R. Anderson), Prentice Hall, 1964.

LENNART ÅQVIST

A NEW APPROACH TO THE LOGICAL THEORY
OF ACTIONS AND CAUSALITY

I. INTRODUCTION

In this article I try to show that the notions of *game-tree* and *game in extensive form*, as explained in Luce and Raiffa (1957), Chapter 3, provide an excellent starting point for the development of a theory of actions and causality that is formally rigorous to a high degree and, moreover, promises to be significant to various fields of application. For instance, the idea of an agent's causing harm by his performance of a given act – important in Tort Law and Criminal Law as a condition for liability or responsibility – turns out to be interestingly analyzable and logically reconstructible within a theoretical framework built on the Luce and Raiffa conception, as I argue (Åqvist, 1973; see also the well known Hart and Honoré (1959) in this context). Now, let me list a few conditions of adequacy to be met by any acceptable theory in the present area, which seems still to be in a state of regrettable conceptual flux:

(i) The theory should do justice to the important insight of von Wright (1963, 1966, and 1968), to the effect that the notion of action involves fundamentally that of *change*, *transformations* of *states*, or *transitions* among such.

(ii) A clear distinction between *individual* acts and *generic* ones should be provided by the theory.

(iii) It should lay down the conditions under which an agent can be said to *perform*, to *omit*, and 'merely' *not* to perform a given act (whether individual or generic) *in* a given situation *at* a given time; as well as those under which an act is *performable for* an agent, or is an *alternative open to* him.

(iv) Justice should be done by the theory to the important insight of a large number of writers who claim that a causal notion of an agent's *bringing* something *about*, or *making* something *happen*, is a central ingredient in the concept of action. Among philosophers trying to develop and apply this idea systematically, we just mention Kanger (1957 and

S. Stenlund (ed.), Logical Theory and Semantic Analysis, 73–91. All Rights Reserved.
Copyright © 1974 by D. Reidel Publishing Company, Dordrecht-Holland.

1972), Chellas (1969), Pörn (1970), and Åqvist (1972), others not to be forgotten.

(v) Justice should however also be done to the insight (we claim it to be one) that the above causal notion derives from a more fundamental one, which is of a 'binary' nature: that of an agent's *bringing* something *about by performing* such and such an *act*. This binary conception has been dealt with predominantly by jurists (who have made impressive efforts to explicate it especially in the areas of Tort and Criminal Law), but seemingly hardly at all by philosophers (those working in the field of performatives and speech-acts certainly constitute an exception here, see Åqvist, 1972; another one may be Danto, 1965). So, our *desideratum* with regard to the notion under discussion is that the theory should enable us to analyze it in a satisfactory manner.

We shall see that the theory of actions and causality elaborated in the present paper readily satisfies conditions (i)–(iii) by virtue of Definitions 3–3.3 below. Definition 6 claims to provide the analysis requested by (v), and (iv) is taken care of by Definition 6.1; we may note that these two definitions appeal to Kripke-style semantical analysis of modal notions in a rather special way, the methodology of which I shall let the reader figure out himself. I ought to add that my notions of *historical necessitation* (Definition 5.1 below) are related to and indeed inspired by certain ideas in Chellas (1969). The theory of conditionals presented in Åqvist (1971) and applied in Åqvist (1972) plays an obvious rôle also in the present contribution.

After discussing an illustrative example that shows our central notions 'at work', we close the paper by outlining a method for the introduction into our theory of so-called *causal act-descriptions*.

Finally, I like to point out that our game-tree approach is such that analyses of *deontic* and *epistemic* notions are easily and naturally carried out on it. Familiarly, such analyses are badly needed in a full reconstruction of the notion of responsibility (liability) e.g. in Tort Law. See Åqvist (1973), Chapter 1.

II. BASIC CONCEPTUAL MACHINERY

DEFINITION 1. By a *finite tree of uniform path-length* we shall understand a structure $Tr = \langle Q, q_0, R, k, rn, T \rangle$ where

LOGICAL THEORY OF ACTIONS AND CAUSALITY 75

(i) Q is a non-empty, finite set of elements called *concrete situations* or *decision points*;

(ii) q_0 is a designated member of Q called the *initial situation* or *starting point*;

(iii) R is an irreflexive binary relation on Q, *has as immediate successor*, satisfying the conditions:

(1) There is no q in Q such that qRq_0;

(2) for each q in Q except q_0 there is exactly one q' in Q such that $q'Rq$; in other words, the converse of R, *has as immediate predecessor*, is a function from $Q-\{q_0\}$ into Q;

(3) for each q in Q we have that $q_0R^s q$, where R^s is the *ancestral* of R, i.e., the smallest reflexive and transitive relation S on Q such that R is included in S;

(iv) k is a positive integer, called the *length* of the tree Tr;

(v) rn is a function which assigns to each concrete situation q in Q a positive integer $rn(q)$ with $1 \leqslant rn(q) \leqslant k$ as its *rank* or *time*(*-point*), and is such that

(1) $rn(q_0)=1$;

(2) for any q, q' in Q with qRq' we have that $rn(q')=rn(q)+1$;

(3) for each q in Q we have that $rn(q)=k$ iff (if and only if) $R(q)=\emptyset$, where $R(q)=\{q' \in Q : qRq'\}$ = the set of all immediate successors to q (emptiness of $R(q)$ obviously amounts to q being an *endpoint* in the tree Tr); and

(vi) $T=\{rn(q):q \in Q\}=\{t: t$ is a positive integer and $1 \leqslant t \leqslant k\}$; T is called *the time in* the tree Tr.

DEFINITION 1.1. Let $Tr=\langle Q, q_0, R, k, rn, T\rangle$ be a finite tree of uniform path-length, and let w be any function from T into $Q(w \in Q^T)$. We say that w is a *path* or a *possible course of events* ('possible world') in Tr, iff, for each t in T with $t>1$ holds that $w(t-1)Rw(t)$; and we let

$$W=\text{the set of all paths in } Tr=\{w \in Q^T : w(t-1)Rw(t) \text{ for each } t \text{ in } T \text{ such that } 1<t \leqslant k\}.$$

DEFINITION 1.2. Let Tr be as above, let w, $w' \in W$, and let $t \in T$. We say that *w coincides with w' at t*, iff, $w(t)=w'(t)$; and we set

$W^{w(t)}$ = the set of all paths in W that coincide with w at $t=$
= $\{w' \in W : w'(t)=w(t)\}$.

Moreover, if $t>1$, we say that *w is an historical alternative to w' at t* just in case w coincides with w' at $t-1$. And we let

HistAlt(w, t) = the set of all historical alternatives to w at $t = W^{w(t-1)}$.

DEFINITION 2. By a *game-tree* we understand a structure $G=\langle Tr, X, N, b, p\rangle$ where
   (i) *Tr* is a finite tree of uniform path-length;
   (ii) *X* is a non-empty, finite set of *agents* or *players*;
   (iii) *N* is a designated member of *X*, the 'spurious' agent Nature, Chance, or what not;
   (iv) *b* is a function which to each x in X assigns a subset $b(x)$ of Q such that $b(x)$ is the set of all concrete situations in Q in which the agent x has to make a choice from among a set of alternatives (which are decision points *for x*, which are '*x*'s move'); we require b to be such that

(1)   for all x, y in X where $x \neq y : b(x) \cap b(y) = \emptyset$; i.e., each situation in Q is assigned to *at most one* agent as a decision point for him; and
(2) $\bigcup_{x \in X} b(x) = Q^-$, where Q^- is the set of all elements in Q that are not endpoints in the tree; in other words, the union of the sets $b(x)$ is to *exhaust* Q^- so that every element in it is assigned to *at least one* agent as his move;

(v) *p* is a probability distribution over the set W of all paths in Tr in the familiar sense of being a function from W into the set of real numbers such that for each w in W:

(1) $0 \leqslant p(w) \leqslant 1$,   and
(2) $\sum_{w \in W} p(w)=1$.

DEFINITION 2.1. Let $G=\langle Tr, X, N, b, p\rangle$ be a game-tree. We say that G is *deterministic*, iff, either $b(N)=\emptyset$, or $b(N)\neq\emptyset$ and for each q in

$b(N)$, $R(q)$ (= the set of immediate successors to q) is identical to the unit set of some member of Q; and we call G *indeterministic* otherwise. We say that G is *fatalistic* iff the path-set W contains *at most one* member.

Note that from the mere fact that a game-tree is deterministic we cannot by any means infer that it is fatalistic. Note also that our definition does not appeal to difficult notions like causality, predictability etc. (We ought to mention here that our conception of determinism, indeterminism and fatalism seems to be suggested by von Wright, 1966 and 1968.)

DEFINITION 3. Let $G = \langle Tr, X, N, b, p \rangle$ be a game-tree. By an *individual act(ion)* (particular *instance* of an action, concrete act) *over G* we shall understand any *member of* the 'tree-relation' R so that

R = the set of all individual acts over G.

And by a *generic act(ion)* (or act-*type*) *over G* we mean any *subset of* the tree-relation R so that

$\mathscr{P}R$ (= the power-set of R) = the set of all generic acts over G.

Remark. Relatively to a game-tree G we thus think of an individual act as an ordered pair $\langle q, q' \rangle$ in R of concrete situations in Q where $rn(q') = rn(q) + 1$, and of a generic act simply as a class of individual ones. Note that our explication agrees nicely with the view of von Wright (1966 and 1968) to the effect that adequate analyses or descriptions of actions must be given in terms of 'states', 'transformations' and 'changes', and will thus have to contain an obvious reference to *at least two consecutive* 'time-points' or 'occasions'.

DEFINITION 3.1. Let G be a game-tree and let $h = \langle q, q' \rangle \in R$ be an individual act over G. The following functions are then readily defined:

 (i)   *The agent of h* = the x in X such that $q \in b(x)$.
 (ii) *The time of h* = the ordered pair $\langle rn(q), rn(q') \rangle$.
 (iii) *The initial situation of h* = q.
 (iv) *The final situation of h* = q'.

It is clear that these functions should be defined for any *individual* act, on any reasonable account of such acts; and it is equally clear that the same thing does not go for generic acts.

DEFINITION 3.2. Let G be a game-tree, let $h \in R$ be an individual act over G, let $H \subseteq R$ be a generic act over G, let $x \in X$, $w \in W$, and $1 < t \leqslant k$. We then say:

(i) *x has just performed h in w at t*, in symbols:

$$\text{Perf}(x, h, w, t), \text{ iff, } w(t-1) \in b(x) \text{ and } \langle w(t-1), w(t) \rangle = h.$$

(ii) *x has just performed H in w at t*, in symbols:

$$\text{Perf}(x, H, w, t), \text{ iff, } w(t-1) \in b(x) \text{ and } \langle w(t-1), w(t) \rangle \in H.$$

(iii) *x has just omitted* (to perform) *h in w at t*, in symbols:

$$\text{Omit}(x, h, w, t), \text{ iff, } w(t-1) \in b(x) \text{ and } \langle w(t-1), w(t) \rangle \neq h.$$

(iv) *x has just omitted* (to perform) *H in w at t*, in symbols:

$$\text{Omit}(x, H, w, t), \text{ iff, } w(t-1) \in b(x) \text{ and } \langle w(t-1), w(t) \rangle \notin H.$$

Remarks. (a) In order for an agent x just to have performed /omitted/ an individual or generic act in w at t it is thus necessary that the situation $w(t-1)$ is a decision point precisely for x. We also claim that this very condition makes for a clearcut distinction between omissions and 'mere' non-performances.

(b) It is readily seen that clauses (i) and (iii) in Definition 3.2 are indeed redundant: given (ii) and (iv), which define performance and omission for *generic* acts, we can replace the defining conditions of (i) and (iii) by the equivalent ones: $\text{Perf}(x, \{h\}, w, t)$ and $\text{Omit}(x, \{h\}, w, t)$, respectively, where $\{h\}$ is of course the unit set of h, and indeed a generic act over G.

DEFINITION 3.3. Let G, h, x, w, and t be as in Definition 3.2. We say that the individual act h *is an alternative open to x in w at* $t-1$, iff, $w(t-1) \in b(x)$, and $h = \langle w(t-1), q \rangle$ for some q in $R(w(t-1))$. An equivalent formulation of the second requirement here is this: there is a possible course of events w' in $\text{HistAlt}(w, t)$ such that $\text{Perf}(x, h, w', t)$. And we let

AltOp$(x, w, t-1) =$ the set of all alternatives open to x in w at $t-1$.

DEFINITION 4. Let $G = \langle Tr, X, N, b, p \rangle$ be a game-tree. By a *state of affairs over G* we understand any subset of Q, and by an *event over G* we understand any subset of W. States of affairs are thus identified with classes of concrete situations, and events (in the sense intended here) with classes of possible courses-of-events, or paths, in the tree. We should bear in mind, however, that other notions of event are current and legitimate as well, e.g. the one of which it is true that all individual acts are events.

DEFINITION 4.1. Let G be a game-tree, let $A \subseteq Q$ be a state of affairs over G, let $w \in W$ and $t \in T$. We say that A *is realized in* w *at* t, iff, the concrete situation $w(t) \in A$.

We also observe that to any state of affairs $A \subseteq Q$ and any $t \in T$ we can assign an event over G in the following way: define

$$|A|_t = \{w \in W : w(t) \in A\} = \text{the set of all paths } w \text{ in } W \text{ such that } A \text{ is realized in } w \text{ at } t.$$

Clearly, then, to say that the state of affairs A is realized in w at t amounts to saying that the path w is a member of the event $|A|_t$.

DEFINITION 4.2. Let G be a game-tree, let $x \in X$, $h \in R$, and $H \subseteq R$. We define the following states of affairs over G:

(i) $\text{perf}_x h = \{w(t) : w \in W, 1 < t \leqslant k, \text{ and } \text{Perf}(x, h, w, t)\}$
(ii) $\text{perf}_x H = \{w(t) : w \in W, 1 < t \leqslant k, \text{ and } \text{Perf}(x, H, w, t)\}$
(iii) $\text{omit}_x h = \{w(t) : w \in W, 1 < t \leqslant k, \text{ and } \text{Omit}(x, h, w, t)\}$
(iv) $\text{omit}_x H = \{w(t) : w \in W, 1 < t \leqslant k, \text{ and } \text{Omit}(x, H, w, t)\}$.

The set defined in (i) is to be understood as *the state of affairs constituted by* x's *having just performed* h, or, somewhat less idiomatically, *the state of affairs that* x *has just performed* h; and analogously for those defined in (ii)–(iv).

Furthermore, assume that $1 < t \leqslant k$. We then define matching *events* over G in the obvious way:

(i') $|\text{perf}_x h|_t = \{w \in W : w(t) \in \text{perf}_x h\} = \{w \in W : w(t-1) \in b(x)$
                                    $\text{and } \langle w(t-1), w(t) \rangle = h\}$.
(ii') $|\text{perf}_x H|_t = \{w \in W : w(t) \in \text{perf}_x H\} = \{w \in W : w(t-1) \in b(x)$
                                    $\text{and } \langle w(t-1), w(t) \rangle \in H\}$.
(iii') $|\text{omit}_x h|_t = \{w \in W : w(t) \in \text{omit}_x h\} = \{w \in W : w(t-1) \in b(x)$
                                    $\text{and } \langle w(t-1), w(t) \rangle \neq h\}$.

(iv') $|\text{omit}_x H|_t = \{w \in W : w(t) \in \text{omit}_x H\} = \{w \in W : w(t-1) \in b(x)$
$\text{and } \langle w(t-1), w(t) \rangle \notin H\}.$

For instance, $|\text{perf}_x H|_t$ is to be thought of as *the event* (over G) *that* x
has just performed the generic act H at time t; and so on for the remaining
events defined.

III. CAUSALITY AND AGENCY

Let us begin with a few preliminary definitions.

DEFINITION 5. Let $G = \langle Tr, X, N, b, p \rangle$ be a game-tree, and let $Y \subseteq W$
be an event over G. Define

$$\text{Maxp}(Y) = \{w \in Y : p(w) \geqslant p(w') \quad \text{for each} \quad w' \text{ in } Y\}$$

i.e., $\text{Maxp}(Y)$ is the set of *most* or *maximally probable* elements in Y
according to the probability distribution p over W in G.

DEFINITION 5.1. Let G be as above, let $Y, Z \subseteq W$ be events over G,
let $w \in W$ and $1 < t \leqslant k$. Relatively to G, then, we define the following
series of quaternary relations:

(i) *Y /strongly/ historically necessitates Z in w at t* (or, *Y is a /strong/
historically sufficient condition for Z in w at t*), iff, $\text{Maxp}(\text{HistAlt}(w, t) \cap$
$\cap Y) \subseteq Z$ /$\text{HistAlt}(w, t) \cap Y \subseteq Z$/.

(ii) *Y is a /strong/ historical conditio sine qua non for Z in w at t*, iff,
$\text{Maxp}(\text{HistAlt}(w, t) \cap -Y) \subseteq -Z$ /$\text{HistAlt}(w, t) \cap -Y \subseteq -Z$/; i.e., iff $-Y$
/strongly/ historically necessitates $-Z$ in w at t. (Here and henceforth
set-complementation is with respect to W, so that $-Y = W - Y$ for any
$Y \subseteq W$.)

(iii) *Z is /strongly/ historically avoidable relatively to Y in w at t*, iff,
$(\text{HistAlt}(w, t) \cap Y) \cap -Z \neq \emptyset$ /$\text{Maxp}(\text{HistAlt}(w, t) \cap Y) \cap -Z \neq \emptyset$/.

(iv) *Z is /strongly/ historically possible relatively to Y in w at t*, iff,
$(\text{HistAlt}(w, t) \cap Y) \cap Z \neq \emptyset$ /$\text{Maxp}(\text{HistAlt}(w, t) \cap Y) \cap Z \neq \emptyset$/.

Remark. Many of the notions just introduced are clearly interdefinable, and various logical relationships hold among them. These matters
can be left to the reader.

We are now able to tackle the notion of causality in relation to agents and their actions. We do this by proposing the following definition, which is probably the most important one laid down in the present paper:

DEFINITION 6. Let G be a game-tree, let $x \in X$, $H \subseteq R$, $A \subseteq Q$, $w \in W$, and let $1 < t \leqslant k$ and $1 \leqslant t' \leqslant k$. Relatively to G we define the following sexternary relation:

By having just performed H in w at t x caused (brought it about, saw to it) that A was realized in w at t', in symbols: ByPerfCaused(x, H, w, t, A, t'), iff, the following conditions are all met:

(i) $\mathrm{Perf}(x, H, w, t)$,
(ii) $w(t') \in A$,
(iii) $\mathrm{Maxp}(\mathrm{HistAlt}(w, t)) \cap |\mathrm{omit}_x H|_t \neq \emptyset$,
(iv) $|A|_{t'}$ is strongly historically avoidable relatively to $|\mathrm{omit}_x H|_t$ in w at t; i.e., by Definition 5.1 (iii), $\mathrm{Maxp}(\mathrm{HistAlt}(w, t) \cap \cap |\mathrm{omit}_x H|_t) \cap -|A|_{t'} \neq \emptyset$,

and

(v) $|\mathrm{perf}_x H|_t$ historically necessitates $|A|_{t'}$ in w at t; i.e., by Definition 5.1 (i), $\mathrm{Maxp}(\mathrm{HistAlt}(w, t) \cap |\mathrm{perf}_x H|_t) \subseteq |A|_{t'}$.

Remarks. (a) Here, condition (i) requires that, as a matter of fact, x has just performed H in w at t, and condition (ii), similarly, that the state of affairs A is indeed realized in w at t'. Condition (iii) requires that x *could 'reasonably' have omitted H in w at t*, and condition (iv) that *by having omitted H in w at t x could 'reasonably' have avoided that A was realized in w at t'* (if you prefer, could 'reasonably' have *made it possible* that A was *not* realized in w at t'). In the context of (iii) and (iv), the word 'reasonably' indicates the strong sense of possibility captured by the Maxp-operation. Condition (v), finally, requires the performance of H by x in w at t to *necessitate* the presence of A in w at t' *historically* (to be *a historically sufficient condition* for it); note that in (v) we do not use our strong notion of historical necessitation, but just the weak one.

(b) Although stated only for generic acts $H \subseteq R$, Definition 6 is easily seen to cover individual acts $h \in R$ *via* the manoeuver described in Remark (b) to Definition 3.2: just appeal to the generic act $\{h\}$ for any $h \in R$.

(c) Conditions (iii) and (iv) can be lumped together into a single one, for their conjunction is equivalent to: $\mathrm{Maxp}(\mathrm{HistAlt}(w,\,t)) \cap |\mathrm{omit}_x H|_t \cap \cap -|A|_{t'} \neq \emptyset$, which differs from (iv) only with respect to the scope of the Maxp-operation. (Åqvist, 1971, Sections 1 and 3.)

(d) The reasons why in Definition 6 we have chosen to adopt precisely the above conditions, of which (iii)–(v) are clearly the crucial ones, emerge from a rather long story which I won't retell here. As it stands, however, Definition 6 is based on my analysis of the notion of *liability for one's own negligence* in Tort Law, which notion familiarly involves that of agent-causation. The analysis itself is given in my 1973 essay on the subject, where it is also applied to a fairly extensive legal material (mostly in the form of cases in Swedish Tort Law) and found to be reasonably adequate with respect to the latter. In the present paper we confine ourselves to give an example (in the next section) intended to illustrate how the conception introduced by Definition 6 works in practice and how it fares with some rival ones.

(e) A well-known intuition about causality requires adequate analyses of the notion to yield the result that "the effect cannot precede the cause in time," and, indeed, to yield it in a *non-trivial* way: for instance, just adding to Definition 6 a clause to the effect that $t' \not< t$ won't satisfy the latter requirement. Fortunately enough, we can prove the following

THEOREM. *Let G, x, H, A, w, t, and t' be as in Definition 6. Then: If* ByPerfCaused $(x,\,H,\,w,\,t,\,A,\,t')$, *then* $t' \not< t$.

Proof. Assume, contrary to the theorem, that we have ByPerfCaused $(x,\,H,\,w,\,t,\,A,\,t')$ as well as $t' < t$ (for some G, x, H, A, w, t, t' as stipulated). By Definition 1.2, $\mathrm{HistAlt}(w,\,t) = W^{w(t-1)}$ where, of course, $w \in W^{w(t-1)}$. By assumption we have $t' < t$; suppose first that $t' = t-1$. Now, since condition (ii) of Definition 6 is satisfied by virtue of our assumption, we obtain $w(t-1) \in A$, $w \in |A|_{t-1}$, and $w' \in |A|_{t-1}$ for all w' in $W^{w(t-1)}$: hence $W^{w(t-1)} \subseteq |A|_{t-1}$, i.e., $\mathrm{HistAlt}(w,\,t) \subseteq |A|_{t'}$, i.e., $\mathrm{HistAlt}(w,\,t) \cap -|A|_{t'} = \emptyset$, from which result we easily derive the negation of condition (iv) as well as that of ByPerfCaused $(x,\,H,\,w,\,t,\,A,\,t')$. This contradiction completes the *reductio ad absurdum* in the case where $t' = t-1$. Suppose next that $t' < t-1$: then, obviously, $t' = t-m$ for some integer m such that $1 < m < t$. Starting from the fact that condition (ii) of Definition 6 is again satisfied by virtue of our counterassumption, we establish that $W^{w(t-m)} \subseteq |A|_{t-m}$

by arguing as above. Also, since we have $W^{w(t-1)} \subseteq W^{w(t-m)}$ by virtue of elementary properties of finite trees, we obtain $\text{HistAlt}(w, t) \subseteq |A|_{t'}$, from where we readily complete the *reductio* in the present case with $t' < t - 1$. Q.E.D.

Let me add that our theorem is of immediate relevance in connection with what tort lawyers call *already realized* or *completed* harms (Åqvist, 1973, Chapter II, Example 8).

IV. AN ILLUSTRATIVE EXAMPLE

Two agents, x and z, are playing the following game. Each has a hand consisting of three cards valued 2, 1, and 0, respectively, and each is supposed to select exactly one card from his hand and play it on a table which is, by an ingenious mechanism, connected with an electric chair where y (a third person) is tied up. The mechanism is such that the current is switched on and kills y, if and only if, the sum of the cards played on the table is equal to or greater than 2. Its mode of operation is a bit delayed, though, inasmuch as it does not start to react until both agents have played their selected cards. The following *order of play* is stipulated: x starts, followed by z. Moreover, it is assumed (i) that z selects and plays his card *independently of* x's previous action, so that the latter does not in any way *influence* or *direct* the choice made by z, and (ii) that the game is 'open' in the sense that z *knows* what x has done whenever he (z) is about to play. Finally, we assume throughout the discussion that the mechanism works perfectly, that the players observe the rules of the game nicely, and perhaps a few more things of the sort.

Evidently, the just described 'system' can be represented by a deterministic (see Definition 2.1) game-tree as follows:

Figure 1 pictures a game-tree $G = \langle\langle Q, q_0, R, k, rn, T \rangle, X, N, b, p \rangle$ where

$W = \{w_1, w_2, \ldots, w_9\}$

$T = \{1, 2, 3, 4\}$

$k = 4$

$Q = \{w_i(t) : i = 1, \ldots, 9 \text{ and } t \in T\}$

$q_0 = w_1(1) (= w_i(1) \text{ for } i = 1, \ldots, 9)$

$R = \{\langle w_i(t), w_i(t+1)\rangle : i = 1, \ldots, 9 \text{ and } t = 1, 2, 3\}$

$rn(w_i(t)) = t \text{ for } i = 1, \ldots, 9 \text{ and } t \in T$

$X = \{x, y, z, N\}$

$b(x) = \{w_1(1)\}$

$b(y) = \emptyset$

$b(z) = \{w_1(2), w_4(2), w_7(2)\}$

$b(N) = \{w_i(3) : i = 1, \ldots, 9\}$, and

$p(w_i) = \frac{1}{9} \text{ for } i = 1, \ldots, 9.$

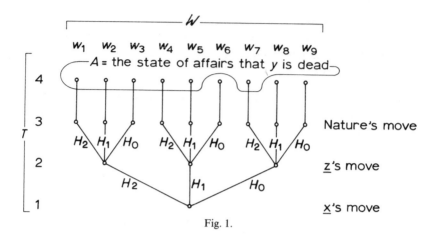

Fig. 1.

Moreover, $H_i(i=0, 1, 2)$ represents the generic act over G of playing the card of value i. Thus,

$$H_2 = \{\langle w_1(1), w_1(2)\rangle, \ \langle w_1(2), w_1(3)\rangle, \ \langle w_4(2), w_4(3)\rangle, \ \langle w_7(2), w_7(3)\rangle\}$$
$$H_1 = \{\langle w_2(2), w_2(3)\rangle, \ \langle w_5(1), w_5(2)\rangle, \ \langle w_5(2), w_5(3)\rangle, \ \langle w_8(2), w_8(3)\rangle\}$$
$$H_0 = \{\langle w_3(2), w_3(3)\rangle, \ \langle w_6(2), w_6(3)\rangle, \ \langle w_9(1), w_9(2)\rangle, \ \langle w_9(2), w_9(3)\rangle\}$$

Exercise: Determine the states of affairs $\text{perf}_x H_i$ and $\text{omit}_x H_i$ for $x \in X$ and $i=0, 1, 2$!

Finally, the set $A = \{w_i(4): i=1, 2, 3, 4, 5, 7\}$ represents the state of affairs over G that y is dead (after having been killed in accordance with the described mode of operation of the mechanism).

As was argued at some length in my 1973 (Chapter II, Example 5), to assume that all the courses of events w_i are equally probable according to our even distribution p (so that $\text{Max}p(W) = W$) may be said to amount exactly to the independence requirement (i) made in the description of the game.

Let us now go on to apply Definition 6 to the present example. We can readily verify that the following statements are *all* true with respect to G:

(1) $\text{ByPerfCaused}(x, H_2, w_i, 2, A, 4)$ for $i=1, 2, 3$.
(2) $\text{ByPerfCaused}(z, H_2, w_i, 3, A, 4)$ for $i=4, 7$.
(3) $\text{ByPerfCaused}(z, H_1, w_5, 3, A, 4)$.

On the other hand, we easily check that *none* of the following statements are true relatively to G:

(4)   ByPerfCaused$(z, H_j, w_i, 3, A, 4)$ where $j=2$ and $i=1$, *or* $j=1$ and $i=2$, *or* $j=0$ and $i=3$.

(5)   ByPerfCaused$(x, H_1, w_i, 2, A, 4)$ for $i=4, 5$.

(6)   ByPerfCaused$(x, H_0, w_7, 2, A, 4)$.

(As for the remaining six possible ByPerfCaused-statements that satisfy condition (i) of Definition 6, we note that they all fail for the trivial reason that $w_i(4) \notin A$ for $i=6, 8, 9$, whence condition (ii) of Definition 6 will be violated in these cases.)

We now wish to comment on the above results somewhat more in detail, and consider in turn what happens in each course of events w_i, where $i=1, 2, 3, 4, 5, 7$ and thus $w_i(4) \in A$.

Cases w_1, w_2 and w_3. In these three cases x starts to play his card of value 2 (and has just performed H_2 at time 2): clearly, *regardless of* what z then does, y will be dead at time 4, because the event $|A|_4$ is indeed strongly historically necessitated in w_1, w_2 and w_3 by the performance of H_2 by x at 2 ($|\text{perf}_x H_2|_2$). The failure of the statements (4) is precisely due to this fact, which entails that condition (iv) in Definition 6 is not met by z: $\text{Maxp}(\text{HistAlt}(w_i, 3) \cap |\text{omit}_z H_j|_3) \cap -|A|_4 = \emptyset$ when i and j are as stipulated. Thus, $|A|_4$ (y's death at time 4) fails to be strongly, and even weakly, historically avoidable relatively to every relevant omission by z at time 3 in w_1, w_2 and w_3; in other words, z could not possibly have avoided that y died by omitting what he in fact did in these courses of events.

On the other hand we have that w_6, w_8, w_9 are all members of $\text{Maxp}(\text{HistAlt}(w_i, 2) \cap |\text{omit}_x H_2|_2) \cap -|A|_4$ for $i=1, 2, 3$, so there is no problem about x's satisfying condition (iv) in Definition 6 or the remaining ones, as fas as the statements (1) are concerned. Hence, they are obviously true with respect to G.

Cases w_4 and w_5. Here, y is dead at 4 after x started to play his card of value 1, followed by z playing his 2 or his 1, as the case may be. The reason why

(2a)   ByPerfCaused$(z, H_2, w_4, 3, A, 4)$

and (3) both come true (conditions (i)–(v) all satisfied) apparently consists in the fact that in the situation $w_4(2)$ ($= w_5(2)$), where x has just performed H_1, the crucial decision about y's life-or-death *is up to z*, because the act just performed by x does not (even weakly) historically necessitate y's death at time 4 and is clearly 'by itself' insufficient to effect the latter. Thus, the failure of the statements (5), relating to x, is due to failure of condition (v) in Definition 6 this time, viz. exactly the following: $w_6 \in \text{Maxp}(\text{HistAlt} \times \times (w_i, 2) \cap |\text{perf}_x H_1|_2)$ for $i = 4, 5$, but $w_6 \notin |A|_4$. With Hart and Honoré (1959) we may say that, in the cases of w_4 and w_5, there has intervened an *independent decision* on the part of z between the original act done by x and the harm suffered by y (see Hart and Honoré, 1959, p. 186).

Case w_7. The truth of

(2b) $\text{ByPerfCaused}(z, H_2, w_7, 3, A, 4)$

as well as the failure of (6) are established and explained in analogy with the two preceding cases.

Further remarks. (a) According to a traditional and familiar view on causation, we ought to replace condition (iv) of Definition 6 by the following one, which, in the presence of (iii), is definitely stronger than (iv):

(iv′) $|\text{perf}_x H|_t$ is an historical *conditio sine qua non* for $|A|_{t'}$ in w at t
          (in the sense of Definition 5.1 (ii)).

In the context of Definition 6, (iv′) requires that the omission of H by x at t ($|\text{omit}_x H|_t$) is to historically *necessitate* the absence of A at t' ($-|A|_{t'}$), whereas (iv) only required the former to *make* the latter *possible*. As argued with some energy in Åqvist (1973, Chapter II, e.g. Examples 1 and 3), (iv′) is much too strong to be admissible in an adequate explication of agent-causation. For one thing, it leads directly to the well known, but altogether unnecessary difficulties in cases involving multiple sufficient causation, which are easily avoided if we merely adopt our weaker condition (iv). Another objection: as applied to our illustrative example, the suggested substitution of (iv′) for (iv) in Definition 6 would yield the undesirable consequence that the statements (1), (2a), and (3) all turn out to be false, while only (2b) remains true. (The verification of this fact can be left to the reader.)

(b) Our result in cases w_4 and w_5 to the effect that z caused y to be dead at time 4 by *his* action, rather than x by *his* one, obviously depends in a crucial fashion on our *even* probability distribution p over W, and over the 'middle tree' $\{w_4, w_5, w_6\}$ in particular. Suppose that p is altered in such a way that the probability of w_4 as well as that of w_5 be greater than that of w_6 (e.g., by putting $p(w_4)=p(w_5)>p(w_6)$): this new distribution embodies the idea that, by having played his card of value 1 at time 2 in w_4 and w_5, x indeed *influenced z in the direction of* playing the 2 or the 1 rather than the 0 card. In other words, according to our new p, the situation in which x has placed z by his action, viz. $w_4(2)$, is such that z is more strongly motivated in it to do H_2 or H_1 rather than to do H_0. Relatively to our game-tree G with such a modified probability distribution, and with the independence-condition (i) thus abandoned, we obtain the following results instead of our earlier ones:

The statements (5) are true, whereas (2a) and (3) fail. The reason for the failure of the latter is violation of (iv) in Definition 6: Maxp(HistAlt × $\times (w_4, 3) \cap |\text{omit}_z H_2|_3) = \{w_5\}$, but $\{w_5\} \cap -|A|_4 = \emptyset$ (and analogously for statement (3)). This result expresses the idea that z could not *reasonably* have avoided y's death at time 4 by acting differently from what he in fact did in w_4 (*cf.* remark (a) to Definition 6). As far as the truth of the statements (5) is concerned, we observe that x now satisfies condition (v) since w_6 no longer counts as maximally (or 'sufficiently') probable according to our modified p. Finally, note that the strong version of (v) is *not* satisfied by x, i.e., the one to the effect that $|\text{perf}_x H_1|_2$ *strongly* historically necessitates $|A|_4$ in w_4, or w_5, at 2, because $w_6 \in \text{HistAlt}(w_i, 2) \cap |\text{perf}_x H_1|_2$ for $i=4, 5$ but $w_6 \notin |A|_4$. In Åqvist (1973) the distinction between our two notions of historical necessitation is nicely illustrated by the two Swedish legal cases NJA 1957 s.139 and NJA 1966 s.30, which essentially follow the pattern of w_1 and that of w_4 in G with modified p, respectively.

(c) In our illustrative example, all results concerning the relation ByPerfCaused depend in a critical way on the stipulated *play order*. If we reverse the latter, we may expect obvious reversed results to hold relatively to the game-tree that is naturally taken to represent the new system. Also, if we stipulate that the agents x and z are to play their cards *simultaneously*, we might expect our previous results to be interestingly affected by that change of play order and a more complicated picture to arise (as lawyers are well aware). A theory of simultaneous agency, using appropriate *sequences of* game-trees instead of single ones, is developed in Chapter II, Example 9, of Åqvist (1973).

V. ON CAUSAL ACT-DESCRIPTIONS

The general problem: *How is an action to be described?* (interestingly discussed e.g. by Rescher, 1966) is of course an extremely complex and fascinating one, and to provide anything like an exhaustive account of all its ramifications would indeed seem to be an overwhelming task. We close the present paper by showing how, within our framework of game-trees, we can use Definition 6 to deal successfully at least with various *causal* descriptions of actions, which are familiar and current in ordinary discourse. First of all, let us supplement Definition 6 by defining the counterpart in our theory to the Kanger-Chellas-Pörn notion of 'plain' *causing* (bringing it about, seeing to it) *that*:

DEFINITION 6.1. Let G, x, A, w, t, t' be as in Definition 6. Relatively to G we then define the following quinternary relation:

> *By his acting in w at t x caused (brought it about, saw to it) that A was realized in w at t'*, or simply, *x caused in w at t A to be realized (in w) at t'*, in symbols: Caused(x, w, t, A, t'), iff, ByPerfCaused $(x, \{\langle w(t-1), w(t)\rangle\}, w, t, A, t')$.

As applied to our illustrative G, Definition 6.1 then gives us results like

> Caused$(x, w_i, 2, A, 4)$ for $i = 1, 2, 3$;   and
> Caused$(z, w_i, 3, A, 4)$ for $i = 4, 5$,   and 7.

We then proceed to

DEFINITION 7. Let G, A, and t' be as above, and define the following binary function:

> Causing$(A, t') = \{\langle w(t-1), w(t)\rangle : w \in W, 1 < t \leqslant k$, and Caused$(x, w, t, A, t')$ for some x in $X\} =$
> $= \{h \in R: $ ByPerfCaused$(x, \{h\}, w, t, A, t')$ for some x in X, some w in W, and some t in $T - \{1\}\}$.

Thus, the function Causing is such that to any state of affairs A over G and any t' in T it assigns as value this generic act over G: the set of those individual acts over G by whose performance in *some* course of events at *some* time by *some* agent the latter *caused* A to be realized at t' (in the same course of events). In short, Causing (A, t') is the set of particular 'causing-A-to-be-realized-at-t''-instances over G, we may say.

As applied to our illustrative example, Definition 7 yields the result that the generic act over G of causing y to be dead at time $4 =$ Causing$(A, 4) = \{\langle w_1(1), w_1(2)\rangle, \langle w_4(2), w_4(3)\rangle, \langle w_5(2), w_5(3)\rangle, \langle w_7(2), w_7(3)\rangle\}$. Note here that Causing$(A, 4)$ is a generic act over G that is distinct from each of the $H_i (i = 0, 1, 2)$.

An obvious result to be checked by the reader: for all G, x, A, w, t, t' as in Definition 6 we have that Perf$(x, $Causing$(A, t'), w, t)$ iff Caused(x, w, t, A, t').

DEFINITION 7.1. Let G, x, A, w, t, t' be as in Definition 6, and define the following series of functions:

(i)   Causing-in-at-by$(A, t', w, t, x) = \{h \in R: $ByPerfCaused$(x, \{h\}, w, t, A, t')\}$.

(ii)   Causing-at-by$(A, t', t, x) = \{h \in R:$
ByPerfCaused$(x, \{h\}, w, t, A, t')$ for some w in $W\} =$
$= \bigcup_{w \in W}$ Causing-in-at-by(A, t', w, t, x).

(iii) Causing-in-by$(A, t', w, x) = \{h \in R: $ByPerfCaused$(x, \{h\}, w, t, A, t')$ for some t in $T - \{1\}\} =$
$= \bigcup_{t \in T - \{1\}}$ Causing-in-at-by (A, t', w, t, x).

(iv)   Causing-in-at$(A, t', w, t) = \{h \in R: $ByPerfCaused$(x, \{h\}, w, t, A, t')$ for some x in $X\} =$
$= \bigcup_{x \in X}$ Causing-in-at-by(A, t', w, t, x).

(v)   Causing-by$(A, t', x) = \{h \in R: $ByPerfCaused$(x, \{h\}, w, t, A, t')$ for some w in W and some t in $T - \{1\}\}$
$\left(= \bigcup_{\substack{w \in W \\ t \in T - \{1\}}} \text{etc.}\right)$.

(vi)   Causing-in$(A, t', w) = \{h \in R: $ByPerfCaused$(x, \{h\}, w, t, A, t')$ for some x in X and some t in $T - \{1\}\}$.

(vii) Causing-at$(A, t', t) = \{h \in R: $ByPerfCaused$(x, \{h\}, w, t, A, t')$ for some x in X and some $w \in W\}$.

The first locution defined in this chain may be read: 'the generic act over G of being a *causing-A-to-be-realized-at-t'-in-w-at-t-by-x*; and so forth for the remaining ones. Here, the temporal cross-references are throughout to be understood in the obvious way: t' is always the time of A's (supposed) realization, and t is always the time of the (supposed) causing.

As applied to our illustrative G, Definition 7.1 gives us results like the following:

$$\text{Causing-in-at-by}(A, 4, w_i, t, x) = \begin{cases} \{\langle w_i(1), w_i(2)\rangle\}, & \text{if } i = 1, 2, 3 \\ & \text{and } t = 2 \quad \text{and } x = x. \\ \{\langle w_i(2), w_i(3)\rangle\}, & \text{if } i = 4, 5, 7 \\ & \text{and } t = 3 \quad \text{and } x = z. \\ \emptyset & \text{otherwise}. \end{cases}$$

$$\text{Causing-at}(A, 4, 2) = \text{Causing-by}(A, 4, x) = \{\langle w_1(1), w_1(2)\rangle\}.$$
$$\text{Causing-at}(A, 4, 3) = \text{Causing-by}(A, 4, z) =$$
$$= \{\langle w_4(2), w_4(3)\rangle, \langle w_5(2), w_5(3)\rangle, \langle w_7(2), w_7(3)\rangle\}.$$

Also, we clearly have that $\text{Causing}(A, 4) = \text{Causing-by}(A, 4, x) \cup \text{Causing}(A, 4, z)$, as well as, in general, that $\text{Causing}(A, t') =$

$$\bigcup_{\substack{w \in W \\ x \in X \\ t \in T - \{1\}}} \text{Causing-in-at-by}(A, t', w, t, x).$$

Finally, we may codify the rôle of the restricting prepositions 'in', 'at' and 'by' in the locutions defined by (i)–(vii) more generally as follows:

DEFINITION 7.2. Let G, x, H, w, t be as in Definition 6. Define

$$\text{By}(H, x) = \{h \in H : \text{Perf}(x, h, w, t)$$
$$\text{for some } w \text{ in } W \text{ and } t \text{ in } T - \{1\}\}$$
$$\text{At}(H, t) = \{h \in H : \text{Perf}(x, h, w, t)$$
$$\text{for some } w \text{ in } W \text{ and } x \text{ in } X\}$$
$$\text{In}(H, w) = \{h \in H : \text{Perf}(x, h, w, t)$$
$$\text{for some } x \text{ in } X \text{ and } t \text{ in } T - \{1\}\}.$$

The first locution here may be read: '*H-as-performed-by-x*', '*H-as-restricted-to-x*', or simply '*H-by-x*'; analogously for the remaining ones. We leave it to the reader to check results like these:

$$\text{Causing-by}(A, t', x) = \text{By}(\text{Causing}(A, t'), x)$$

$$\text{Causing-at-by}(A, t', t, x) = \text{At}(\text{By}(\text{Causing}(A, t'), x), t) = \text{By}(\text{At}(\text{Causing}(A, t'), t), x)$$

etc., etc.

University of Uppsala

BIBLIOGRAPHY

Chellas, Brian F., *The Logical Form of Imperatives*, Perry Lane Press, Stanford, 1969.
Danto, Arthur C., 'Basic Actions', *American Philosophical Quarterly* 2 (1965), 141–148.
Hart, H. L. A. and Honoré, A. M., *Causation in the Law*, Oxford 1959.
Kanger, Stig, *New Foundations for Ethical Theory*, Stockholm 1957. Reprinted in Hilpinen (ed.), *Deontic Logic: Introductory and Systematic Readings*, Dordrecht, Holland, 1970, pp. 36–58.
Kanger, Stig, 'Law and Logic', *Theoria* **XVIII** (1972), 105–132.
Luce, R. D. and Raiffa, H., *Games and Decisions: Introduction and Critical Survey*, New York 1957.
Pörn, Ingmar, *The Logic of Power*, Oxford 1970.
Rescher, Nicholas, 'Aspects of Action', in *The Logic of Decision and Action* (ed. by N. Rescher), Pittsburgh 1966, pp. 215–219.
von Wright, G. H., *Norm and Action*, London 1963.
von Wright, G. H., 'The Logic of Action – a Sketch', in *The Logic of Decision and Action* (ed. by N. Rescher), 1966, pp. 121–136.
von Wright, G. H., *An Essay in Deontic Logic and the General Theory of Action*, Amsterdam 1968.
Åqvist, Lennart, *Modal Logic with Subjunctive Conditionals and Dispositional Predicates*, Uppsala 1971. Reprinted in *Journal of Philosophical Logic* 2 (1973), 1–76.
Åqvist, Lennart, *Performatives and Verifiability by the Use of Language*, Uppsala 1972.
Åqvist, Lennart, *Kausalitet och Culpaansvar inom en logiskt rekonstruerad skadeståndsrätt: en studie i analytisk rättsfilosofi (Causation and Liability for Negligence in a logically reconstructed Law of Torts: a study in analytic philosophy of law)*, Uppsala 1973.

INGMAR PÖRN

SOME BASIC CONCEPTS OF ACTION*

1.   This paper presents the elements of a causal theory of action. I use the term 'causal' here because the principal construction employed in my analysis of the role of agents as authors or originators pertains to agent causality. The construction that I have in mind is 'a brings it about that p'. It is not certain that this can be analysed in terms of anything simpler or more fundamental than itself. But it can be elaborated, it seems to me, in terms that make it possible to set out the principles of our reasoning with it. It is terms of this sort which i refer to when I speak of basic concepts of action.

2.   I will formulate the theory within a logically well-written language. We therefore let $L(Pr, Co, Mo)$ or L, for short, be the language determined by a set Pr of predicate letters, a set Co of individual constants, and a set Mo of symbols for modalities. L employs the symbols that determine it and, in addition, symbols drawn from the following standard logical categories: individual variables, quantifiers, connectives, and punctuation symbols.
   A well-formed formula or wff not including members of Mo is defined in the same way as in a first-order language. As for wffs including members of Mo, we assume that Op is a wff whenever $O \in Mo$ and p is a wff. A modal operator $O \in Mo$ may or may not be supplied with an index $a \in Co$; if it is, it will be referred to by O_a and said to denote a relative modality.
   A convenient way to articulate the modality denoted by an operator $O \in Mo$, is to give the truth condition of a wff of the kind Op. By means of this method I will characterise the relative modalities that are relevant for my purpose in this paper. So we proceed to the semantics of L.

3.   A model for L is defined as a triple $M = (W, U, V)$ where W, the domain of the model, is a nonempty set of points of reference or possible situations, U is a universe function which assigns to each member $u \in W$ a nonempty universe $U(u)$, and V is a valuation function which assigns a

S. Stenlund (ed.), Logical Theory and Semantic Analysis, 93–101. All Rights Reserved.
Copyright © 1974 by D. Reidel Publishing Company, Dordrecht-Holland.

denotation or extension to each one of the symbols that determine L. More precisely, setting $U(W) = \bigcup_{u \in W} U(u)$ and assuming that $U(W)$ is of the same size as Co or less, V is such that, for each $u \in W$, $V(P, u) \subseteq U(W)^k$, for each k-place predicate letter $P \in Pr$; $V(a, u) \in U(W)$, for each $a \in Co$, in such a way that the members of Co between them denote the members of $U(W)$; and, finally, for each $O \in Mo$, $V(O, u) \subseteq W^2$. We assume that $V(O, u) = V(O, u')$ and, hence, no ambiguity arises if we call $V(O, u)$ simply $V(O)$.

We next define inductively the relation that obtains between a point of reference u in (the domain of) a model M and any closed wff p when p holds in M at u, which in symbols is expressed by $M|=p$. The basis of the definition of the relation $|=$ is given by the clause

(C.Pr) $M|\overline{\overline{u}} P(a_1, a_2, ..., a_k)$ if and only if
$(V(a_1, u), V(a_2, u), ..., V(a_k, u)) \in V(P, u)$.

The inductive clauses cover the connectives in the standard fashion, 'local' quantification as illustrated by the clause

(C.∀) $M|\overline{\overline{u}} \forall xp$ if and only if $M|\overline{\overline{u}} S_a^x p|$ for each $a \in Co$ such that, for some v, $V(a, v) \in U(u)$,

and they cover modalities of the kind that interests us here by means of conditions of the type

(1C.O$_a$) $M|\overline{\overline{u}} O_a\, p$ if and only if $V(a, u) \in U(u)$ and $M|\overline{\overline{v}} p$ for each v such that $(u, v) \in V(O_a)$,

and, in one case, by means of a condition of the type

(2C.O$_a$) $M|\overline{\overline{u}} O_a\, p$ if and only if $V(a, u) \in U(u)$ and $M|\overline{\overline{v}} {\sim} p$ for each v such that $(u, v) \in V(O_a)$.

As is well-known, once the relation $|=$ has been defined, a number of other crucial semantic notions may be made available.

In particular, an open wff is said to hold in M at u if and only if its universal closure holds in M at u. With $|=$ now totally defined, the standard notion of logical consequence is easily formulated. By the logic of L we understand the class of all consequence relationships such that $p_1, p_2, ..., p_n |= q$ $(n \geqslant 0)$.

4. We assume that L contains wffs of the kind $D_a p$, translated as 'it is necessary for something which a does that p'. In Pörn (1970, pp. 9–11) the semantics of $D_a p$ was articulated under the reading 'a brings it about that p'. Following Kanger (1972, p. 108 and p. 111), I will now re-articulate it with the present reading in mind. At the same time I take up two other concepts of action.

Assume that we wish to say that a state of affairs is necessary for something which a does in a situation u. Evidently, the meaning intended here cannot be explicated by reference to u alone. It is well known that notions of necessity cannot be exhausted by considering only what is the case; consideration must also be given to what might be the case, or what is the case in certain hypothetical situations. In the case at hand we must consider all those hypothetical situations u' such that everything that a does in u is the case in u'. If v is such a situation, it may be said to be possible relative to what a does in u. We express this by writing $(u, v) \in V(D_a)$.

In these terms the nature of the necessity in question can now be specified. For if p is necessary for something that a does in u, then there cannot be a situation which is possible relative to what a does in u and which lacks the state of affairs that p. In other words, (1C.O_a) for $O = D$ is the truth condition for wffs of the kind $D_a p$. The precise import of this condition depends of course on the properties of $V(D_a)$. A natural minimal assumption is that the relation is reflexive in W.

We next let $V(A_a)$ be a subrelation of $V(D_a)$ such that $(u, v) \in V(A_a)$ if and only if everything that a supports in u is the case in v. As we do not wish to say that everything supported by a in u comes about in u, we cannot make the subrelation reflexive. But, allowing a certain amount of idealization, we shall assume that everything which a supports is realisable. We therefore require, minimally, that the subrelation be serial in W. If in (1C.O_a) we now set $O = A$, we get a condition which we may identify as the truth condition of wffs of the kind $A_a p$, read as 'p is necessary for the realisation (success) of something that a supports'.

Our third notion concerns counter-action conditionality and turns up in wffs of the kind $D'_a p$. We read these as 'but for a's action it would not be the case that p'. In their truth condition we consider all those situations in which everything that a does in u is absent. That is, for the truth of $D'_a p$ at u we require all hypothetical situations u' such that the opposite of everything that a does in u is the case in u'.[1] If v is such a situation, we write $(u, v) \in V(D'_a)$ and, setting $O = D'$ in (2C.O$_a$), the desired truth condition is obtained. We further define this condition by requiring the relation $V(D'_a)$ to be, at least, irreflexive and serial.

5.   In terms of the three modalities now available others may be defined. We first introduce the following convenient rewrites of the duals of $D_a p$ and $D'_a p$:

(Df1) $C_a p = {\sim} D_a {\sim} p$
(Df2) $C'_a p = {\sim} D'_a {\sim} p$

The first says that it is compatible with everything which a does that p, the second that without a's action it might not be the case that p.

It is a plain truth that if a brings it about that p, then p is necessary for something that a does. To maintain the converse, as I did in Pörn (1970, 1971), has its disadvantages. The ascription of agent causality to a normally suggests either that without a's action it would not be the case that p or, without a's action, it might not be the case that p. Of these counter-action conditional sentences, the former is stronger than the latter, since $(D'_a p \rightarrow C'_a p)$ belongs to the logic of L. Intuitively, the stronger sentence is not always an element of 'a brings it about that p'. This does seem to be true of the weaker sentence, however. So we shall take it that if a brings it about that p, then p is necessary for something that a does and but for a's action it might not be that p, and, accepting also the converse, we therefore introduce the definition

(Df3) $E_a p = (D_a p \ \& \ C'_a p)$

for the agent-causal construction 'a brings it about that (effects, causes it to be the case that) p'.[2] And, in analogy with (Df3), we introduce

(Df4) $F_a p = (A_a p \ \& \ C'_a p)$

for the weaker 'a supports that p', intended to cover, e.g., cases of interpersonal influence in which the question of whether the influence is effective is left open, or cases concerning the support which the action of an agent participating in a group lends to the action of this group. Finally, we make available the following rewrites:

(Df5) $Np = \forall x (D_x p \ \& \ D'_x {\sim} p)$
(Df6) $Mp = \exists x (C_x p \lor C'_x {\sim} p)$

Np is read as 'it is unavoidable (inevitable) that p' and Mp as 'it is possible that p' or 'it is not unavoidable that $\sim p$'. The latter is appropriate in view of the fact that $|=(Mp \leftrightarrow \sim N \sim p)$. N and M, as per (Df5) and (Df6), obey in fact (at least) the logical laws for necessity and possibility in Feys's system T.

6. There is a distinction to be made between agent-causal predicates and act predicates and, accordingly, between agent-causal relations and act relations. In this section the class of agent-causal predicates will be defined. To this end we call a wff which exhibits n $(n \geqslant 0)$ free occurrences of individual variables an n-place predicate or a predicate of degree n. For example, 'x kills y', 'x loves x', and 'x sends y to John' are 2-place predicates.

If p is a 0-place predicate, a is a constant, and $E_a p$ is true, then $E_a p$ is a 0-place agent-causal predicate. That is clear enough, so we have here a sufficient condition (for a special case). Is it necessary? To say so would give us, it seems to me, an unduly strong criterion; all we need to ascertain, for classifying $E_a p$ as a 0-place agent-causal predicate, is that $E_a p$ can be true, not that it actually is true of or applies to the agent a. If this is correct, the truth of $ME_a p$ will do. The generalisation of this idea is obvious. We have:

(C.ag)   Let p be a wff, a a constant, and $y_1, y_2, ..., y_n$ $(n \geqslant 0)$ the free occurrences of individual variables in p.
(i) If $M \exists y_1 \exists y_2 ... \exists y_n E_a p$ is true, then $E_a p$ is an n-place agent-causal predicate.
(ii) If $M \exists x \exists y_1 \exists y_2 ... \exists y_n E_x p$ is true, then $E_x p$ is an $(n+1)$-place agent-causal predicate.

The range of (C.ag), however, does not cover the class of agent-causal predicates. For example, (C.ag) determines 'x brings it about that y is dead' as an agent-causal predicate, but not 'x kills y', though, of course, any adequate definition of the class of agent-causal predicates ought to do so. In order to be able to define exhaustively the class of agent-causal predicates, we must therefore somehow supplement (C.ag). And it is not hard to see what is needed here. The reason why 'x kills y', under one interpretation, is an agent-causal predicate is that, under this interpretation, it is equivalent to 'x brings it about that y is dead', which is an agent-causal predicate. In other words, a notion of equivalence is required.

As regards this, we note that it is not the case that $\models((p\leftrightarrow q)\rightarrow(E_a p\leftrightarrow E_a q))$. To use material equivalence would therefore give rise to trouble. For instance, we could not then make 'a brings it about that b kills c' and 'a brings it about that b brings it about that c is dead' interchangeable. On the other hand, it is true that $\models(E_a p\leftrightarrow E_a q)$ if $\models(p\leftrightarrow q)$.[3] But $\models(p\leftrightarrow q)$ is too strong as a general requirement; we cannot by this route get the interchangeability just mentioned, since the material equivalence of 'b kills c' and 'b brings it about that c is dead' is not logically true, only analytically true. There is an intermediate position, however. This is the one suggested by the fact that $\models(N(p\leftrightarrow q)\rightarrow(E_a p\leftrightarrow E_a q))$. More elaborately, I suggest that we use the notion of an unavoidable (material) equivalence of predicates and that we understand this in the following way:

(C.eq) Let $p(x_1, x_2, ..., x_n)$ be an n-place predicate in k variables and $q(x_1, x_2, ..., x_m)$ an m-place predicate in the same variables $(m, n \geqslant 0; k \leqslant m, n)$. Then the predicates are equivalent if and only if $N(\forall x_1 \forall x_2 ... \forall x_k(p(x_1, x_2, ..., x_n)\leftrightarrow q(x_1, x_2, ..., x_m)))$ is true.

If we now stipulate, as I suggested above, that a predicate, which is equivalent in the sense of (C.eq) to an agent-causal predicate, is itself an agent-causal predicate, then we have in fact provided an inductive definition of the class of agent-causal predicates. The definition may be restated as follows:

(Df7) (i) A predicate of the form $E_a p$ is an n-place agent-causal predicate if it satisfies condition (i) of (C.ag).
(ii) A predicate of the form $E_x p$ is an $(n+1)$-place agent-causal predicate if it satisfies condition (ii) of (C.ag).
(iii) A predicate which is equivalent as per (C.eq) to an agent-causal predicate is itself an agent-causal predicate.
(iv) A predicate is an agent-causal predicate if and only if it is required to be so by applications of (i)–(iii).

By means of (Df7) we pick out agent-causal predicates from the total class of predicates of L. In so doing we pair predicates with each other and, in particular, we pair predicates that are agent-causal predicates in virtue of (iii) with agent-causal predicates of the form $E_a p$ or $E_x p$ and, hence, with predicates p of degree n. Familiar pairings of this sort are, for example, 'x kills y' with 'y is dead', 'x moves y' with 'y is in motion', 'x is cooking y' with 'y is cooking', and 'x shows y to z' with 'y is seen by z'.

7. We are now in a position to define the class of act predicates of L.

(Df8)   Let p be an n-place predicate; let $x_1, x_2, ..., x_n$ ($n \geqslant 0$) be the free occurrences of individual variables in p and $a_1, a_2, ..., a_m$ the occurrences of constants in p; and let the equivalence of predicates be understood as in (C.eq). Then p is an n-place act predicate if and only if
(i) p is equivalent to $E_{a_i} p$ for some $i = 1, 2, ..., m$ and $E_{a_i} p$ is an n-place agent-causal predicate; or
(ii) p is equivalent to $E_{x_i} p$ for some $i = 1, 2, ..., n$ and $E_{x_i} p$ is an $(n+1)$-place agent-causal predicate; or
(iii) p is equivalent to q for some act predicate q.[4]

In view of (i), 'John is growing old' is a 0-place act predicate if it is equivalent to 'John brings it about that John is growing old' and this is an agent-causal predicate. Similarly, 'John kisses Jane' is a 0-place act predicate if it is equivalent to 'John brings it about that John kisses Jane' and this is an agent-causal predicate, or equivalent to 'Jane brings it about that John kisses Jane' and this is an agent-causal predicate. In view of (ii), 'x is coughing' is a 1-place act predicate if it is equivalent to 'x brings it about that x is coughing' and this is an agent-causal predicate. In view of (i) and (ii) 'x is coughing and John kisses x' is a 2-place act predicate if it is equivalent to 'John brings it about that (x is coughing and John kisses x)' and this is an agent-causal predicate, or equivalent to 'x brings it about that (x is coughing and John kisses x)' and this is an agent-causal predicate. And in view of (iii), 'x influences y to vote Labour' is an act predicate if it is equivalent to 'x influences y to bring it about that y votes Labour' and this is an act predicate. And so on. Clearly, authorship as per (Df8) is self-involving agency. But agency, as per (Df7), is not necessarily authorship.

One more illustration. A predicate of the form $F_a p$ is an act predicate if it is equivalent to the corresponding predicate of the form $E_a F_a p$. If p in an act predicate $F_a p$ expresses a's authorship, the predicate says that a attempts to act in a certain way. We note that, on this analysis, acting does not entail attempting to act, although bringing about a state of affairs does entail supporting this state of affairs.

The relation expressed by an n-place act predicate is an n-place act relation. The elements of this relation, i.e. the n-tuples that satisfy it, are act individuals or individual acts. The relation itself may be termed an act category (type) or a generic act.[5] A generic act may be conceived of as a property of moments in time or, perhaps more appropriately, as a property of intervals. For instance, the generic act of helping is then the property of any interval t such that x helps y during t. Under this articulation of generic acts it is natural to call the individual elements act instances.

8.   It is not possible, within the limits of this essay, to discuss in full the important applications of the theory of action outlined above. For example, I cannot take up the notion of an intentional act because this would raise complex issues concerning the relation between belief and action. I therefore conclude by indicating in brief the usefulness of the suggested theory in one area.

Consider the following rule for a modal operator O:

(R.conseq) If $p_1, p_2, ..., p_n |= q$,   then $Op_1, Op_2, ..., Op_n |= Oq \, (n \geqslant 0)$.

It may be shown that the rule holds for D_a, A_a, and N. It fails for D'_a, E_a, and F_a, however. In particular, it is not the case that $E_a p |= E_a (p \vee q)$. Now, let it be that L contains an operator *Shall*, which, as is customary in standard normative logic, is made subject to (R.conseq). Then, because of the failure of the rule for E_a, *ShallE$_a$p* does not yield *ShallE$_a$* $(p \vee q)$. So if we take 'Post the letter' to be of the form *ShallE$_a$p* and 'Post the letter or burn it' of the form *ShallE$_a$* $(p \vee q)$, the oddity of the so-called Ross's Paradox may be explained simply as a fallacious inference.

Or assume, in much the same vein, the presence in L of an operator *Ought*. And consider the argument advanced in Chisholm (1963) against the use of *Ought* $(\sim p \rightarrow q)$ for the expression of contrary-to-duty imperatives, namely that the formula is a logical consequence of *Oughtp* in standard deontic logic. It seems reasonable to think that *Ought* operates on act descriptions, at least in the context of contrary-to-duty imperatives. $(\sim p \to q)$ should accordingly be understood as equivalent to $E_a(\sim p \to q)$, for some suitable choice of a, and p as equivalent to $E_a p$. Since the former is not a logical consequence of the latter, it will not be the case that $Ought E_a p \mid= Ought E_a(\sim p \to q)$, even if (R.conseq) is assumed to hold for *Ought*. Thus, the criticism in Chisholm (1963) of the standard development of deontic logic need not be as destructive as many logicians have taken it to be.

University of Birmingham

NOTES

* I am indebted to my colleague Mr. A. J. I. Jones for his comments on an earlier version of this paper.
[1] Cf. the treatment of *Dò* in Kanger (1972, p. 121).
[2] Intuitions and purposes vary. In Chellas (1969, Ch. III, Sect. 4) there is a definition of '*a* sees to it that *p*' which, like the one given in Pörn (1970) and readopted for certain purposes in Pörn (1971), makes the construction equivalent to the present $D_a p$. A definition similar to (Df3) may be found in Needham (1971, p. 154). Essentially the same idea is suggested in Hilpinen (1973, §VI). Kanger (1972, p. 108) gives a definition which, when translated into L, would require $C'_a p$ in (Df3) to be replaced by $D'_a p$.
[3] Hence $E_a p$ is intensional with respect to p, in the sense of Carnap (1956, Ch. I, Sect. 11).
[4] Cf. Kanger (1972, p. 123) on the characterization problem for acting.
[5] Cf. von Wright (1951, p. 2) and von Wright (1963, p. 36).

BIBLIOGRAPHY

Carnap, R., *Meaning and Necessity*, Chicago 1956.
Chellas, B. F., *The Logical Form of Imperatives*, Standford 1969.
Chisholm, R. M., 'Contrary-to-Duty Imperatives and Deontic Logic', *Analysis* **24** (1963), 33–36.
Hilpinen, R., 'On the Semantics of Personal Directives', *Ajatus* **35** (1973).
Kanger, S., 'Law and Logic', *Theoria* **38** (1972), 105–132.
Needham, P. L., *A Semantic Approach to Causal Logic*, M. A. thesis deposited in the Birmingham University Library, 1971.
Pörn, I., *The Logic of Power*, Oxford 1970.
Pörn, I., *Elements of Social Analysis*, Uppsala 1971.
von Wright, G. H., 'Deontic Logic', *Mind* **60** (1951), 1–15.
von Wright, G. H., *Norm and Action*, London 1963.

KAREL DE BOUVÈRE

SOME REMARKS CONCERNING
LOGICAL AND ONTOLOGICAL THEORIES

The present paper consists of two parts. The first part describes some pertinent features of the metatheory of theories, most of which is contained, explicitly or implicitly, in the work of A. Tarski.[1] The second part is an experiment in shifting from the logical to the ontological order by searching for physical models of the same metatheory.[2] The experiment ends up with classical and medieval physics and metaphysics throwing some light on the theories under consideration and the patterns followed by the human mind in conceiving them.

The considerations in this paper start with *formal languages*. For the purpose in mind we can confine ourselves to first-order languages with identity containing no other non-logical constants than countably many of finitary rank. If we speak of a language $\mathscr{L}$ we refer to a language of this kind. For a given language $\mathscr{L}$ we can define formulas and sentences of finite length in the usual way. By $S(\mathscr{L})$, or where confusion is excluded simply S, we shall understand the set of all sentences of $\mathscr{L}$. If $A \subseteq S$, then by $\mathrm{Cn}(A)$ we shall understand the closure of A under logical deduction with respect to S:

$$\mathrm{Cn}(A) = \{s : s \in S \ \& \ \exists s_1 \ldots s_n \, (s_1, \ldots, s_n \in A \ \& \ s_1, \ldots, s_n \vdash s)\}.$$

If $A \subseteq S(\mathscr{L})$ and A contains exactly the logical axioms of $\mathscr{L}$ and the identity axioms of $\mathscr{L}$, then we shall call $\mathrm{Cn}(A)$ the *smallest $\mathscr{L}$-theory*, denoted by $L(\mathscr{L})$, where confusion is excluded by L. If $L(\mathscr{L}) \subseteq T \subseteq S(\mathscr{L})$ and $T = \mathrm{Cn}(T)$, then T is called an *$\mathscr{L}$-theory*, or a *theory of $\mathscr{L}$*, or, where confusion is excluded, simply a *theory*. If T is an $\mathscr{L}$-theory and $T \subset S(\mathscr{L})$ (proper subset), then T is a *consistent* theory. If T is an $\mathscr{L}$-theory and for every $s \in S(\mathscr{L})$ either $s \in T$ or $\bar{s} \in T$ but not both ($\bar{s}$ being the negation of s), then T is a *complete* theory. Clearly, $L(\mathscr{L})$ is a subset (*subtheory*) of every $\mathscr{L}$-theory, or, every $\mathscr{L}$-theory is an extension of $L(\mathscr{L})$ containing the same non-logical constants as $L(\mathscr{L})$.

Given a language $\mathscr{L}$ and an $\mathscr{L}$-theory T we can consider $\mathbf{T}(T)$, or

S. Stenlund (ed.), Logical Theory and Semantic Analysis, 103–112. All Rights Reserved.
Copyright © 1974 by D. Reidel Publishing Company, Dordrecht-Holland.

simply $\mathbf{T}$, which is the class of all $\mathscr{L}$-theories which are extensions of T:

$$\mathbf{T} = \{X : T \subseteq X \subseteq S(\mathscr{L}) \ \& \ X = \mathrm{Cn}(X)\}.$$

This way, for every given $\mathscr{L}$-theory T there is a corresponding algebra $\langle \mathbf{T}, \cap, \cup, \dot{-}, T, S \rangle$, where for all $X, Y \in \mathbf{T}$:

$X \cap Y = X \cap Y$, (intersection);

$X \cup Y = \mathrm{Cn}(X \cup Y)$, (logical union);

$\dot{-} X = \underset{s \in X}{\bigcap} (T \cup \{\bar{s}\})$, (pseudo-complementation);

here $\cap$, $\cup$ and $\bigcap$ are the familiar set-theoretical operations, T and S are zero-element and unit-element respectively. Like a Boolean algebra this algebra can be enriched with infinite operations for intersection and (logical) union, but for our purpose the finite operations are sufficient. On the other hand, one difference with the analogous algebras of sets becomes clear immediately. Notice that the definition of pseudo-complement implies that for $X \in \mathbf{T}$, theories X and $\dot{-} X$ are disjoint modulo T, i.e., $X \cap (\dot{-} X) = T$ (assume there is a sentence $t \in S$ such that $t \notin T$, $t \in X$ and $t \in (\dot{-} X)$, then for every $s \in X$, $t \in T \cup \{\bar{s}\}$, and hence $t \in T \cup \{\bar{t}\}$ or $T \vdash \bar{t} \to t$ or $T \vdash t$ or $t \in T$ contrary to the assumption). It follows that, if $X \neq T$ and X is consistent, $\dot{-} X$ is consistent also. Now, let $X \neq T$ and let X be consistent but not complete (which is a familiar situation), then there is a sentence $s \in S$ such that $s \notin X$, $\bar{s} \notin X$; however at least one of s, $\bar{s}$ does not belong to $\dot{-} X$, since $\dot{-} X$ is consistent. Hence it happens to be possible that there are sentences of S which belong neither to a theory nor to the pseudo-complement of that same theory.

Tarski[3] noticed already that the algebra associated with a theory, let us call it a theory algebra, is an algebra of the same kind as Heyting's intuitionistic sentential calculus[4], a class of algebras nowadays often called Brouwer algebras (or Brouwerian algebras). In Brouwer algebras, as in Boolean algebras, the binary operations are idempotent, commutative and associative and obey the absorption laws and distributive laws; moreover, the zero-element and unit-element are minimum and maximum element, respectively. But unlike complementation in Boolean algebras, the unary operation in Brouwer algebras does not obey the additive complementation law. For a theory algebra $\langle \mathbf{T}, \cap, \cup, \dot{-}, T, S \rangle$ this means that for $X \in \mathbf{T}$ not necessarily $X \cup (\dot{-} X) = S$ and all consequences thereof.

The following summary of some pertinent facts may clarify the matter:

(i) $\dot- T = S$ and $\dot- S = T$. Clearly, just for the record,
       $T \cup (-T) = S$ and $S \cup (-S) = S$ and $\dot- T \neq T$ whenever $T \neq S$;

(ii)   for $X \in \mathbf{T}$ and $T \subset X \subset S$,

    (a) $X \cup (\dot- X) = S$ if, and only if, X contains a sentence, say t, such
             that $X = T \cup \{t\}$ (in which case $\dot- X = T \cup \{\bar{t}\}$);

    (b)   in all cases where $X \cup (\dot- X) \neq S$ we have $\dot- X = T$ except in
             the case where there is a sentence, say t, $t \in S$, such that
             $X \subset T \cup \{t\} \subset S$, (in which case $\dot- X$ contains a sentence, say
             u, $u \in S$, $u \notin T$, such that $\dot- X = T \cup \{u\}$).

As an example of our intentions we wish to consider a very simple
theory T (of a language $\mathscr{L}$). We shall say that T^* is a *complete extension*
of T if, and only if, $T^* \in \mathbf{T}(T)$ and T^* is complete. We shall say that T^* is
a *finite extension* of T if, and only if, $T^* \in \mathbf{T}(T)$ and T^* contains a sentence
t such that $T^* = T \cup \{t\}$. We shall say that theory T is *virtually complete*[5]
if, and only if, T is consistent and all complete extensions of T are finite
extensions. It can be proved easily[6] that a virtually complete theory has
only a finite number of complete extensions and conversely, if a theory
is consistent and has only a finite number of complete extensions, then it
is virtually complete (Tarski[7]). It follows that the theory algebra of a
theory T is Boolean (i.e., $X \cup (\dot- X) = S$ for every $X \in \mathbf{T}$) if, and only if, T
is virtually complete. The less obvious part of the latter statement amounts
to the fact that not only the complete extensions of a virtually complete
theory T are finite extensions of T, but all incomplete extensions of T as
well. Assume there is an incomplete extension X of T which does not
contain a sentence u such that $X = T \cup \{u\}$. Then $T \subset X \subset S$ and there is a
sentence $s_1 \in X$, $s_1 \notin T$ and $\bar{s}_1 \notin T$. Consider $T_1 = T \cup \{s_1\}$ and $T_1' = T \cup \{\bar{s}_1\}$,
both consistent extensions of T and $T_1 \subset X$. Then there is a sentence
$s_2 \in X$, $s_2 \notin T$, and $\bar{s}_2 \notin T_1$. Consider $T_2 = T_1 \cup \{s_2\}$ and $T_2' = T_1 \cup \{\bar{s}_2\}$, both
consistent extensions of T_1 and hence of T and $T_2 \subset X$. Then there is a
sentence $s_3 \in X, \ldots$ and so on, ad infinitum. Considering the theories
$T_1', T_2', \ldots$ we notice that they are all consistent but pairwise incompatible,
which implies that there are infinitely many complete extensions of T
(by the wellknown theorem of Lindenbaum) contrary to the fact that T
is virtually complete. Now, for our simple example we choose a virtually
complete theory T, thus having a finite number of complete extensions

of the form $T \cup \{t\}$ and an associated theory algebra which is Boolean. To fix our thoughts we assume T to have precisely *four* complete extensions viz. $T_1 = T \cup \{t_1\}$, $T_2 = T \cup \{t_2\}$, $T_3 = T\{t_3\}$ and $T_4 = T \cup \{t_4\}$. We can make the following tree:

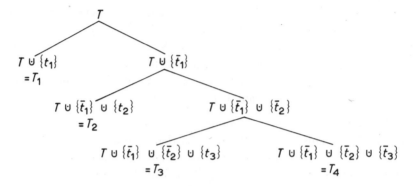

The last theory appearing in the tree, $T \cup \{\bar{t}_1\} \cup \{\bar{t}_2\} \cup \{\bar{t}_3\}$ must be $= T_4$ otherwise there would be more than four complete extensions of T, (which implies that t_4 is equivalent in T with $\bar{t}_1$ & $\bar{t}_2$ & $\bar{t}_3$). It can be seen readily that the tree can be re-written as follows:

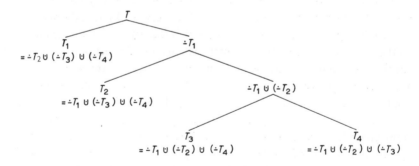

From this tree it may be clear why it seems appropriate to call $\div T_1$, $\div T_2$, $\div T_3$ and $\div T_4$ the *atoms* of the proper extensions of T, quite in accordance with the terminology used in Boolean algebra; all theories which are proper extensions of T are *sums* (short for logical unions) of these four atoms. Notice that these extensions are exhibited in the following tetraeder:

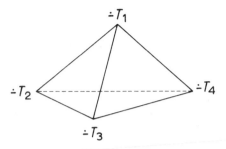

The vertices constitute the four one-term sums. The edges constitute the six two-term sums: $\dot{-}\,T_1 \cup (\dot{-}\,T_2)$, $\dot{-}\,T_1 \cup (\dot{-}\,T_3)$, etc. The faces constitute the four three-term sums: $\dot{-}\,T_1 \cup (\dot{-}\,T_2) \cup (\dot{-}\,T_3)$, $\dot{-}\,T_1 \cup (\dot{-}\,T_2) \cup (\dot{-}\,T_4)$, etc. The whole tetraeder constitutes the one four-term sum $\dot{-}\,T_1 \cup (\dot{-}\,T_2) \cup \cup (\dot{-}\,T_3) \cup (\dot{-}\,T_4)$, which is the inconsistent extension. Calling T itself the zero-term sum we could identify T with the empty figure (or with the center of mass, or such), this way obtaining all extensions of T nicely arranged by binomial coefficients. The less obvious matter that there are no other extensions of T than the 16 exhibited in the tetraeder can be seen readily in two steps:

(i)   if $s \in S$ is compatible with T without being valid in T, and neither s nor $\bar{s}$ is equivalent in T with one of t_1, t_2, t_3, t_4, then s belongs to exactly two different complete extensions of T;

(ii)   if $s \in S$ is as described in (i) and $s \in T_1$ and $s \in T_2$, then not only $T \cup \{s\} \subseteq T_1 \cap T_2$ but also $T_1 \cap T_2 \subseteq T \cup \{s\}$ and hence $T \cup \{s\} = T_1 \cap T_2 = \dot{-}\,T_3 \cup \dot{-}\,T_4$.

Notice that we have 4 completing sentences t_1, t_2, t_3, t_4, 4 atoms $\dot{-}\,T_1$, $\dot{-}\,T_2$, $\dot{-}\,T_3$, $\dot{-}\,T_4$ and $1+4+6+4+1=2^4$ extensions of T. If we had another number of complete extensions we would have a simplex of another dimension without basic differences. In general, n completing sentences $t_1, \ldots, t_n$ generate 2^n extensions exhibited in an $(n-1)$-dimensional simplex.

Leaving alone the connection between theory algebras and simplicial theory we next wish to have some better understanding of the non-Boolean case. Comparing theory algebras with algebras of sets it is obvious that for $X \in T$ such that $X \cup (\dot{-}\,X) \subset S$ the defect is not due to the notion of logical union (which is an extension of the set-theoretical union) but to the concept of pseudo-complementation. The question might arise whether a better definition of some kind of complementation is possible. The answer is negative. The explanation involves two properties, each others duals; referring to $X \cap (\dot- X) = T$ as *disjointness* and to $X \cup (\dot- X) = S$ as *exhaustiveness* we claim that every definition preserving one of the two ruins the other (except, as expounded above, in the case that T is a virtually complete theory where the given definition of pseudo-complementation preserves both properties).

It is sufficient to consider the preservation of disjointness, i.e., we assume that a unary operation, say $\sim$, is defined on $\mathbf{T}$ in such a way that for $X \in \mathbf{T}$, $X \cap (\sim X) = T$, while $\dot- X$ is still the pseudo-complement as defined above. The following remark is pertinent:

If X, $Y \in \mathbf{T}$ and $X \cap Y = T$, then $Y \subseteq \dot- X$.

(For the proof of this remark: let $t \in Y$, then for every $s \in X$ we have $s \vee t \in X \cap Y = T$ or $T \vdash s \vee t$ or $t \in T \cup \{\bar{s}\}$; hence for every $t \in Y$ we have $t \in \dot- X$, or $Y \subseteq \dot- X$).

Another way of stating the pertinent remark is the following: if $X \in \mathbf{T}$, then $\dot- X$ is the largest member of $\mathbf{T}$ which is disjoint $(\mathrm{mod}\, T)$ from X. Applying the remark to our case we obtain:

$$\sim X \subseteq \dot- X \text{ and it is obvious that } X \cup (\sim X) \subset S \text{ whenever}$$
$$X \cup (\dot- X) \subset S.$$

As an example one could define $\sim$ trivially as follows: $\sim T = S$, $\sim S = T$ and $\sim X = T$ for every $X \in \mathbf{T}$ such that $T \subset X \subset S$. In this example it is obvious that disjointness is preserved and exhaustiveness is not. The trivial example has been mentioned mainly because of its counterpart, where $\sim$ is defined by: $\sim T = S$, $\sim S = T$ and $\sim X = S$ for every $X \in \mathbf{T}$ such that $T \subset X \subset S$; here exhaustiveness is preserved and disjointness is not. The situation of the latter example emerges if one tries to imitate set-theoretical complementation. Let $X \in \mathbf{T}$ and consider $Y = X - T$ (or $\{s : s \in X \,\&\, s \notin T\}$, as usual); consider further $-X = S - Y$, i.e., the set-theoretical complement $(\mathrm{mod}\, T)$ of X. Obviously, $-T = S$ and $-S = T$ as in the above examples. However, for $X \in \mathbf{T}$ such that $T \subset X \subset S$ we obtain $-X$ just as a set of sentences, not as a theory. The least one can do to correct this failure is defining $\mathrm{Cn}(-X)$ as the logical complement. But since $-X$ is an inconsistent set of sentences, $Cn(-X)=S$ and one arrives at the situation of the second example.

Having some familiarity with the metatheory of deductive theories one might ask the question whether this theory allows for some interpretation outside the realm of logic. In other words, leaving alone the fact that a theory algebra is a model of a certain kind of Brouwer algebra in the sense of model theory, one might ask whether the algebra associated with a certain T of a certain $\mathscr{L}$ can be seen as a mathematical model of some extraneous theory, e.g. of a physical or sociological theory, in the sense modern sciences use mathematics as a descriptive tool. Purposedly trying to connect logic and ontology, whatever the outcome, we try an interpretation of the metatheory under consideration as a description of the qualitative physics of some world (even if it turns out to be a rather strange world).

In such an interpretation, instead of the language $\mathscr{L}$ one could speak of the *universe* $\mathscr{L}$, instead of formulas of $\mathscr{L}$ one could speak of *particles* of $\mathscr{L}$, some prime and some compound and such that even prime particles may consist of smaller units as some prime formulas do. Thus one describes a world in which the smallest units have relevance only in so far as they serve to form particles (according to certain rules). It is not unusual to call certain particles *elementary particles*, although they are not so elementary after all; pursuing this way of speech one could speak of S as the set of elementary particles of $\mathscr{L}$ rather than the set of sentences of $\mathscr{L}$. This way one selects (according to certain rules) certain particles, the elementary ones, which are intended to serve as building stones for higher levels, whereas the other particles have relevance only in so far as they form elementary particles. Instead of the negation $\bar{s}$ of s one could speak of the *antiparticle* $\bar{s}$ of s, instead of the implication $s \rightarrow t$ one could speak of the *induction* $s \rightarrow t$. Instead of reading $s_1, \ldots, s_n \vdash s$ as 's follows from $s_1, \ldots, s_n$' one could read 's is *concurrent* with $s_1, \ldots, s_n$' meaning that s occurs whenever $s_1, \ldots, s_n$ occur (or, s is available whenever $s_1, \ldots, s_n$ are simultaneously available); thus $\vdash s$ could be read as 's occurs (is available) in all situations'. If A is a set of elementary particles, then by $Cn(A)$ one could understand the closure of A under concurrence, or again

$$Cn(A) = \{s : s \in S \ \& \ \exists s_1 \ldots s_n (s_1, \ldots, s_n \in A \ \& \ s_1, \ldots, s_n \vdash s)\}.$$

Instead of the equivalence $s \leftrightarrow t$ one could speak of the *identity* $s \leftrightarrow t$, not so strange if one thinks of a Lindenbaum algebra. At this point phantasy has to take a barrier; unlike the situation in the ordinary physics of neutrons, protons, electrons and such, it is useless to use more than one particle of the same kind to construct the same higher-level unit; if $s \in A \subseteq S$, then $A = A \cup \{s\} = A \cup \{s\} \cup \{s\} = \ldots$. On the other hand, the same particle may be used to construct different higher-level units; if $A \subseteq S$, $B \subseteq S$ and $A \neq B$, then $s \in A$ and $s \in B$ is quite possible. Instead of the smallest $\mathscr{L}$-theory one could speak of the *smallest $\mathscr{L}$-element*, denoted by $L(\mathscr{L})$ or L (defined in a certain way), and instead of an $\mathscr{L}$-theory one could speak of an *$\mathscr{L}$-element* or *element* (*element* here to be understood as analogous to a chemical element and not in the set-theoretical sense of member). Instead of a consistent theory T (i.e. $T \subset S$) one could speak of an *orderly* element, instead of the inconsistent theory S one could speak of the *disorderly* element S (or the chaos S). Instead of complete, virtually complete and incomplete theories one could speak of *complete*, *virtually complete* and *incomplete* elements. If X is an element and $T \subseteq X$, then X is an *extension* of T, eventually a *proper extension* of T in the usual sense. One could speak of the *element algebra* of T, viz. $\langle \mathbf{T}, \cap, \cup, \dot{-}, T, S \rangle$, where $\mathbf{T}$ is the class of all $\mathscr{L}$-elements which are extensions of T. Since $X \cap Y$ is the set-theoretical intersection one might continue to speak of intersection, whereas instead of the logical union $X \cup Y$ one could speak of the *fusion $X \cup Y$* and instead of the speudo-complement $\dot{-} X$ the *pseudo-antielement* $\dot{-} X$. Notice that $L(\mathscr{L})$ is a subset (*subelement*) of every $\mathscr{L}$-element. Obviously $L(\mathscr{L})$ contains exactly those elementary particles of $\mathscr{L}$ which occur in all situations.

It could be remarked that the abnormal interpretation sketched above is not more than a suggestive game of re-naming things and that there is nothing around to justify it. Especially a world of particles without mass and extension, as suggested by $A \cup \{s\} \cup \{s\} = A \cup \{s\}$, seems rather alien. But in the historic endeavors of mankind to understand its world, serious efforts have been made which more or less seem to fit in with the description suggested.

Once again a simple example may clarify the matter. Out of many possible universes a certain universe $\mathscr{L}$ is chosen. Out of many possible $\mathscr{L}$-elements a certain element T is chosen. If again T is called *zero-element* then notice the double meaning of this word; alternatively one could call T a *basis element* or *basis*. Let T be virtually complete and let T have precisely four complete extensions, viz. T_1, T_2, T_3 and T_4. The associated algebra is Boolean and hence one could call the pseudo-antielements just antielements; fusion of an element and its antielement causes chaos. The atoms of the Boolean algebra are $\div T_1$, $\div T_2$, $\div T_3$ and $\div T_4$ which in this context could be called the *urelements* (of the universe $\mathscr{L}$ with basis T); one could call them earth, water, air and fire. All elements of the universe $\mathscr{L}$ with basis T are fusions of the four urelements, except T itself which is the intersection of the urelements, that what makes them elements.

Thus the classical world built from earth, water, air and fire could be seen, at least in a general sense, as one of the possible worlds of the suggested interpretation of the metatheory of theories. In order to obtain a wider context one could supplement classical physics by its corresponding metaphysics, as was customary in the old days anyway, in this case by the Aristotelian theory of matter and form called hylemorphism. For a given $\mathscr{L}$ and T one could call the basis T the *prime matter* and the orderly proper extensions of T *substances*. Thus every substance is made up of prime matter and something that turns prime matter into a substance, called the *substantial form*. If $t \notin T$ and $T \cup \{t\}$ is orderly, then the substance $T \cup \{t\}$ is the fusion of the prime matter T and the substantial form induced by adding t. There is room for a type-like gradation in the way substances are built; the simpler ones may be fused into more complex ones, e.g., if X and Y are substances such that $X \nsubseteq Y$, $Y \nsubseteq X$ and $X \cup Y \subset S$, then $X \cup Y$ is a substance also.

There is, however, a most important point in the theory of hylemorphism which is not covered by the metatheory of theories, viz. the way there is room for individual substances of the same species differentiated by their matter (the so-called quantification of matter). On the contrary, every member of $\mathbf{T}(T)$ constitutes its own species and there are no more individuals of the same species. But even this negative result stimulates to re-thinking some aspects of classical theories. As a first example, the anomaly mentioned might indicate that in hylemorphism the quantification of matter is a third fundamental principle independent of the principles of matter and form, as indeed is stressed by the medieval version. As a second example, there is one medieval application where entities are considered which constitute their own species, viz. the theory of angels; in the light of the analogy developed this lack of individualization could be attributed to the absence of quantification rather than to the principles of prime matter and substantial form.

The University of Santa Clara

NOTES

[1] Cf. [4], [5] and [6]. Numbers between brackets refer to the Bibliography.
[2] Cf. [2].
[3] Cf. [6], p. 352 of the English translation.
[4] Cf. [3].
[5] Cf. [1], p. 12.
[6] Cf. [1], pp. 12, 13.
[7] Cf. [6], p. 371 of the English translation.

BIBLIOGRAPHY

[1] de Bouvère, K. L., 'Remarks on Classification of Theories by their Complete Extensions', *Notre Dame Journal of Formal Logic* **X** (1969), 1–17.
[2] de Bouvère, K. L., 'Logical and Ontological Models' (Abstract), *The Journal of Symbolic Logic* **34** (1969), 544.
[3] Heyting, A., 'Die formalen Regeln der intuitionistischen Logik', *Sitzungsberichte der Preussischen Akad. der Wiss., Phys.-math. Klasse* (1930), 42–56.
[4] Tarski, A., 'Ueber einige fundamentale Begriffe der Metamathematik', *Comptes Rendus des séances de la Société des Sciences et des Lettres de Varsovie* **23** (1930), iii, 22ff. (English translation in *Logic, Semantics, Metamathematics*, papers from 1923 to 1938 by Alfred Tarski, translated by J. H. Woodger, Oxford, 1956, 30ff.)
[5] Tarski, A., 'Fundamentale Begriffe der Methodologie der deduktiven Wissenschaften I', *Monatshefte fuer Mathematik und Physik* **37** (1930), 361ff. (English translation as in [4], 60ff.)
[6] Tarski, A., 'Grundzuege des Systemenkalkuels', Erster Teil, *Fundamenta Mathematicae* **25** (1935), 503–526, Zweiter Teil, *Fundamenta Mathematicae* **26** (1936), 283–301. (English translation of both parts as in [4], 342ff.)

IAN HACKING

COMBINED EVIDENCE*

How is the force of different items of evidence to be combined? Modern probability theory and statistics can tell you how to combine evidence of the same kind, but there has been little study of how different kinds of evidence interact. Yet it is an old problem. Jacques Bernoulli (1654–1705) has a good discussion of it.[1] One of his solutions was rejected by J.-H. Lambert (1728–1777)[2]. Their disagreement provides a good test case for any theory about the combination of evidence.

It is convenient to follow much of Bernoulli's own presentation. He thought that probability is degree of certainty. He called probabilities 'subjective', but he was not a subjectivist like B. de Finetti or L. J. Savage. He would have agreed with students of 'objective' inductive probability who maintain that probability is relative to the evidence available to the subject who is assessing the probability.

Bernoulli thinks of inconclusive evidence as being at least conceptually divisible into parts, so that we may say, for example, that a parts of the evidence support h, and b parts support $\sim h$. He assumes that the several parts are of equal force. It is not at all necessary to follow Bernoulli here but I shall do so, in order to make it easier for the reader to compare Bernoulli's own presentation with what follows.

In most modern inductive logic it is assumed that the evidence, relative to which probability is determined, is itself known for certain. Bernoulli observed that there are really three different cases of partial support of hypothesis h by evidence e. First, e may be known for certain. In that case e is 'necessary' relative to our state of knowledge, and indicates h 'contingently' – i.e., even if e is true, it is not thereby certain that h is true. But there are also cases in which the very evidence is not itself known with certainty. It is called 'contingent', and it may indicate h 'necessarily' (i.e., entail h) or only contingently. When e is contingent it may be better to speak not so much of evidence for h but, as Bernoulli does, of an argument for h. Thus there are three kinds of arguments that may be adduced: those that have necessary premisses and indicate h contingently, and

S. Stenlund (ed.), Logical Theory and Semantic Analysis, 113–123. All Rights Reserved.
Copyright © 1974 by D. Reidel Publishing Company, Dordrecht-Holland.

those that have contingent premises and indicate h either necessarily or contingently. For simplicity I shall largely ignore this trio of distinctions, but any realistic application of what follows would have to employ it.

Bernoulli has another distinction that cuts across this first one. He divides evidence or arguments into 'pure' and 'mixed'. Mixed evidence is of the sort that divides in two, with a parts indicating h while b parts indicate $\sim h$. Pure evidence, in contrast, divides in three, with x parts indicating h, z parts indicating $\sim h$, and y parts being simply neutral. Again, for simplicity, I shall disregard z, and chiefly consider examples exhaustively dividing into x parts that indicate h and y that are neutral. Moreover I shall only consider evidence that is necessary, and which indicates h (or $\sim h$) contingently.

Pure evidence is rather unfamiliar, and requires an example. On a Monday early this April I was on the overnight train from Washington D.C. to Chicago. I had left sun, azaleas and cherry blossom and was firmly entrenched in thoughts of early summer. In the parlor car I found a scrap of paper saying, 'Blizzard due in Chicago tomorrow'. The dateline bore the legend, 'Monday...' but the actual date was torn off. There were two possibilities. Either this was the morning paper, or it was of earlier date. In the latter case, the scrap tells me nothing whatever about tomorrow's weather. It is quite neutral. But in the former case, I may well trust such a categorical forecast of sudden cold. If I were certain the scrap of paper were up-to-date, I could be virtually certain of a cold arrival in Chicago.

The parlor car is kept tidy and my fellow passengers do not seem the sort of people who litter with old scraps of paper. The scrap is clean and fresh. I assess the probability, that the scrap is from today's paper, as 90%. Hence I become 90% certain of a cold arrival. Note that I am not thereby 10% certain of a temperate arrival, because the evidence stated so far is simply neutral about the 10% of remaining cases.

A modern probabilist would say that I must be at least 90% certain of a cold arrival, and at most 10% certain of a temperate one. He would say that 0.9 and 0.1 are upper and lower bounds, and my actual degree of certainty in cold must be $0.9 + q$, while my actual degree of certainty in the opposite is $0.1 - q$. That is because he is committed to the additivity of probability. Bernoulli is not so committed, and even, in one instance, thinks that the probabilities of both h and of $\sim h$ could be well over $\frac{1}{2}$.[3] This is because he takes seriously the notion of probability being part of certainty. The argument based on finding the scrap of paper makes me 90% certain of a cold arrival, and makes me no more certain than that; it does not make me 10% certain of a temperate arrival. In the thesis cited in note 1, Glen Shafer develops this non-additive notion of probability, but I shall not need it here. I myself tend to agree with Bernoulli and Shafer, and deny that probabilities have to be additive, but you may say, if you prefer, that the evidence of the scrap of paper confers some probability of $0.9 + q$ on a cold arrival, and $0.1 - q$ on a temperate arrival.

Our problem is not additivity but combination. Suppose that as well as pure evidence I have mixed evidence. I know enough about continental weather patterns to say that the probability of severe cold on an April morning in Chicago is only 20%. Let C denote the proposition that it will be cold on arrival. On this data the probability of C is only 0.2, while the probability of $\sim C$ is 0.8. This sort of 'statistical' argument is mixed, for I think that 20% of the time it is cold, early in April, and 80% of the time it is not.

Now I possess two arguments. One is pure, conferring 90% probability on C, and one is mixed, conferring 20% probability on C. How are they to be combined? It is natural to say that the two arguments are independent. At any rate they are causally independent: the scrap of paper does not produce Chicago weather, nor does future weather affect the distribution of paper in parlor cars. The two arguments may not be epistemologically independent – a matter I shall postpone until later.

We should first see how to combine several mixed arguments or several pure arguments. Every school of probability gives the same answer for combining mixed evidence. Bernoulli himself reasoned as follows. Let there be two items of mixed evidence, e and e', dividing into a and a' parts that entail h, and b and b' parts that entail $\sim h$. Each of the a parts is incompatible with each of the b' parts, so in the orthogonal cross-product ee' we have $aa' + bb'$ consistent parts, of which aa' parts entail h. In general, with $e_1, e_2, ..., e_k$ mixed items, each dividing into a_i parts entailing h and a_i' parts entailing $\sim h$, the probability of h on all k arguments is,

$$\frac{\prod a_i}{\prod a_i + \prod b_i}.$$

Every theory of probability gives this answer. Few theories of probability even recognize pure evidence so we shall not be able to find such agreement for the second kind of case. Bernoulli's own way to combine independent pure evidence seems plausible. Suppose e and e' divide into x and x' parts entailing h and into y and y' parts that are neutral. Then e gives us $x/(x+y)$ parts of certainty, with a remaining region of $y/(x+y)$ for agnosticism. The second item, e', cannot increase our certainty in the first region, and so can affect only the $y/(x+y)$ parts where we are ignorant. To these it brings $x'/(x'+y')$ parts of certainty. Using this method of reasoning for k items of independent pure evidence, we obtain as the resultant probability of h,

$$1 - \frac{\prod y_i}{\prod (x_i + y_i)}.$$

Since this is a resultant of pure evidence, it does not follow, in Bernoulli's opinion, that the probability of $\sim h$ has to be $\prod y_i / \prod (x_i + y_i)$.

We now reach the perplexing combination of pure and mixed evidence. First resolve all items of pure evidence into a single fraction, with x parts entailing h and y parts neutral. Resolve all the mixed evidence into a single fraction with a parts entailing h and b parts entailing $\sim h$. Bernoulli reasons as in the pure case. The mixed evidence pertains only to those y parts of the pure argument that left us agnostic, and we obtain for the probability of h,

$$1 - \frac{by}{(a+b)(x+y)}.$$

In this case, however, the remaining $by/(a+b)(x+y)$ is the probability of $\sim h$, regardless of any general qualms about additivity.

Lambert thought that Bernoulli is wrong. Suppose that a tends to 0. That is, the statistical data show that h is the sort of thing that virtually never happens. On Bernoulli's formula, the probability of $\sim h$ will then tend to $y/(x+y)$. Thus, even if the probability of a cold arrival in April were, on meteorological grounds, virtually zero, the Bernoulli formula would give us a probability of cold of 90%. That, said Lambert, is absurd.

In arguing for a solution different from Bernoulli's, and more in accord with Lambert's intuitions, Shafer employs the following illustrative diagrams. We use an orthogonal representation, with $(+)$ denoting those parts of the evidence that entail h, $(-)$ those that entail $\sim h$, and $(?)$ those that are neutral. The square denotes 'the whole of certainty'; one item of evidence is marked on the horizontal axis, and one on the vertical.

Mixed case:

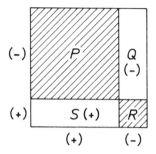

The shaded areas denote inconsistent parts that must be eliminated before evaluating the combined evidence. Bernoulli's formula for the mixed case consists in saying that the probability of h, on two mixed items of evidence, is as the ratio of S to $S+Q$.

Pure case:

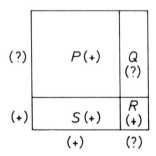

The previous solution for the pure case makes the probability of h to be $(P+R+S)/(P+Q+R+S)$. These two cases are beyond dispute. But here are two possible solutions for the pure-mixed case:

Both agree that S, the intersection of the pure and the mixed cases favorable to h, should be positive. Bernoulli says that the pure evidence makes us certain of $P+S$, leaving the mixed evidence to work in $Q+R$, resulting in Q being against h and R for h. This gives us $(P+S+R)/(P+Q+R+S)$ for h. However, a Lambert may object that in the mixed

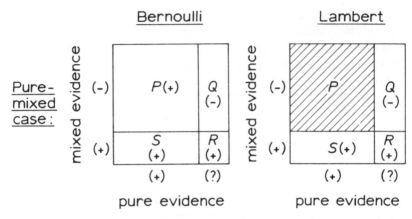

case above we crossed out cases that are incompatible. So we should cross out P because the negative part of the mixed evidence is incompatible with the positive part of the pure evidence. On that analysis, the probability of h is $(R+S)/(Q+R+S)$. This has the consequence that Lambert desired, that as the positive mixed evidence goes to 0, $R+S$ becomes small and the probability of h itself tends to 0.

The Lambert-style solution, which is advocated by Shafer, does not, however, end the matter. Herschel L. Gottlieb has sent me a vindication of Bernoulli's position, using another assumption which, in some cases, will seem appropriate.[4] We have already assumed that we are dealing with infallible newspaper reports. Let us suppose further that the chance of cold, within a given period of time t, is constant, and that we may take for granted that any newspaper we find is issued during t. Naturally t might be the whole year (though that would be unrealistic for Chicago) or we might be speculating about a cold April, and t be the past couple of centuries. Then consider the following four propositions.

F: Exactly one piece of paper including a weather report has been found in the parlor car, and this scrap must be from period t.

C: We are now in t, and it will be cold tomorrow in Chicago.

N: The newspaper mentioned in F predicts cold on the day following publication.

T: It is today's newspaper.

In our example, $P(C)=0.2$, and $P(T/F)=0.9$.

The assumed infallibility of newspapers instructs us that,

$$P(C/NTF) = P(N/CTF) = 1.$$
$$P(N/\sim CTF) = P(\sim C/NTF) = 0.$$

As for independence, out-of-date newspapers do not affect the weather, nor does cold tomorrow affect out-of-date newspapers:

$$P(C/NTF) = P(C), \ P(N/\sim TCF) = P(N/F).$$

The weather is independent of whether a newspaper is timely:

$$P(C/\sim TNF) = P(C/\sim T \sim NF) = P(C/F) = P(C).$$
$$P(T/CF) = P(T/\sim CF).$$

Finally, out-of-date newspapers, being infallible and drawn from the period of time t, predict cold as frequently as cold does in fact occur in the period t. We shall mark this assertion with an asterisk for future reference:

$$(*) \qquad P(N/\sim TCF) = P(N/\sim T \sim CF) = P(C).$$

By the probability calculus,

$$P(N/CF) = P(N/CTF) \, P(T/CF) + P(N/\sim TCF) \, P(\sim T/CF),$$

and similarly for $P(N/\sim CF)$. Hence,

$$P(N/CF) = P(T/F) + P(C) \, P(\sim T/F)$$

and

$$P(N/\sim CF) = P(N/F) \, P(\sim T/F).$$

By Bayes' theorem,

$$\frac{P(C/NF)}{P(\sim C/NF)} = \frac{P(C/F) \, P(N/CF)}{P(\sim C/F) \, P(N/CF)}.$$

So $P(C/NF) = 1 - P(\sim C) \, P(\sim T/F)$. This is exactly Bernoulli's solution. Evidently the assumption marked $(*)$ is essential to this derivation. It asserts, roughly speaking, that the probability, that an infallible weather forecast taken at random from t predicts cold, is the same as the probability, that a day in t taken at random should be cold. That seems unexceptionable. What then of Lambert's objection?

To answer we must break down the proposition F, on which we conditioned throughout the above argument. F has two parts, namely:

H: Exactly one piece of newspaper including a weather forecast has been found in the parlor car.

G: This scrap of newspaper is from the period of time t.

The period t is the period in which the probability of cold, $P(C)$, got from weather records, is constant, and which includes the day of the journey to Chicago. Now suppose I am travelling in August, so that $P(C)$ is almost 0. Then if the scrap of newspaper predicts cold, it *must* be out-of-date. Thus the prediction given in the newspaper may itself be evidence against the newspaper being timely. The paper can testify against itself.

When I am travelling in August, and am secure in my knowledge of weather patterns, I devalue my pure argument based on finding a scrap of newspaper predicting cold: the paper must be out-of-date. But I could reason differently. I am pretty ignorant of weather in the Tierra del Fuego. If I were asked I might, out of a subjectivist blue, come up with a rate at which to bet on the occurrence of snow there in September. I will, let us say, give odds of 7:1. But a randomly found recent-looking scrap of Argentinian newspaper will completely outweigh that initial betting rate. It will do so, not merely by combining with it, but by making me realize that my odds of 7:1 were themselves quite unfounded. It is not just that I combine my beliefs about weather patterns with my beliefs about newspaper scraps. I revise my beliefs about the weather in the light of the newspaper.

'Tierra del Fuego' and 'August in Chicago' are two extreme examples. In the latter, no amount of newspaper scraps will make me expect cold, for I know too much about the weather. In the former, I am so ignorant of Southern Argentina that my hunch based on weather lore at once collapses before the newspaper. Let us have yet one more extreme, which I shall call the case of complete information.

Imagine that I have a fair coin. A trial on this coin consists in tossing it, fairly, k successive times. On a particular occasion I wish to know the outcome, but cannot actually observe the outcome. I do, however, have access to a random recorder. 90% of the time, say, this recorder tells me the actual outcome of the trial of interest. The other 10% of the time, it gives me the actual outcome of some other trial, which it picks at random. In this case, all the assumptions of Gottlieb's argument are valid, and Bernoulli's method of combining evidence will be accepted. Thus, if the recorder tells me that the trial yielded nothing but heads, the probability of 'all heads' on the trial of interest will, *pace* Lambert, be assessed at barely over 90%. This is true no matter how large k may be, that is, no matter how high the initial improbability of 'all heads'.

In this case we have incorporated Gottlieb's assumption (∗), that the probability distribution of 'neutral' answers from the recorder is the same as that from the coin. Even if we delete this, and have no knowledge about what the recorder does in its 10% of neutral answers, we should still have over 90% of certainty, that the outcome of interest is all heads. I call these cases of perfect information, because we *know* the probability of a non-neutral record, and we *know* the probability distribution of the coin.

We began with a pure and a mixed argument for C. They were based, say, on data U and M respectively. We made an assessment of $P(C/U)$ and $P(C/M)$ and sought some way of combining these to give $P(C/MU)$. Bernoulli offered us one algorithm. Lambert found a counterexample, and this suggested another algorithm. My solution is different. I believe that Bernoulli gives the correct answer – regardless of assumption (∗) – in a case of complete information. That is, he is right when we are completely certain of our assessments of the probabilities. I contend that pure and mixed arguments may interact in two quite different ways. In the case of complete information, we simply combine pure and mixed arguments in the manner of Bernoulli. Otherwise, however, one of the two arguments to be combined may lead us to revise our very judgements of probability used in the other argument. Thus, in the Tierra del Fuego case, the newspaper convinces me that my hunch about weather is plain wrong. This is shown by the fact that, after getting the scrap of newspaper purportedly about tomorrow's weather, I revise not only my expectations about tomorrow's weather, but also about next year's weather at the same time of year. Likewise, in the case of August in Chicago, I revise my assessment of the probability that newspaper scraps are timely. Thus, if after finding my scrap of weather report I also find a different newspaper fragment about 'new U.S. bombing raids in Cambodia', I am no longer 90% confident that this (or any other fragment) is from today's paper.

Talk about reassessing probabilities will be anathema to the contemporary Bayesian, personalist, school of statistical inference. The Bayesian will restructure any 'reassessment' as follows. I have a big space of events, including snow in Chicago in August, bombings in Cambodia, and the like. In the end, I acquire a personal probability for the proposition, 'Bombing Cambodian civilians has started up again'. The data on which I base this are: I found a scrap of paper predicting cold. I found another scrap stating that new bombings have occurred. It is August, and I possess vaguer data about weather and about the regularity of cleaning up parlor cars and the tidiness of the current crop of travellers. By Bayesian multiplication I can work out this personal probability, and show that it will be much lower than the probability based on the following subset of the data: scrap of paper states that bombing has occurred, together with facts about the parlor car and tidiness. Very well: the Bayesian, as we know, can do anything. But this calculation is completely unrealistic and has, I think, almost nothing to do with the formation of rational belief. The rational man need have no truck with this welter of imaginary betting rates over otherwise quite disconnected spheres of interest. He simply changes his assessment of the probability that a scrap of newspaper, found in a parlour car, will be of recent date. Then he reasons on the basis of this new assessment.

I conclude, then, that Bernoulli did have a correct rule for combining pure and mixed evidence. It is applicable, however, only so long as the pure and mixed arguments are epistemologically independent. Each argument carries a probability. If an argument of one kind leads us to reassess the probability associated with an argument of the other kind, then we cannot blindly apply Bernoulli's algorithm to the old, unmodified probabilities. Lambert's seeming counterexample arises from an unwillingness to reassess probabilities. That is always a possibility, except in the case of perfect information. In that case, Bernoulli's algorithm is inviolate.

Cambridge, England

NOTES

* This work is a continuation of a course of lectures given in Uppsala in Easter, 1971, at the kind invitation of Stig Kanger. Most of the material given in those lectures is now in my book, *The Emergence of Probability*, Cambridge University Press, 1974.

[1] *Ars conjectandi*, Basel, 1713, Part IV. For bibliography and a survey of the whole of this work, see my paper, 'Jacques Bernoulli's *Art of Conjecturing*', *British Journal for the Philosophy of Science* **22** (1971) 209. The significance of Bernoulli's discussion of the combination of evidence was first pointed out to me by Glen Shafer, who discusses it, and presents his own theory, in his important PhD. dissertation, in preparation for the Department of Statistics, Princeton University, 1973.

[2] See, for example, I. Todhunter, *A History of the Mathematical Theory of Probability*, London, 1865 and New York, 1949, p. 71. Todhunter supports Lambert's objection, saying of Bernoulli that his 'formula is inaccurate'.

[3] *Ars conjectandi*, Pt. IV, Ch. iii, Sec. 7.

[4] In a letter from Chicago dated 16 April, 1973.

CLAES ÅBERG

SOLUTION TO A PROBLEM RAISED BY STIG KANGER AND A SET THEORETICAL STATEMENT EQUIVALENT TO THE AXIOM OF CHOICE

0. Let us say that a set is a *fragment of an ordinal* if it can be obtained from an ordinal by removing certain sets (which are necessarily ordinals) from the ordinal and/or from the members of the ordinal and/or from the members of the members of the ordinal etc. As an example

$$\{\{\{\{\ \}\}\}\}$$

is a fragment of an ordinal since it can be obtained in the manner indicated below:

$$\{\cancel{\{}\ \cancel{\}\cancel{\{}}\ \{\cancel{\{}\ \{\{\ \}\}\}\}$$

Professor Kanger has raised the following problem: Is it true that

*   *Every set is a fragment of an ordinal*

We prove the answer to be affirmative. Moreover we prove that the statement * when formalized as below in the language of set theory, is equivalent to the axiom of choice.

1. First we must straighten out the imprecision in the statement of the problem. We fix *ZF*, not including *AC*, as our set theory. * can be interpreted in two ways: the absolute sense and the relativized sense. In the absolute sense * says that every set in a model for *ZF* can be obtained from an ordinal of the model by removing elements (elements in the sense of the model), elements of elements etc. of the ordinal, where we do not require the removal to take place *in* the model in question but are free to use 'outside' means in the process. In the absolute sense * is not a statement which can be (formalized and) true or false *in* the model for *ZF* in question. It is rather a statement *about* the model, comparable in this respect to the statement that a model is pointwise definable. In the relativized interpretation of * on the other hand, we require that the process of cutting the ordinal in question down to the set in question can be performed *in* the given model. It is the relativized interpretation

we have in mind when speaking intuitively about the sets in the 'actual' set theoretical universe. It is obvious that ∗ in its relativized sense implies ∗ in the absolute sense (since it is a stronger condition that the process of cutting ordinals down takes place inside the model).

Our route will be as follows: We give a certain formalization $\forall x OF(x)$ of the relativized interpretation of ∗. We then prove $ZF + AC \vdash \forall x OF(x)$. By the last remark in the above paragraph this gives an affirmative answer to the initial question in both its interpretations. To prove that $ZF \vdash (AC \leftrightarrow \forall x OF(x))$ it only remains to prove $ZF \vdash (\forall x OF(x) \rightarrow AC)$. That proof together with a couple of remarks concludes this note.

2.   We start by defining a binary relation x is a fragment of y by induction on max$\{$rank x, rank $y\}$. Assume z is a fragment of u has been defined for all z, u, where max$\{$rank z, rank $u\} < \alpha$. Then if max$\{$rank x, rank $y\} = \alpha$ define x is a fragment of y to be true if and only if:

> $x \subseteq y$ or there is a one-one function f on the whole of x into y such that for all $z \in x$ holds z is a fragment of $f(z)$.

Since rank z, rank $f(z) < \alpha$ for all $z \in x$ this definition is admissible. The function f is introduced into the definition (rather than defining x is a fragment of y by the condition

$$(x \subseteq y) \vee \forall z \in x \exists v \in y \, (z \text{ is a fragment of } v))$$

to make sure (as is necessary) that all $z \in x$ can be produced simultaneously from different sets in y in the process of taking fragments.

We can now define $\forall x OF(x)$ as:

> For all x there is an ordinal α such that x is a fragment of α.

$\forall x OF(x)$ is (disregarding of course the fact that for readability we have not formalized the statement fully) a statement in the language of set theory and has a truth value in every model for this language.

THEOREM 1. $ZF + AC \vdash \forall x OF(x)$
Proof. We first give a simple

LEMMA. *Let* α, β *be ordinals. If* x *is a fragment of* β *and* $\beta \leqslant \alpha$ *then* x *is a fragment of* α.
Proof. Obvious since $\beta \subseteq \alpha$. (If $x \subseteq \beta$ then $x \subseteq \alpha$ so x is a fragment of α.

If x is a fragment of β by the function f then the same f shows that x is a fragment of α.)

We now prove that $OF(x)$ holds for all x by induction on rank x. Assume $OF(z)$ holds for all z with rank $z < \alpha$ and let rank $x = \alpha$. Then by assumption, for all $z \in x$ there is a β such that z is a fragment of β. We can define a function $g : x \to On$ by letting $g(z) =$ the least ordinal β such that z is a fragment of β. By the replacement axiom the ordinals $g(z)$ for $z \in x$ form a set. Let β_0 be the supremum of this set. Use AC to get an enumeration $(z_0, z_1, \ldots, z_\xi, \ldots)$ of x of order type $\bar{\bar{x}}$. Define $f : x \to \beta_0 + \bar{\bar{x}}$ by letting $f(z_\xi) = \beta_0 + \xi$. By the choice of β_0 and the lemma z_ξ is a fragment of $\beta_0 + \xi$ for all $z_\xi \in x$. The $\beta_0 + \xi$ are all different so f is a one-one function. By the definition of x *is a fragment of* y this shows that x is a fragment of the ordinal $\beta_0 + \bar{\bar{x}}$ so we have $OF(x)$ and the proof of Theorem 1 is completed.

THEOREM 2. $\forall x OF(x)$ *is equivalent to AC (relative to ZF).*

Proof. It only remains to show that $\forall x OF(x)$ implies AC. Let x be a set. We show that $\forall x OF(x)$ implies that x can be well-ordered. By $\forall x OF(x)$ x is a fragment of some ordinal α. Then either $x \subseteq \alpha$ and then x is automatically well-ordered. Or there is a one-one function $f : x \to \alpha$. Then we well-order x by defining, for all $z, v \in x$, $z < v$ if and only if $f(z) \in f(v)$.

Remark 1. In the proof of Theorem 1 the existence of an ordinal with the properties of β_0 plays a crucial role. It is the (relativized interpretation of $*$ and the) fact that the whole construction of fragments takes place inside the set theoretical universe which guarantees the existence of β_0. Otherwise *a priori* nothing would prevent the least ordinals of which the elements of x are fragments to occur cofinally in the class of ordinals.

Remark 2. In the proof that $ZF + AC \vdash \forall x OF(x)$ we used the axiom of regularity (since we assumed that every set has a rank). That this can not be avoided can be seen as follows: We observe that if x is a fragment of y and y is well-founded then x is also well-founded. Then since the ordinals are well-founded $\forall x OF(x)$ implies that every set is well-founded. So in fact $\forall x OF(x)$ is equivalent to the conjunction of AC and the axiom of regularity (with respect to ZF minus the axiom of regularity).

Univ. of Uppsala and Gothenburg

PER LINDSTRÖM

ON CHARACTERIZING ELEMENTARY LOGIC

This is an expository paper. My aim is to explain in a way accessible to the non-specialist a number of results that amount to characterizations of elementary logic (*EL*), i.e. first order predicate logic with identity. The characterizations that I have in mind can be described as follows: First I define the very general concept abstract logic (*AL*). Then I define an inclusion relation $\subseteq$ between *AL*s. Intuitively $L \subseteq L'$ means that everything that can be expressed in *L* can also be expressed in *L'* although perhaps in a different way. For example, in *EL* it can be said of a binary relation that it is transitive. Thus if $EL \subseteq L$, this can also be expressed in *L*. (I assume, of course, that *EL* is an *AL*.) *L* and *L'* are equivalent, $L \equiv L'$, if $L \subseteq L'$ and $L' \subseteq L$. The next step consists in choosing a number of properties $P_1, \ldots, P_n$ of *AL*s such that *EL* has $P_1, \ldots, P_n$. An example of an interesting property of this type is the following which may be called the Löwenheim property, since it means that the original Löwenheim theorem holds for *L*: If a sentence of *L* has a model, then it has a countable (finite or denumerable) model. Finally, a characterization of *EL* is a (true) statement of the form: If *L* is an *AL*, $EL \subseteq L$, and *L* has $P_1, \ldots, P_n$, then $L \equiv EL$. Since all reasonable *AL*s contain *EL*, this may also be expressed by saying that *EL* is the strongest *AL* having $P_1, \ldots, P_n$. Of course, one can also speak of characterizations of logics other than *EL* and there are, in fact, results of this type but they will not be discussed here. (See [1].) Most of the results presented here are proved in [6]. They were later rediscovered by Friedman [3]. Theorem 5 is proved in [7].

Let me point out once again that I have taken some trouble to make this paper readable to the non-specialist with some background in logic and set theory. Formal definitions and results are, in all cases where I considered this necessary, accompanied by informal, intuitive explanations. In the following I have also made a number of simplifying assumptions. Unless the contrary is explicitly stated, these will not lead to any essential loss of generality.

Before introducing the inevitable technicalities, let me give some ex-

S. Stenlund (ed.), Logical Theory and Semantic Analysis, 129–146. All Rights Reserved.
Copyright © 1974 by D. Reidel Publishing Company, Dordrecht-Holland.

amples of ALs all of which are proper extensions of EL. The reason why extensions of EL are considered at all is, of course, that there are mathematically and logically interesting conditions that cannot be expressed in EL. The simplest example is this: In EL we cannot say of a set, represented by a 1-place predicate, that it is finite. A natural way of removing this deficiency is to construct a new logic $L(Q_0)$ by adding to EL the quantifier Q_0, there are infinitely many.[1] Then $\neg Q_0 v P_v$ means that 'P is finite'. Of course, in $L(Q_0)$ it is possible to say many other things not expressible in EL as well. For example, we can say of a linear ordering that it is isomorphic to the natural numbers in order of magnitude. Another and perhaps less *ad hoc* way of constructing a logic in which it can be said of a set that it is finite is based on the observation that this can be expressed by an infinite disjunction of sentences of EL. Indeed, a set is finite if it has at most 1 or at most 2 or at most 3 or... members. Thus, for this, and many other, reasons it is natural to consider the logic $L_{\omega_1\omega}$ obtained from EL by allowing conjunctions and disjunctions of denumerable sets of formulas. ($L_{\varkappa\lambda}$ is the logic obtained from EL by allowing conjunctions and disjunctions of fewer than $\varkappa$ formulas and existential and universal quantification of sets (sequences) of fewer than λ variables. Thus $L_{\omega\omega}$ is EL.) Clearly, $L(Q_0) \subseteq L_{\omega_1\omega}$. On the other hand, $L_{\omega_1\omega}$ is not contained in $L(Q_0)$. A simple example of something that can be expressed in $L_{\omega_1\omega}$ but not in $L(Q_0)$ is that in $L_{\omega_1\omega}$ it can be said of an equivalence relation that it has finitely many equivalence classes. This cannot even be expressed by a, possibly infinite, set of sentences of $L(Q_0)$. There are other more interesting but unfortunately also more complicated examples of this. However, in $L_{\omega_1\omega}$ we still cannot say, for example, of a set that it is uncountable or of a linear ordering that it is a well-ordering. Thus we may contemplate adding the quantifier Q_1, there are uncountably many, or the quantifier W such that $WxyPxy$ means that 'P is a well-ordering' or passing to $L_{\omega_1\omega_1}$. Indeed, in the latter we can say that a linear ordering $<$ is a well-ordering, since this is true if and only if

$$\neg \exists v_0 v_1 v_2 \ldots (v_1 < v_0 \wedge v_2 < v_1 \wedge v_3 < v_2 \wedge \ldots)$$

is true. Thus $L(W) \subseteq L_{\omega_1\omega_1}$. Note also that $L(Q_1) \subseteq L_{\omega_1\omega_1}$, since $Q_1 v P v$ is equivalent to

$$\forall v_0 v_1 v_2 \ldots \exists v (Pv \wedge \neg v = v_0 \wedge \neg v = v_1 \wedge \ldots).$$

In none of the logics defined so far can it be said of two sets that the one has more members than the other. (This is supposed to include the case where one of the sets is or both are infinite.) Again the problem of constructing a logic in which this can be expressed can be solved in a trivial way, namely by introducing the quantifier M such that Mx, $y(Fx, Gy)$ simply means that 'there are more F's than G's'. In terms of M we can define the Chang or equi-cardinal quantifier C; $CvPv$ is equivalent to $\neg Mx, y(x=x, Py)$. Of course, it is also possible to add more than one quantifier to EL thus forming, for example, $L(Q_1, M)$. One can also add new quantifiers to, for example, $L_{\omega_1\omega}$. All the quantifiers mentioned here have familiar definitions in second order logic which, incidentally, is another example of an AL. These examples should give the reader an idea of the vast variety of possible ALs. However, they by no means exhaust the ALs that have been studied in the literature.

Intuitively speaking, an AL L is determined by two things namely its set of sentences and its truth relation. The latter is a relation between sentences of L and what these sentences are about namely structures. Thus it is reasonable to identify L with a pair $(S, |=)$, where $S=S_L$ is the set of *sentences* of L and $|= =|=_L$ is the *truth relation* of L. However, clearly not every pair $L=(S, |=)$ can be regarded as a logic. One condition that is absolutely fundamental is that

(i)   if a sentence φ of L is true in a structure $\mathfrak{A}$, $\mathfrak{A}|=\varphi$, and the structure $\mathfrak{B}$ is isomorphic to $\mathfrak{A}$, then $\mathfrak{B}|=\varphi$.

To complete the definition of the concept AL I need some preliminary definitions. First, a *non-logical constant* is either a predicate, a function constant, or an individual constant. I assume that each predicate and function constant has a fixed finite number of places. A *signature* (language) s is simply a set of non-logical constants. Next, a *structure* for (of signature) s is a pair $\mathfrak{A}=(A, f)$, where A, the domain of $\mathfrak{A}$, is a non-empty set, and f is an assignment of values over A to the members of s. Thus f is a function on s such that (i) if $P \in s$ is an n-place predicate, then $f(P)$ is an n-ary relation over A, i.e. a set of ordered n-tuples of members of A, (ii) if $F \in s$ is an n-place function constant, then $f(F)$ is an n-ary function on A with values in A, and (iii) if $c \in s$ is an individual constant, then $f(c)$ is a member of A. The following relation between structures will be needed later. Let $\mathfrak{A}=(A, f)$ and $\mathfrak{B}=(B, g)$ be structures for the same signature s. $\mathfrak{A}$ is a *substructure* of $\mathfrak{B}$, $\mathfrak{A}\subseteq\mathfrak{B}$, if $A\subseteq B$ and f is obtained from g by restricting every value of g to A. Thus if $P\in s$ is an n-place predicate, then $f(P)$ is the set of n-tuples of members of A which are in $g(P)$, $f(P)=g(P)\cap A^n$; if $F\in s$ is an n-place function constant, then the function $g(F)$ applied to an n-tuple of members of A yields a member of A and $f(F)$ is obtained from $g(F)$ by restricting the domain of $g(F)$ to A, $f(F)=g(F)\cap A^{n+1}$; finally, if $c\in s$ is an individual constant, then $f(c)=g(c)$.

Next, it must be specified what it means that a non-logical constant occurs in a sentence of L. Now, instead of complicating things by introducing one more new concept, viz. occurs in, it is preferable to restrict oneself to the case where the sentences of L are sequences of entities, abstract or concrete, and say that a nonlogical constant *occurs in* a sentence exactly when this is literally true. A sentence φ of L is a *sentence in s* if every non-logical constant occurring in φ is a member of s.

Three more defining conditions of the concept AL can now be formulated.

(ii)   Every sentence of L is a sentence in some finite signature.

(iii)   If $\mathfrak{A}$ is a structure for s, φ is a sentence of L, and $\mathfrak{A}\models\varphi$, then φ is a sentence in s.

(iv)   If $s\subseteq s'$, φ is a sentence of L in s, $\mathfrak{A}=(A,f)$ is a structure for s', and g is the restriction of f to s, then $\mathfrak{A}\models\varphi$ if and only if $(A,g)\models\varphi$.

(iii) means that in order that a sentence φ be true in a structure $\mathfrak{A}$ it is necessary that $\mathfrak{A}$ contains an interpretation of every non-logical constant occurring in φ; otherwise the truth valued of φ in $\mathfrak{A}$ is simply undetermined. (iv) means that whether or not a sentence φ is true in a structure depends solely on the values assigned by the structure to the non-logical constants that actually occur in φ and not on the values assigned to non-logical constants not occurring in φ. (ii) and (iv) together imply that the truth value of a sentence in a structure depends solely on the values assigned to a certain fixed finite number of non-logical constants. This is a real restriction. It appears, however, that nothing of much interest is excluded if we adopt (ii), at least not in the present context. Moreover, this restriction allows me to somewhat simplify the statement of some of the results below. But note that it follows that, strictly speaking, the logics $L_{\varkappa\lambda}((\varkappa, \lambda)\neq(\omega, \omega))$ are not ALs, since sentences of these logics may contain infinitely many non-logical constants. On the other hand, the fragments of these logics consisting of those sentences that contain only finitely many non-logical constants are, of course, ALs.

The following condition means, roughly speaking, that any individual constant (predicate, function constant) occurring in a sentence may be replaced by any other individual constant (predicate, function constant, with the same number of places) without changing the 'structure' of the sentence. Instead of formulating the appropriate abstract condition I shall, for simplicity, assume that the formulation just given is essentially correct. A more exact version is as follows.

(v)   Let φ be a sentence of L in s, $\mathfrak{A}$ a structure for s, and suppose P and P' are n-place predicates, $P \in s$ and $P' \notin s$. Let φ', s', $\mathfrak{A}'$ be obtained from φ, s, $\mathfrak{A}$ by replacing P by P'. Then φ' is a sentence of L in s' and $\mathfrak{A}|=\varphi$ if and only if $\mathfrak{A}'|=\varphi'$; and similarly for function constants and individual constants.

Finally, the following conditions, expressing that L is closed under negation and conjunction, will be needed.

(vi)   Let φ be any sentence of L. There is then a sentence ψ of L such that for every structure $\mathfrak{A}$, $\mathfrak{A}|=\psi$ if and only if not $\mathfrak{A}|=\varphi$.

(vii)   Let φ and ψ be any sentence of L. There is then a sentence θ of L such that for every structure $\mathfrak{A}$, $\mathfrak{A}|=\theta$ if and only if $\mathfrak{A}|=\varphi$ and $\mathfrak{A}|=\psi$.

The definition of the concept AL can now be stated. An *abstract logic* is a pair $L=(S, |=)$ such that conditions (i)–(vii) are satisfied. This definition is very nearly the same as and perhaps somewhat more natural than the definition of a generalized first order logic in [6]. Taking the conjunction of (i) and (iii)–(v) we obtain Barwise's concept of a system of logics [1]. This is clearly a natural concept. Since, however, the conditions (vi) and (vii) are required in all the results stated here, it is, for the purposes of this paper, better to include them in the definition. In addition, it would be natural to assume that L is closed under (universal and existential) quantification and possibly also closed under 'substitution of formulas for predicates' (a strengthening of (v)). These conditions will, however, not be needed. But note that together they imply the condition (+) below.

Clearly, EL and all the other logics mentioned in the introduction, with the above reservation in connection with the $L_{\varkappa\lambda}$, are ALs. In the following I will assume that L and L' are ALs. Moreover, I will assume that if φ is a common sentence of L and L', then φ has the same 'meaning' in L and L', i.e., $\mathfrak{A}|=_L \varphi$ if and only if $\mathfrak{A}|=_{L'} \varphi$ for all $\mathfrak{A}$. The subscript 'L' in '$|=_L$' can then be dropped. If $\mathfrak{A}|=\varphi$, I will say that $\mathfrak{A}$ is a *model* of φ.

The inclusion relation $\subseteq$ between ALs mentioned in the introduction can now be defined. $L\subseteq L'$ if and only if for every sentence φ of L, there is a sentence ψ of L' such that φ and ψ have the same models. L and L' are *equivalent*, $L\equiv L'$, if $L\subseteq L'$ and $L'\subseteq L$. A relation closely related to $\subseteq$ which is sometimes useful is the following. $L\subseteq_{inf}L'$ if and only if for every sentence φ of L, there is a sentence ψ of L' such that φ and ψ have the same infinite models. $L\equiv_{inf}L'$ if $L\subseteq_{inf}L'$ and $L'\subseteq_{inf}L$.

Before I introduce the first four of the properties that will be used to characterize EL let me state some well-known and fundamental results about EL. In the last two of these I speak about the cardinality of a structure by which I mean that of its domain. A structure is a model of a set of sentences if it is a model of each one of its members.

COMPACTNESS THEOREM. *Let T be any set of sentences of EL. If every finite subset of T has a model, then T has a model.*

THE DOWNWARD LÖWENHEIM-SKOLEM-TARSKI (LST) THEOREM. *Let T be any set of sentences of EL of cardinality $\varkappa$ and let λ and μ be infinite cardinals such that $\varkappa\leqslant\lambda<\mu$. If T has a model of cardinality μ, then T has a model of cardinality λ.*

THE UPWARD LST THEOREM. *Let T be any set of sentences of EL of cardinality $\varkappa$ and let λ and μ be infinite cardinals such that $\varkappa\leqslant\lambda<\mu$. If T has a model of cardinality λ, then T has a model of cardinality μ.*

The upward LST theorem, although superficially quite similar to the downward LST theorem, is actually a result of a quite different nature. Together these two theorems imply that if T is a set of sentences of EL and T has an infinite model of cardinality not smaller than that of T, then it has models of all infinite cardinalities not smaller than that of T. Actually somewhat more is true: The same conclusion follows from the weaker assumption that T has an infinite model.[2]

In view of these results it might seem quite natural to consider the corresponding properties of *AL*s. However, it turns out that in most situations certain weaker properties will suffice. The appropriate properties are the following.

Compactness. L is *compact* if for every set *T* of sentences of *L*, if every finite subset of *T* has a model, then *T* has a model.

Countable compactness. L is *countably compact* if for every countable set *T* of sentences of *L*, if every finite subset of *T* has a model, then so does *T*.

The Löwenheim property. L has the *Löwenheim property* if for every sentence φ of *L*, if φ has an infinite model, then φ has a denumerable model.

The Tarski property. L has the *Tarski property* if for every sentence φ of *L*, if φ has an infinite model, then φ has an uncountable model.

A basic result from which many characterizations of *EL* follow as easy corollaries is the following

THEOREM 1. *Suppose* $EL \subseteq L$, $L \nsubseteq_{inf} EL$, *and L has the Löwenheim property. Then there is a sentence* φ *of L containing a* 1-*place predicate P and such that (i) if* $\mathfrak{A} = (A, f)$ *is a model of* φ, *then* $\mathfrak{A}$ *is infinite and* $f(P)$ *is finite and (ii) for every natural number n, there is a denumerable model* $\mathfrak{A}$ *of* φ *such that* $f(P)$ *has exactly n members.*[3]

An immediate consequence of Theorem 1 is the following:

COROLLARY 1. *Suppose* $EL \subseteq L$, $L \nsubseteq EL$, *and L has the Löwenheim property. Then there is a sentence* φ *of L containing a* 1-*place predicate P and such that (i) if* $\mathfrak{A} = (A, f)$ *is a model of* φ, *then* $f(P)$ *is finite and (ii) for every natural number n, there is a model* $\mathfrak{A}$ *of* φ *such that* $f(P)$ *has exactly n members.*

From Corollary 1 we obtain at once the following characterization of *EL*.

THEOREM 2. *Suppose* $EL \subseteq L$, *L has the Löwenheim property, and L is countably compact. Then* $L \equiv EL$.

Indeed, suppose $EL \subseteq L$, *L* has the Löwenheim property, and $L \nsubseteq EL$. Let φ be a sentence of *L* as described in Corollary 1. Since $EL \subseteq L$, there is for every *n*, a sentence ψ_n of *L* saying that '*P* has at least *n* members'.

Consider the set $T=\{\varphi\}\cup\{\psi_n: n=0, 1, 2, ...\}$. By Corollary 1 (ii), every finite subset of T has a model and, by Corollary 1 (i), T itself has no model. Thus L is not countably compact.

Theorem 2 cannot be improved by omitting the assumption that L has the Löwenheim property or the assumption that L is countably compact. $L(Q_1)$ is an example of a countably compact proper extension of EL, as has been shown by Fuhrken [4]. In fact, Shelah [9] has shown that there are (fully) compact proper extensions of EL. An example of a proper extension of EL which has the Löwenheim property is $L(Q_0)$. Indeed, the full downward LST theorem holds for $L_{\omega_1\omega}$. But note that in the proof of Theorem 2 compactness was applied only to a very simple set. Clearly, in any reasonable AL, this set is recursive. This is an instance of the following general observation: For any AL L that has been defined so far, if L is not countably compact, then there is a recursive counterexample to compactness for L.

To obtain a characterization of EL using the Löwenheim and Tarski properties I have to introduce the following artificial looking condition $(+)$. I will state this condition only for the case that the signature involved consists of predicates only. The extension to the general case which is, of course, necessary if complete generality is to be achieved is not difficult but somewhat messy. Thus let s be a set of predicates. For each $P\in s$, let P^+ be a new predicate which is $n+1$-place if P is n-place. Let s^+ be the set of the P^+. Next, let $\mathfrak{A}=(A, f)$ be a structure for s^+. For each $a\in A$, I define the structure $\mathfrak{A}^{(a)}=(A^{(a)}, f^{(a)})$ of signature s as follows: $A^{(a)}=A$ and $f^{(a)}(P)=\{\langle a_1,...,a_n\rangle:\langle a, a_1,...,a_n\rangle\in f(P^+)\}$ for $P\in s$.

$(+)$ For every sentence φ of L in s, there is a sentence φ^+ of L in s^+ such that for every structure $\mathfrak{A}$ of signature s^+, $\mathfrak{A}|=\varphi^+$ if and only if $\mathfrak{A}^{(a)}|=\varphi$ for all $a\in A$.

Intuitively φ^+ is obtained from φ in the following way. Let v be an individual variable not in φ. Replace $Pv_1...v_n$ by $P^+vv_1...v_n$. Let the result be $\varphi'(v)$. Then φ^+ is $\forall v\varphi'(v)$. Of course, this description may not be applicable to sentences of a given L even though L satisfies $(+)$. Since, however, it is applicable to the ALs mentioned above, it is clear that all these ALs do satisfy $(+)$.

Combining Theorem 1 and $(+)$ we get

COROLLARY 2. *Suppose* $EL \subseteq L$, $L \not\equiv_{\inf} EL$, L *has the Löwenheim property, and* L *satisfies* $(+)$. *Then there is a sentence* φ *of* L *containing a 2-place predicate* P *and such that (i)* φ *has a model and (ii) if* $\mathfrak{A} = (A, f)$ *is a model of* φ, *then* $\langle A, f(P) \rangle$ *is isomorphic to* $\langle \omega, \leqslant \rangle$, *where* $\leqslant$ *is the usual ordering of the set* ω *of natural numbers.*

Obviously, the sentence φ in Corollary 2 cannot have an uncountable model. Thus we obtain at once

THEOREM 3. *Suppose* $EL \subseteq L$, L *has the Löwenheim and Tarski properties, and* L *satisfies* $(+)$. *Then* $L \equiv_{\inf} EL$.

The AL $L(Q_0)$ shows that the assumption that L has the Tarski property cannot be omitted from Theorem 3. An example of a proper extension of EL which has the Tarski property and satisfies $(+)$ is $L(C)$. Indeed, any sentence of $L(C)$ which has a denumerable model has a model of each infinite cardinality [4]. Finally, to see that $(+)$ cannot be dispensed with either, consider the 'least' AL L_0 obtained from EL by adding the sentence $Q_0 v P v$. L_0 is a proper extension of EL and has the Löwenheim and Tarski properties. In fact, it satisfies the full downward and upward LST theorems. Thus L_0 is much weaker than $L(Q_0)$.

$\forall x \neg Q_0 y P' x y$ is an example of a sentence of $L(Q_0)$ which is not (equivalent to) a sentence of L_0.

Two structures $\mathfrak{A}$ and $\mathfrak{B}$ are *equivalent* in L, $\mathfrak{A} \equiv_L \mathfrak{B}$, if every sentence of L which is true in $\mathfrak{A}$ is true in $\mathfrak{B}$ and conversely. Combining Theorem 3 with the downward and upward LST theorems for EL we obtain the following characterization of EL.

THEOREM 4. *Suppose* $EL \subseteq L$, L *satisfies* $(+)$, *and for all* $\mathfrak{A}$, $\mathfrak{B}$, *if* $\mathfrak{A} \equiv_{EL} \mathfrak{B}$, *then* $\mathfrak{A} \equiv_L \mathfrak{B}$. *Then* $L \equiv_{\inf} EL$.

To prove this, suppose L is as assumed. Then L has the Löwenheim property. Indeed, let φ be any sentence of L and let $\mathfrak{A}$ be an uncountable model of φ. We can assume that the signature of $\mathfrak{A}$ is finite. By the downward LST theorem applied to the set T of sentences of EL true in $\mathfrak{A}$, there is a denumerable structure $\mathfrak{B}$ such that $\mathfrak{B} \equiv_{EL} \mathfrak{A}$. By hypothesis, this implies that $\mathfrak{B} \equiv_L \mathfrak{A}$. But then $\mathfrak{B} \models \varphi$ and so φ has a denumerable model. Similarly, it can easily be shown, using the upward LST theorem, that L has the Tarski property. Theorem 4 now follows from Theorem 3.

Strictly speaking, Theorems 3 and 4 are not characterizations of EL

since their conclusion is not $L \equiv EL$. (The same applies to Theorem 8 below.) One way of obtaining this conclusion is to add the assumption that every sentence of L which has arbitrarily large finite models has an infinite model. Another and perhaps more natural way is to assume that L *relativizes* in the following sense: For every sentence φ of L in s and every 1-place predicate P not in φ, there is a sentence $\varphi^{(P)}$ of L in $s \cup \{P\}$ such that for every structure $\mathfrak{A} = (A, f)$ and every $X \subseteq A$, $(A, f \cup \{\langle P, X \rangle\})$ $\models \varphi^{(P)}$ if and only if there is a substructure $\mathfrak{B}$ of $\mathfrak{A}$ with domain X such that $\mathfrak{B} \models \varphi$. If φ is a sentence of EL, then $\varphi^{(P)}$ is obtained thus. First, relativize all quantifiers to P, i.e., replace $\exists v \psi(v)$ by $\exists v (Pv \wedge \psi(v))$ and $\forall v \psi(v)$ by $\forall v (Pv \rightarrow \psi(v))$. Let φ_P be the result. Then $\varphi^{(P)}$ is the conjunction of φ_P, $\exists v Pv$, $\forall v_1 \ldots v_n (Pv_1 \wedge \cdots \wedge Pv_n \rightarrow PFv_1 \ldots v_n)$ for every n-place function constant in φ, and, finally, Pc for every individual constant in φ. Thus EL relativizes. In fact, this is true of all the ALs described in the introduction with the exception of those containing the quantifier W or the quantifier C.

It is known that there are compact proper extensions of EL. (See [9].) In view of this it is natural to ask if there is a simple property, preferably one corresponding to some basic theorem about EL, which together with compactness yields a characterization of EL. It turns out that this is, indeed, the case. The result that I have in mind is the Tarski union lemma which I will formulate presently after having introduced the necessary terminology.

A set K of structures of the same signature s is a *chain* if for all $\mathfrak{A}, \mathfrak{B} \in K$, either $\mathfrak{A} \subseteq \mathfrak{B}$ or $\mathfrak{B} \subseteq \mathfrak{A}$. Given a chain K the *union* $\bigcup K$ of K can be formed in the natural way. Intuitively $\bigcup K$ is the least common extension of the members of K. More exactly, $\bigcup K$ is the structure (C, h) of signature s such that $C = \bigcup \{A : \mathfrak{A} \in K\}$, $h(P) = \bigcup \{f(P) : \mathfrak{A} \in K\}$ for every $P \in s$, $h(F) = \bigcup \{f(F) : \mathfrak{A} \in K\}$ for every $F \in s$, and, finally, for every $c \in s$, $h(c)$ is the common value of the $f(c)$ for $\mathfrak{A} \in K$. Note that $h(F)$ is a function, since K is a chain. To formulate the Tarski union lemma and the corresponding property of ALs I need two more notions. $\mathfrak{A}$ is an *L-substructure* of $\mathfrak{B}$, $\mathfrak{A} <_L \mathfrak{B}$, if $\mathfrak{A} \subseteq \mathfrak{B}$ and if f^* is any function on a set C^* of new individual constants into A, then $(A, f \cup f^*) \equiv_L (B, g \cup f^*)$. The meaning of this can be explained as follows. Let φ be any sentence of L in $s \cup C^*$, where s is the common signature of $\mathfrak{A}$ and $\mathfrak{B}$, and let $c_1, \ldots, c_n$ be the members of C^* occurring in φ. Then φ can be thought of as expressing a condition on n-tuples in the following way. Let $\mathfrak{C} = (C, h)$ be a structure for s, suppose $a_1, \ldots, a_n \in C$ and let f^* be a function on C^* such that $f^*(c_i) = a_i$, $i = 1, \ldots, n$, i.e., let us for the moment regard $c_1, \ldots, c_n$ as names of $a_1, \ldots, a_n$ respectively. Then $\langle a_1, \ldots, a_n \rangle$ satisfies in $\mathfrak{C}$ the condition expressed by φ if and only if $(C, h \cup f^*) \models \varphi$. Thus $\mathfrak{A} <_L \mathfrak{B}$ means that $\mathfrak{A} \subseteq \mathfrak{B}$ and that for every condition expressible in L and every n-typle x of members of A, x satisfies the condition in $\mathfrak{A}$ if and only if x satisfies the same condition in $\mathfrak{B}$. Clearly, $\mathfrak{A} <_L \mathfrak{B}$ implies $\mathfrak{A} \equiv_L \mathfrak{B}$. A set K of structures is an *L-chain* if for all $\mathfrak{A}, \mathfrak{B} \in K$, either $\mathfrak{A} <_L \mathfrak{B}$ or $\mathfrak{B} <_L \mathfrak{A}$.

TARSKI'S UNION LEMMA. *Let K be any EL-chain. Then $\mathfrak{A} <_{EL} \bigcup K$ for every $\mathfrak{A} \in K$.*[4]

This result, although quite elementary, is still very useful in the development of the theory of models of *EL*.

The property corresponding to the above result is

The union property. L has the *union property* if for every L-chain K, $\mathfrak{A} <_L \bigcup K$ for every $\mathfrak{A} \in K$.

In terms of the union property we have the following characterization of *EL*.

THEOREM 5. *Suppose $EL \subseteq L$, L is compact, and L has the union property. Then $L \equiv EL$.*[5]

It is not known if compactness in Theorem 5 can be replaced by some weaker property, for example, countable compactness. There is, however, a property somewhat stronger than but closely related to the union property which together with countable compactness yields a characterization of *EL*. This property is defined as follows. Let K be any set of structures for some signature s. Consider the following conditions on K.

(a)   If $A, \mathfrak{B} \in K$ and f^* is any function on a set C^* of new individual constants into $A \cap B$, then $(A, f \cup f^*) \equiv_L (B, g \cup f^*)$,

(b)   for any finite subset X of $\bigcup \{A : \mathfrak{A} \in K\}$, there is an $\mathfrak{A} \in K$ such that $X \subseteq A$.

If K satisfies (a) and (b), we can form the union $\bigcup K$ of K in the natural way. L is said to have the *strong union property* if for any set K of structures satisfying (a) and (b), $\mathfrak{A} <_L \bigcup K$ for every $\mathfrak{A} \in K$. *EL* has the strong union property. Moreover, countable compactness together with the strong union property yields a characterization of *EL*. In fact, the strong union property obviously implies the union property and together with countable compactness it implies full compactness. Thus the result just stated follows from Theorem 5.

In addition to the theorems about *EL* already mentioned there is another equally well-known and fundamental result namely the

COMPLETENESS THEOREM. *There is a complete proof procedure for EL.*[6]

This requires some explanation. Let X be a finite set of symbols and let X^* be the set of finite sequences of members of X. Let Y be a subset of X^*. A proof procedure for Y (relative to X) is a completely effective procedure (algorithm) which applied to any member x of X^*, which may be thought of as representing the question '$x \in Y$?', yields the answer YES if and only if x is in fact a member of Y. Note that nothing is said about what happens if x is not a member of Y. To be able to speak about proof procedures in connection with an *AL L* I have to assume that

(∗)　　　the sentences of L are finite sequences of symbols from some finite set X_L.

Clearly all the *AL*s mentioned above with the exception of the $L_{\varkappa\lambda}$ with $(\varkappa, \lambda) \neq (\omega, \omega)$ and extensions of these satisfy this condition. Note that any *AL L* which is countable in the sense that the set of sentences of L is countable is equivalent to an *AL* satisfying (∗). A sentence of L in s is *valid* (logically true) if it is true in all structures for s. A *proof procedure* for an *AL L* satisfying (∗) is a proof procedure for the set of valid sentences of L (relative to X_L). Proof procedures for logics are sometimes described as complete, as, for example, in the above formulation of the completeness theorem, to emphasize that the procedure is a proof procedure not only in the sense that it allows us to prove that sentences of L are valid but also in the sense that it yields *all* valid sentences of L.

The property of *AL*s corresponding to the completeness theorem can now be defined.

Completeness. L is *complete* if there is a (complete) proof procedure for L; in other words, if the set of valid sentences of L is recursively enumerable.

Let me say that L is *effectively closed under negation and conjunction* if

(i) there is an effective method by means of which to any sentence φ of L a sentence ψ of L can be found such that for every structure $\mathfrak{A}$, $\mathfrak{A} \models \psi$ if and only if not $\mathfrak{A} \models \varphi$ and (ii) there is an effective method whereby for any sentences φ and ψ of L a sentence θ of L can be found such that for every $\mathfrak{A}$, $\mathfrak{A} \models \theta$ if and only if $\mathfrak{A} \models \varphi$ and $\mathfrak{A} \models \psi$. This means that sentences ψ and θ as described in parts (vi) and (vii) of the definition of the concept AL not only exist but can be effectively constructed given φ and φ, ψ, respectively. L is *effectively contained* in L', $L \subseteq_{\text{eff}} L'$, if there is an effective method by means of which given any sentence φ of L a sentence ψ of L' can be found such that φ and ψ have the same models. $L \equiv_{\text{eff}} L'$ if $L \subseteq_{\text{eff}} L'$ and $L' \subseteq_{\text{eff}} L$. Clearly all the above mentioned ALs satisfying (∗) are effectively closed under negation and conjunction. Moreover, if L is any one of these ALs, then $EL \subseteq_{\text{eff}} L$ for the trivial reason that any sentence of EL is also a sentence of L.

After these preparations the following characterization of EL can now be stated.

THEOREM 6. *Suppose* $EL \subseteq_{\text{eff}} L$, L *has the Löwenheim property and* L *is complete and effectively closed under negation and conjunction. Then* $L \equiv_{\text{eff}} EL$.

The proof of this uses Corollary 1 in combination with the well-known result of Trakhtenbrot [11] that there is no complete proof procedure for the set of sentences of EL true in all finite structures.

As was to be expected, the assumption that L is complete cannot be omitted from Theorem 6; all the other conditions are satisfied by $L(Q_0)$. An example showing that the assumption that L has the Löwenheim property likewise cannot be left out is $L(Q_1)$, since Vaught [12] has proved that $L(Q_1)$ is complete.

In conclusion I would like to present two new characterizations of EL. They are both in terms of properties related to Beth's theory of semantic tableaux. Thus I shall have to generalize Beth's concept semantic tableau to ALs other than EL. This can be done in many ways. As it turns out, the generalization needed in the present context is a fairly simple-minded one. But before I do this, let me say a few words about some of the ideas behind Beth's theory.

Let φ be any sentence of EL. Suppose φ is valid. Then φ is true in every structure for the set s of non-logical constants occurring in φ. Now the validity of φ can hardly be verified by going through all such structures and verifying for each one of them that φ is true in it. A more practical way would be to look systematically for a counterexample to φ, i.e. a structure in which φ is false. The problem is then if there is a general method which applied to any φ will lead to a counterexample to φ whenever there is one. This method should be completely effective and enable us to recognize effectively that it has failed to produce a counterexample whenever this is the case. Finally, it should lead to the construction, in some sense, and not to the mere existence of a counterexample whenever there is one.

For *EL* Beth [2] has described a method satisfying these conditions. It consists in the construction of what is called a semantic tableau for the sentence in question. Let φ be a sentence of *EL*, let s be the set of non-logical constants occurring in φ, and let C be a denumerable set of new individual constants. A semantic tableau for φ may be described as a(n inverted) tree

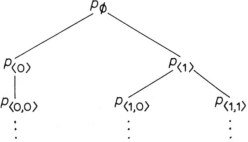

where each p_σ, σ a finite sequence of 0's and 1's, is a pair (X_σ, Y_σ) of finite sets of sentences of *EL* in $s \cup C$. Furthermore, $P_\emptyset = (\emptyset, \{\varphi\})$ and, for simplicity, $X_\sigma \subseteq X_{\sigma'}$ and $Y_\sigma \subseteq Y_{\sigma'}$ whenever σ is an initial segment of σ'. The construction of the tableau is completely effective. Each pair $p = (X, Y)$ appearing in it is to be thought of as a condition on structures $\mathfrak{A}$, namely the condition that all members of X are true in $\mathfrak{A}$ and all members of Y are false in $\mathfrak{A}$. Thus what we are looking for is a structure satisfying the condition $p_\emptyset$. The tableau represents a systematic search for a structure satisfying this condition. The fact that it branches off in two directions at certain points comes from the fact that, for example, X may contain a disjunction $\varphi \vee \psi$ and so a structure satisfying (X, Y) must satisfy either $(X \cup \{\varphi\}, Y)$ or $(X \cup \{\psi\}, Y)$. But as we cannot in general tell which we have to consider the two possibilities separately. Thus each branch represents an alternative that has to be taken into account. In view of this interpretation of the tableau it is certainly natural to give up the search for a counterexample to φ along a certain branch if we have reached a pair (X, Y) such that X and Y have a sentence in common. A branch containing such a pair is said to be *closed*. If every branch of a tableau is closed, then the tableau itself is said to be closed. Finally, consider any non-closed branch b starting with $p_\emptyset$ and extending as far as possible. Let X_b be the set of atomic sentences belonging to some set X_σ which is the left member of some pair belonging to b and define Y_b similarly from the right members of pairs in b. Then there is a structure $\mathfrak{A} = (A, f)$ of signature $s \cup C$ such that (i) for every member a of A, there is a $c \in C$ such that $f(c) = a$, (ii) every member of X_b is true in $\mathfrak{A}$, and (iii) every member of Y_b is false in $\mathfrak{A}$. Moreover, any such structure is a counterexample to φ. Semantic tableaux in the sense of Beth have several other highly interesting and important properties but they are not relevant here.

The fundamental theorem concerning semantic tableaux established by Beth is the

SEMANTIC TABLEAU THEOREM. *To every sentence φ of EL a semantic tableau can be effectively constructed such that φ is valid if and only if the tableau is closed.*

To see that the goal described above has been achieved it only remains to verify that if the semantic tableau for φ does not lead to a counterexample to φ, i.e. if the tableau is closed, then this can be effectively recognized. Now, if every branch is closed, then every branch is finite and so, by König's lemma, the tableau contains altogether only finitely many pairs. But then it can certainly be effectively verified that it yields no counterexample to φ.

One definition of the notion *semantic tableau* for an *AL L* other than *EL*, and the one which I will adopt here, can be obtained from the above description of the semantic tableaux for *EL* by simply replacing '*EL*' by '*L*'. However, it is not necessary to define 'closed' in exactly the same way as before as long as the property of being closed is an effective one, and it is not necessary to assume that every pair in the tree has at most two immediate descendants as long as there are only finitely many. But these are matters of little importance. Note, however, that it must be assumed that L satisfies (∗). In addition to this, it must be specified what is to count as an atomic sentence of L. For simplicity I shall assume that *the atomic sentences of EL are sentences of L and have the same meaning in L as in EL.*

In terms of the present notion semantic tableau the property of ALs corresponding to the semantic tableau theorem is the

Uniform semantic tableau (s.t.) property. L has the *uniform s.t. property* if there is an effective method whereby given any sentence φ of L a semantic tableau for φ can be constructed which is not closed unless φ is valid.

A slightly weaker property is the

S.t. property. L has the *s.t. property* if for every sentence φ of L, there is a semantic tableau for φ which is not closed unless φ is valid.

Suppose L has the uniform s.t. property. Then L is complete for reasons that are apparent from what has already been said. A complete proof procedure for L is as follows. Let φ be any sentence of L. Construct a semantic tableau for φ. φ is valid if and only if after a finite number of steps every branch of this tableau is closed. Moreover, the (uniform) s.t. property clearly implies the Löwenheim property, since any structure associated with a non-closed branch of a semantic tableau in the manner described above is certainly countable. Thus, in view of Theorem 6, we have the following

THEOREM 7. *Suppose* $EL \subseteq_{\mathrm{eff}} L$, *$L$ is effectively closed under negation and conjunction and L has the uniform s.t. property. Then* $L \equiv_{\mathrm{eff}} EL$.

If L has the s.t. property but fails to have the uniform s.t. property, then the proof just given does not work, since, although there exists a semantic tableau for every sentence of L and although each one of these tableaux can be constructed by means of an effective method, these methods cannot be brought together into one single effective method. Nevertheless we have the following

THEOREM 8. *Suppose* $EL \subseteq L$, *L satisfies* $(+)$, *and L has the s.t. property. Then* $L \equiv_{\mathrm{inf}} EL$.[7]

The proof can be outlined as follows. Let ψ be any sentence of L and suppose ψ has a model. If L has the s.t. property, then it can be shown, by considering a non-closed tableau for a 'negation' of ψ and using König's lemma, that ψ has a model $\mathfrak{A} = (A, f)$ such that either A is finite or A is the set of natural numbers and $f(P)$ and $f(F)$ for all predicates and functions constants in ψ belong to some fixed level of the arithmetical hierarchy; Δ_3^0 to be exact. If, on the other hand, $L \nsubseteq_{\inf} EL$, then, using the sentence φ described in Corollary 2, it is possible to construct a sentence of L which has a model but none satisfying the above description. Thus the assumption that Theorem 8 is false leads to contradiction. This derivation of Theorem 8 from Corollary 2 is essentially the same as Kleene's proof of Skolem's theorem that the natural numbers with the successor function cannot be characterized in EL. (Theorem 44 [5].)

University of Gothenburg

NOTES

[1] Logics with generalized quantifiers were first studied by Mostowski [8].
[2] For proofs of these results see [10].
[3] I take this opportunity to point out that Theorem 1 and Corollary 2 in [6] are not quite correct as they stand. This has been brought to my attention by several people. One out of many ways of putting things right is to replace, as is done here, the assumption $EL \subseteq_{\inf} L$ by the stronger assumption $EL \subseteq L$. The mistake in the proof occurs on p. 6 where I conclude that $K_1 \in C_L$.
[4] For a proof of this see [10].
[5] This result was stated in [7] for logics obtained from EL by adding quantifiers only. However, the same proof yields the more general result stated here.
[6] This is an abstract version of the results ordinarily referred to as completeness theorems for EL. These results usually state the completeness of some particular 'natural' proof procedure. Proofs of results of this type can be found in [5, 10]. See also [2].
[7] Cf. the remark immediately following the proof of Theorem 4.

BIBLIOGRAPHY

[1] K. J. Barwise, 'Absolute Logics and $L_{\infty\omega}$', *Annals of Math. Logic* **4** (1972), 309–340.
[2] E. W. Beth, *Semantic Entailment and Formal Derivability*, 1955. Reprinted in *The Philosophy of Mathematics* (ed. by J. Hintikka), Oxford 1969, pp. 9–41.
[3] H. Friedman, *Why First-Order Logic?*, Mimeographed, 1970.
[4] G. Fuhrken, 'Skolem-Type Normal Forms for First Order Languages with a Generalized Quantifier', *Fund. Math.* **54** (1964), 291–302.
[5] S. C. Kleene, *Introduction to Metamathematics*, Amsterdam 1962.
[6] P. Lindström, 'Extensions of Elementary Logic', *Theoria* **35** (1969), 1–11.
[7] P. Lindström, 'A Characterization of Elementary Logic', in *Modality, Morality and Other Problems of Sense and Nonsense*, Essays dedicated to Sören Halldén, Lund, 1973, pp. 189–191.
[8] A. Mostowski, 'On a Generalization of Quantifiers', *Fund. Math.* **44** (1957), 12–36.
[9] S. Shelak, *Generalized Quantifiers and Compact Logic*, to appear.

[10] J. R. Shoenfield, *Mathematical Logic*, Addison-Wesley, 1967.

[11] B. A. Trakhtenbrot, 'On Recursive Separability', *Dokl. Akad. Nauk SSSR* **88** (1953), 953–956.

[12] R. L. Vaught, 'The Completeness of Logic with the Added Quantifier 'There Are Uncountably Many' ', *Fund. Math.* **54** (1964), 303–304.

DANA SCOTT

RULES AND DERIVED RULES

I. INTRODUCTION

It is very easy to confuse rules with axioms or even theorems. Consider for example this equation from arithmetic:

$$4 \cdot 11 = 44.$$

We may regard this as a truth about integers; or we may consider it a suggestion for an even more general rule about how easy it is to multiply a one-digit number by 11. From the first point of view we are concerned with *content*; while from the second, *form*. In the case of arithmetic the confusion is not particularly troublesome, but in logic such mixups have wasted considerable time. The endless discussions of *modal* logic form a prime example. In [3] the author tried to argue that there was a point that had been generally overlooked about C.I. Lewis' introduction of strict implication which turned on the distinction between rules of inference and tautologies. The conclusion reached there was that the Lewis System S4 was more interesting than it might seem even with the benefit of modern semantics. The crux of the argument was a formal metatheorem relating derived rules to derived theorems (Cf. [3], p. 803), but lack of space and time resulted in the exclusion of the proof of the result. The purpose of the present paper is to supply the details along with some general definitions about rules and derivations.

The assumed background for the investigation is the Gentzen-style formalization which uses the conditional assertion:

(*) $A_0, A_1, ..., A_{n-1} \vdash B_0, B_1, ..., B_{m-1}$.

In *proof* theory the systems of *natural deduction* have been found to be much more useful than the ⊢-systems, but conditionals of the form (*) with the premises fully written out are very well suited to *truth* theory – that is, to semantics and model theory. When we are mainly interested in what is valid (in a class of structures or interpretations), we care more

S. Stenlund (ed.), Logical Theory and Semantic Analysis, 147–161. *All Rights Reserved.*
Copyright © 1974 *by D. Reidel Publishing Company, Dordrecht-Holland.*

about knowing just what is deriv*able* from the axioms than any partic- ular *path* of derivation. This does not mean that we will not ask about the forms of rules which preserve validity, but we shall not look too closely at whole proofs (i.e. the rules in combination). Nevertheless, even on this level, *some* attention to the proper choice of rules is worthwhile; this has been argued in [2] and [4] and the discussion will not be repeated here. Neither will the full consideration of the aims of modal logic be rehearsed in this paper, and the reader is referred to [3].

There is one common confusion about the meaning of (∗) that must be cleared up from the start. The problem is well illustrated by the question of *modus ponens*. In Table I four versions of this well-known rule are

TABLE I

Four forms of modus ponens

$A, A \Rightarrow B \vdash B$	$\dfrac{\vdash A \Rightarrow B}{A \vdash B}$	$\dfrac{\vdash A}{\dfrac{\vdash A \Rightarrow B}{\vdash B}}$	$\dfrac{\vdash A}{\dfrac{A \vdash B}{\vdash B}}$
(i)	(ii)	(iii)	(iv)

given. We ask: which is the one deserving the name? The correct answer seems to be (iii), for this is the metatheoretic statement that the validities of the system are closed under the rule allowing for the detachment of the conclusion of an implication (provided it and its antecedent are valid). *Modus ponens* is a rule about the *connective* of implication. Rule (iv), however, is a rule about the *relationship* of implication. The confusion between connectives and relations resting on the confusion between object language and metalanguage is one of long standing. We shall not debate it again here. The point is that use of ⊢ accepted in this paper is such that rule (iv) is correct for *all* systems. On the other hand (iii) expresses a special property of implication; its correctness depends on the kind of implica- tion being discussed and therefore on the particular system. Two features of this list of rules are furthermore confusing: they are all correct for the system of material implication, and in *any* system each implies the next (assuming the standard meaning of ⊢; obviously (iii) implies (iv)). Thus (i), which we might call a conditional tautology, *suggests* a rule, namely: (iii). But the tautology and the rule are not the same. For example, in the Łukasiewicz many-valued logic (i) fails while (ii) (and (iii) and (iv)) holds.

There is no difficulty distinguishing (iii) and (iv), for we can easily think of a system in which (iii) fails (e.g. make $A \Rightarrow B$ *always* true). To distinguish (ii) and (iii) take a familiar modal system, say S4, which employs material implication (written with $\supset$) and necessity (written with $\square$). Now for this system there are two forms for a rule of necessitation as shown in Table II.

TABLE II

Two forms of necessitation

$A \vdash \square A$	$\vdash A$
	$\vdash \square A$

The second is correct, the first not. Now define a new kind of implication by the equation:

$$(A \Rightarrow B) = (\square A \supset B).$$

Using familiar properties of material implication (e.g. modus ponens and $\vdash \square A \supset \square A$), we see that (iii) of Table I holds (use the correct form of necessitation), but (ii) fails (take the case $B = \square A$).

The above remarks have assumed a 'standard' meaning for $\vdash$. What meaning is this? Answer: the semantical one. We are supposing that every system *has* a semantical interpretation or model theory. This is not to say that we know or fully understand the semantics, but the *possibility* is our assumption. For a given system, then (*) is valid iff *whenever* all the A_i are true, *then* at least one of the B_j is also true (in the *same* model or instance). To say $\vdash A$ is to say that A is *always* true. Thus, since in modal logic contingent truth does not imply necessity, we see the difference between the properties of $\square$ in Table II. What is confusing about semantics, of course, is that the *same* formal system may have quite *different* interpretations; indeed two classes of models may have the same collection of valid (conditional) assertions. Thus the mere writing of an assertion does not tell us what we are asserting it about. A formal system standing alone is an incomplete entity: it needs its interpretation. This circumstance does not keep us from studying the formal properties of formal systems, but it should restrain us from ascribing importance to our results independent of any interpretation.

Another possibility of confusion is illustrated in Table III. Two rules are given and Curry, for example in [1] p. 98, often says they are to mean the same. (Here, we should treat the A_i and B as schematic for compound expressions as in the other examples.) We do not accept this view of ⊢ as has already been explained, but what is unfortunate is that *certain* systems allow for the confusion. In classical propositional calculus, for example, if a rule of the second kind (right hand side of Table III) is a derived rule, then the conditional tautology can also be derived. (The converse goes in any system.) *But* if we extend the system with new con-

TABLE III

Two rules

$$A_0, A_1, ..., A_{n-1} \vdash B \qquad \begin{array}{l} \vdash A_0 \\ \vdash A_1 \\ \vdots \\ \vdash A_{n-1} \\ \hline \vdash B \end{array}$$

nectives – like □ – and new rules, this equivalence no longer holds. Thus, we argue here that the Curry view is not only inconvenient but misleading – though of course it is possible to be consistent about it. On the positive side, our metatheorem will show general conditions under which this kind of equivalence *is* correct and when it is retained under *extensions*. But first we must have more precise definitions about systems, rules, and derivations.

II. RULES AND DERIVATIONS

For simplicity we shall restrict attention to propositional systems. These are determined by a 'language' which has a set $\mathscr{S}$ of 'sentences' or 'statements' together with a relation ⊢ between finite subsets of $\mathscr{S}$, the relation of conditional assertion or 'entailment'. The semantical point of view presupposes a set $\mathscr{V}$ of (two-valued!) truth valuations on $\mathscr{S}$ which delimits the ways in which the statements can be made *true* or *false*. The use of $\mathscr{V}$ makes ⊢ precise, but the trouble is that we may not be able to know $\mathscr{V}$ in advance. However if we assume that some $\mathscr{V}$ exists, then ⊢ must satisfy some general conditions no matter what $\mathscr{V}$ is. These are shown in Table IV. These rules are well known from the work of Gentzen and many others. As indicated in the three other papers cited, the author prefers to regard ⊢ as a generalized sort of partial ordering on $\mathscr{S}$ (the generalization in particular allows ⊢ to be a multi-ary relation). The names for the rules are then: (R) or the Reflexive Law, (M) or the Monotonic Law, and (T) or the Transitive Law. The last one is of course the Cut Rule. We take it as basic since in general it is *not* eliminable. In [4] (cf. §1) the standard arguments are given establishing the connection between ⊢ relations, consequence relations in the sense of Tarski, and sets of valuations. In particular any system satisfying (R), (M) and (T) has some semantical interpretation *via* truth valuations. That is about all there is to

TABLE IV

The three basic rules of entailment

$A \vdash A$	$\dfrac{\mathfrak{A} \vdash \mathfrak{B}}{\mathfrak{A}, \mathfrak{A}' \vdash \mathfrak{B}, \mathfrak{B}'}$	$\dfrac{\mathfrak{A} \vdash B, \mathfrak{C} \quad \mathfrak{A}, B \vdash \mathfrak{C}}{\mathfrak{A} \vdash \mathfrak{C}}$
(R)	(M)	(T)

say for ⊢ in general (except for the compactness results and the usual kinds of theorems on relations between different ⊢-relations, cf. [4]). The more interesting discussion of rules will involve connectives.

Again for simplicity let us consider for the time being only one connective ⇒. This will be taken as a binary connective under which $\mathscr{S}$ is closed. (Cf. [2] for a discussion of the reasonableness of this format.) In the next section we shall have to employ more connectives, but the definitions carry over to a more complex syntax without change of essentials. As an example, consider again the rule (MP) of *modus ponens* (rule (iii) of Table I). We know many systems for which this rule is *correct*. By this we mean that we have definitions of $\mathscr{S}$, ⇒, and ⊢ in mind such that for all $A, B \in \mathscr{S}$, if we have

$$\vdash A \quad \text{and} \quad \vdash A \Rightarrow B$$

both holding for the relation ⊢, then we also have ⊢ B. (Recall that ⊢ A means $\emptyset \vdash \{A\}$ stated more rigorously in terms of finite subsets of $\mathscr{S}$.) But what *is* the rule (MP). Certainly it is not this particular fact about this particular system $\mathscr{S}$, ⇒, ⊢. No, it is a meta-notion, something schematic that can be meaningfully applied to *all* systems – and sometimes it is correct for a system, and sometimes not.

What we need to consider then are metavariables $A, B, C, \ldots$ and compound 'polynomials' of these, like $A \Rightarrow B$, $A \Rightarrow (B \Rightarrow C)$, etc. These are then formed into *sequents* such as:

$$\Gamma = A,\ A \Rightarrow B,\ (A \Rightarrow B) \Rightarrow (A \Rightarrow (B \Rightarrow C))$$
$$\Delta = C$$

We then consider such 'direct' rules (or: conditional tautologies) as:

(**) $\forall A, B, C, \ldots [\Gamma \vdash \Delta]$

Or such syllogistic rules as (MP) more formally stated in this way:

(MP) $\forall A, B, C, \ldots [\vdash A \wedge \vdash A \Rightarrow B \rightarrow \vdash B]$.

We are thus in the process of reflecting on the logic of our metatheory ('You have to know some logic to do some logic') and we can ask if the rule is correct for (or: satisfied in) a particular system. Now (**) may or may not be correct for a given $\mathscr{S}$, $\Rightarrow$, $\vdash$, and even if (MP) is correct, then (**) need not be. However, if the conditional form of the rule:

(CMP) $\forall A, B[A,\ A \Rightarrow B \vdash B]$

is correct for $\mathscr{S}$, $\Rightarrow$, $\vdash$, then so is (**). This can be seen by the following derivation given in Table V.

TABLE V

A derivation

(1)	$A \Rightarrow B, (A \Rightarrow B) \Rightarrow (A \Rightarrow (B \Rightarrow C)) \vdash A \Rightarrow (B \Rightarrow C)$	by (CMP)
(2)	$A, A \Rightarrow (B \Rightarrow C) \vdash B \Rightarrow C$	by (CMP)
(3)	$A, A \Rightarrow B, (A \Rightarrow B) \Rightarrow (A \Rightarrow (B \Rightarrow C)) \vdash A \Rightarrow (B \Rightarrow C), B \Rightarrow C$	by (1) and (M)
(4)	$\Gamma, A \Rightarrow (B \Rightarrow C) \vdash B \Rightarrow C$	by (2) and (M)
(5)	$\Gamma \vdash B \Rightarrow C$	by (3), (4) and (T)
(6)	$A, A \Rightarrow B \vdash B$	by (CMP)
(7)	$\Gamma \vdash B, C$	by (6) and (M)
(8)	$\Gamma, B \vdash B \Rightarrow C, C$	by (5) and (M)
(9)	$B, B \Rightarrow C \vdash C$	by (CMP)
(10)	$\Gamma, B, B \Rightarrow C \vdash C$	by (9) and (M)
(11)	$\Gamma, B \vdash C$	by (8), (10) and (T)
(12)	$\Gamma \vdash \Delta$	by (7), (11) and (T)

Clearly we are not bothering here about *short* proofs, since the rules can be made more efficient. One concession has been allowed, however, the so-called *structural rules* have not been made explicit. We think of the sequents as shorthand names for finite *sets*, so the terms can be permuted, duplicated, and condensed at will. In any case, we have shown *why* (∗∗) follows from (CMP), and this insight can be applied to *any* system.

In Table V we see that each line is either an *instance* of (CMP) or follows from previous lines by instances of the general rules (M) or (T). Finally we get the general instance of (∗∗). This is not quite so simple for syllogistic rules like (MP) and we would have to treat everything in the way we have done (M) and (T).

So by a *rule* (**R**) we mean a universally quantified conditional with premises and a conclusion as in the illustrations. We can think of it as a figure (or general syllogism) for passing from several ⊢-assertions to the final one. It is schematic and is defined *independently* of any system. But when a system $\mathscr{S}, \Rightarrow, \vdash$ *is* specified, then the rule is either correct for that system or not. Next, we say that a rule (**R**) *follows from* rules (**R₀**), (**R₁**), ... (**Rₙ₋₁**) just in case (**R**) is correct for *all systems* for which the (**Rᵢ**) are correct. Since we only allow systems satisfying (R), (M) and (T), the correctness of the basic rules is tacit. So far derivations have not entered.

The obvious definition of derivability seems to be this: (**R**) is *derivable from* (**R₀**), (**R₁**), ..., (**Rₙ₋₁**) just in case there is a sequence of (schematic) ⊢-assertions such that each 'line' is either one of the premises of (**R**) or derives from earlier lines, in the sense that we can find an *instance* of one of the rules (**R₀**), (**R₁**), ..., (**Rₙ₋₁**), (R), (M), (T) such that the earlier lines are the premises and the line in question is the conclusion of the instance. Further, the last line must be the conclusion of (**R**).

Warning: There is an ambiguity in our notion of rule! The rules (R), (M), and (T) are of a different kind from, say, (MP). In the latter we have only specific sequents but in (T) we see the set *variables* $\mathfrak{A}$ and $\mathfrak{C}$. What we shall have to do is to replace these variables (which are of a different kind from the *A*, *B*, *C*-variables) by specific sequents. Thus we must regard (M) and (T) as an infinite *bundles* of related rules. This is somewhat tiresome, but the author does not know at the moment how to define derivability without this restriction to rules without set variables. (There is no difficulty in defining *follows from* even for these more general rules.) The problem can be illustrated by the example shown in Table VI. Here we can suppose $\Gamma, \Delta, \Gamma^*, \Delta^*$ are four specific sequents; while X is a sentense variable not in any of them. $\mathfrak{A}$ and $\mathfrak{A}'$ are two set variables. Now the third rule clearly follows from the other two because the set $\mathfrak{A}'$ is either empty or not. But do we want to have this passage as a principle

TABLE VI
Three rules

$\dfrac{\Gamma \vdash \Delta}{\Gamma^* \vdash \Delta^*}$	$\dfrac{\mathfrak{A}, X, \Gamma \vdash \Delta}{\mathfrak{A}, X, \Gamma^* \vdash \Delta^*}$	$\dfrac{\mathfrak{A}', \Gamma \vdash \Delta}{\mathfrak{A}', \Gamma^* \vdash \Delta^*}$

of derivation? And are there others? The situation is not clear to the author, and so we make the restriction to rules without set variables. Is it an interesting problem to remove the restriction? Can it be removed?

THE COMPLETENESS THEOREM FOR RULES. *A rule (without set variables) follows from given rules iff it is derivable from them.*

Proof: The method is well known. Of course, from right to left the result is obvious, but a rigourous proof can be given by induction on the lengths of derivations. Suppose then **(R)** is *not* derivable from **(R₀)**, **(R₁)**, ..., **(R$_{n-1}$)**. We specialize $\mathscr{S}$, $\Rightarrow$ to the 'free algebra' of polynomial sentential 'expressions' generated from 'atomic' statements by an operation $\Rightarrow$ that is essentially a pairing function. We then define $\vdash$ to be the *least* entailment relation satisfying the rules **(R₀)**, **(R₁)**, ..., **(R$_{n-1}$)** and which contains the general instances (i.e. with original variables) of the premises of **(R)**. An inductive analysis of $\vdash$ shows that it just follows the derivations, and so the conclusion of **(R)** cannot hold for this minimal $\vdash$. Thus **(R)** does not follow from the given rules. $\square$

There is a great temptation to do all logic on the free algebra, but the temptation should be resisted as it is conclusive to sterile formalism.

III. LOGICAL IMPLICATION

We shall not enter here into the squabble about the paradoxes (so called) of implication. The proposed solutions to the problems of relevance (which are real problems!) have not been sufficiently tried out, and the recent semantical interpretations have as yet no adequate philosophical justification. The $\vdash$-relations have quite clear semantics as *material* entailment relations, on the other hand, even though one can question whether they capture the 'laws of thought'. The question that interests us here is the connections between the properties of such relations and the properties of implication as a connective. The genesis of the problem was discussed at length in [3] where a positive result about the formal properties of rules was indicated. Our purpose here is to make the result more precise and to show how to prove it.

One feature of the discussion in [3] that was not sufficiently clear was the distinction between particular systems and collections of rules (which apply to a whole class of systems). The distinction was mentioned in [3] pp. 803–4, but the notions about rules in Section 1 allow us to state what we mean more rigourously. Before we do so, however, we list some specific rules that seem to be needed to make the proof work. They are not very alarming rules, though, for they are just those for conjunction and disjunction. We give two versions: the more general in Table VII and the more specific in Table VIII. Strictly speaking the rules of Table VII are not allowed because they involve set variables. Note they are double-sided rules and should be read as pairs of rules going from top to bottom and from bottom to top. If we like we could interpret Table VII as an infinite collection of rules by replacing the $\mathfrak{A}$ and $\mathfrak{B}$ by specific sequents. Fortunately this is not necessary, since the rules of Table VII (taken together) are equivalent to the eight (direct) rules of Table VIII. All the specific cases of what is in Table VII are deducible from those in Table VIII. From now on we assume that we are considering systems of the type:

$$\mathcal{S}, \top, \wedge, \bot, \vee, \Rightarrow, \vdash,$$

which satisfy rules $(\top)$, $(\wedge)$, $(\bot)$, $(\vee)$.

TABLE VII
The general rules for conjunction and disjunction

$\dfrac{\mathfrak{A} \vdash \mathfrak{B}}{\mathfrak{A}, \top \vdash \mathfrak{B}}$	$\dfrac{\mathfrak{A}, A, B \vdash \mathfrak{B}}{\mathfrak{A}, A \wedge B \vdash \mathfrak{B}}$	$\dfrac{\mathfrak{A} \vdash \mathfrak{B}}{\mathfrak{A} \vdash \bot, \mathfrak{B}}$	$\dfrac{\mathfrak{A} \vdash A, B, \mathfrak{B}}{\mathfrak{A} \vdash A \vee B, \mathfrak{B}}$
$(\top)$	$(\wedge)$	$(\bot)$	$(\vee)$

TABLE VIII
The specific rules for conjunction and disjunction

$\vdash \top$	$A, B \vdash A \wedge B$	$\bot \vdash$	$A \vee B \vdash A, B$
	$A \wedge B \vdash A$		$A \vdash A \vee B$
	$A \wedge B \vdash B$		$B \vdash A \vee B$
$(\top)$	$(\wedge)$	$(\bot)$	$(\vee)$

In a way the use of the rules of conjunction and disjunction obviates the problem of set variables, for if we assume them, then the two rules of Table IX become equivalent. The reason is that every finite set can be

TABLE IX
Equivalent versions

$\mathfrak{A}, \Gamma \vdash \Delta, \mathfrak{B}$	$A, \Gamma \vdash \Delta, B$
$\mathfrak{A}, \Gamma^* \vdash \Delta^*, \mathfrak{B}$	$A, \Gamma^* \vdash \Delta^*, B$

replaced by a conjunction or disjunction depending on which side the variable occurs. (If a set variable were used on *both* sides of $\vdash$ in the same rule, we would not know what to do. So the method is not completely general.) We shall make constant use of conjunctions and disjunctions in what follows. If Γ is a sequent, let $\hat{\Gamma}$ be the conjunction of all its terms ($\top$ in case of the empty sequent) with, say association to the left. Similarly let $\check{\Gamma}$ be the disjunction ($\bot$ in the empty case).

What about $\Rightarrow$? What is its rôle? The vague idea is that this is a new connective for 'logical' implication as distinguished from material implication. At the level at which we are working the only way we have to express logical implication is as a relation: $A \vdash B$. We cannot confuse $A \Rightarrow B$ with this directly since that would violate the separation of object and metalanguage. But a *coherent* rule of confusion can be stated as shown in Table X.

TABLE X
The rule of confusion

(C) $$\frac{A \vdash B}{\vdash A \Rightarrow B}$$

Note that rule (C) also allows all conditional tautologies to be equivalently stated as ordinary tautologies.

Let us call a collection of rules *normal* if it contains $(\top)$, $(\wedge)$, $(\bot)$, $(\vee)$, (C). Two collections are called *equivalent* if each rule of one is derivable from rules in the other. Finally, before we state our metatheorem, we need names for some special $\Rightarrow$-rules as given in Table XI.

TABLE XI

Three rules of implication

(MP$_\Rightarrow$)	$A \Rightarrow B, (A \Rightarrow B) \Rightarrow (C \Rightarrow D) \vdash C \Rightarrow D$
(T$_\Rightarrow$)	$A \Rightarrow B, C \Rightarrow D \vdash (B \Rightarrow C) \Rightarrow (A \Rightarrow D)$
(T$_{\wedge\vee}$)	$A \Rightarrow (B \vee C), (A \wedge B) \Rightarrow C \vdash A \Rightarrow C$

METATHEOREM. *A normal collection of rules is such that whenever a rule of the vertical form:*

(V)
$$\Gamma_0 \vdash \Delta_0$$
$$\Gamma_1 \vdash \Delta_1$$
$$\vdots$$
$$\frac{\Gamma_{n-1} \vdash \Delta_{n-1}}{\Gamma_n \vdash \Delta_n}$$

is derivable, then the horizontal form:

(H) $\hat{\Gamma}_0 \Rightarrow \check{\Delta}_0, \hat{\Gamma}_1 \Rightarrow \check{\Delta}_1, ..., \hat{\Gamma}_{n-1} \Rightarrow \check{\Delta}_{n-1} \vdash \hat{\Gamma}_n \Rightarrow \check{\Delta}_n$

is also derivable, **if and only if** *it can be replaced by an equivalent normal collection containing aside from* (C) *only horizontal rules including* (MP$_\Rightarrow$). (T$_\Rightarrow$), *and* (T$_{\wedge\vee}$).

Proof: The necessity of the three $\Rightarrow$-rules was established by easy arguments in [3], pp. 802–3. If a collection allows the passage from (V) to (H) in all cases, then clearly all its rules can be written as conditional tautologies. And from these with the aid of (C) and the rules of conjunction of disjunction we can rederive the original rules.

In the other direction, suppose we have a normal collection containing the stated rules. Suppose that (V) is a derived rule. We must show that (H) is also. The idea is to mimic the deduction in horizontal form. We require a few lemmata. In the statements of some of them we use $A \equiv B$ as an abbreviation of $A \vdash B$ *and* $B \vdash A$ taken together.

LEMMA 1. *A derived rule is:* $\vdash A \Rightarrow A$.

Proof: This is trivial in view of (R) and (C). $\square$

158 DANA SCOTT

LEMMA 2. $A \Rightarrow B, B \Rightarrow C \vdash A \Rightarrow C$

(In other words, the displayed formula is a derived rule for the given normal collection; and similarly in the following lemmata.)

Proof: An instance of $(T_\Rightarrow)$ is:

$$A \Rightarrow B, B \Rightarrow C \vdash (B \Rightarrow B) \Rightarrow (A \Rightarrow C)$$

An instance of $(MP_\Rightarrow)$ is:

$$B \Rightarrow B, (B \Rightarrow B) \Rightarrow (A \Rightarrow C) \vdash A \Rightarrow C$$

The desired conclusion now follows from Lemma 1 and several applications of (M) and (T). □

LEMMA 3
$$A \equiv A'$$
$$\frac{B \equiv B'}{A \Rightarrow B \equiv A' \Rightarrow B'}$$

Proof: An instance of $(T_\Rightarrow)$ is:

$$A' \Rightarrow A, B \Rightarrow B' \vdash (A \Rightarrow B) \Rightarrow (A' \Rightarrow B').$$

The result now follows by several applications of (C), (M), and (T). □

LEMMA 4
$$A \equiv A'$$
$$\frac{\Gamma \vdash \Delta}{\Gamma' \vdash \Delta'}$$

where $\Gamma' \vdash \Delta'$ results from $\Gamma \vdash \Delta$ by substituting A' for A.

Proof: Our only connectives are $\wedge$, $\vee$, $\Rightarrow$. The analogues of Lemma 3 for $\wedge$ and for $\vee$ are easily shown to be derivable. This general principle then results by induction on the complexity of Γ, Δ. □

We say two sequents Γ, Γ' are *congruent* $(\Gamma \cong \Gamma')$ if they contain the same terms except possibly in different order or in a different multiplicity.

LEMMA 5. *If $\Gamma \cong \Gamma'$ and $\Delta \cong \Delta'$, then $\hat{\Gamma} \Rightarrow \check{\Delta} \equiv \hat{\Gamma}' \Rightarrow \check{\Delta}'$.*

Proof: We use Lemma 3 together with the fact that the laws of conjunction and disjunction are sufficient for deriving: $\hat{\Gamma} \equiv \hat{\Gamma}'$ and $\check{\Delta} \equiv \check{\Delta}'$. □

LEMMA 6. $A \Rightarrow B \quad \top \Rightarrow (A \Rightarrow B)$

Proof: An instance of $(\top_\Rightarrow)$ is:

$$A \Rightarrow A, A \Rightarrow B \vdash (A \Rightarrow A) \Rightarrow (A \Rightarrow B).$$

By Lemma 1 we derive

$$A \Rightarrow B \vdash (A \Rightarrow A) \Rightarrow (A \Rightarrow B).$$

But $\top \equiv A \Rightarrow A$ also by Lemma 1, so we apply Lemma 4. Next an instance of $(\text{MP}_\Rightarrow)$ is:

$$A \Rightarrow A, (A \Rightarrow A) \Rightarrow (A \Rightarrow B) \vdash A \Rightarrow B.$$

We proceed as usual to derive:

$$\top \Rightarrow (A \Rightarrow B) \vdash A \Rightarrow B. \quad \square$$

LEMMA 7. $A \Rightarrow B \vdash A \wedge A' \Rightarrow B \vee B'$

Proof: By (C) we can derive:

$$\vdash A \wedge A' \Rightarrow A \quad \text{and} \quad \vdash B \Rightarrow B \vee B'.$$

We then employ the obvious instances of Lemma 2. $\quad \square$

Proof of Metatheorem (Continued): Consider a deduction of (V) which has as lines:

$$\Gamma_0^* \vdash \Delta_0^*, \Gamma_1^* \vdash \Delta_1^*, ..., \Gamma_k^* \vdash \Delta_k^*,$$

where the last line is the same as $\Gamma_n \vdash \Delta_n$. We must show by induction on $j \leqslant k$ that a derived rule is:

$$\hat{\Gamma}_0 \Rightarrow \check{\Delta}_0, \hat{\Gamma}_1 \Rightarrow \check{\Delta}_1, ..., \hat{\Gamma}_{n-1} \Rightarrow \check{\Delta}_{n-1} \vdash \hat{\Gamma}_j^* \Rightarrow \check{\Delta}_j^*.$$

When we get to $j = k$ we have (H) as derivable. We argue by cases.

(1) $\Gamma_j^* \vdash \Delta_j^*$ is one of the premises of (V). No problem.

(2) $\Gamma_j^* \vdash \Delta_j^*$ is one of the direct rules of the normal collection. We apply rules of conjunction and disjunction together with (C) to derive $\vdash \hat{\Gamma}_j^* \Rightarrow \check{\Delta}_j^*$, which is more than we need.

(3) $\Gamma_j^* \vdash \Delta_j^*$ follows from $\Gamma_i^* \vdash \Delta_i^*$ with $i < j$ by one of the directions of (C). We use Lemma 6 to prove $\hat{\Gamma}_i^* \Rightarrow \check{\Delta}_i^* \vdash \hat{\Gamma}_j^* \Rightarrow \check{\Delta}_j^*$ and then apply the induction hypothesis.

(4) $\Gamma_j^* \vdash \Delta_j^*$ follows from an earlier line by (M). We use Lemmas 5 and 7 and the induction hypothesis.

(5) $\Gamma_j^* \vdash \Delta_j^*$ follows from two earlier lines by (T). We use $(T_{\wedge \vee})$ here and the induction hypothesis.

As these five cases are the only ways lines can be entered in a derivation, the proof is complete. ☐

As applications of this result we can take three familiar collections of rules: strict implication (S4), intuitionistic implication, material implication. All of these satisfy the conditions of the theorem. This seems to explain why *in these systems* there is no harm in confusing tautologies with rules: all you ever wanted to know about derived rules is already contained in the tautologies of the collection (granting (C), (M), and (T), of course). Hence, in a certain sense, rules can be eliminated. This need not be so if we add other connectives and other rules – unless the new rules are all tautologies.

TABLE XII

Rules for material implication

$(\supset)$	$A, A \supset B \vdash B$
	$B \vdash A \supset B$
	$\vdash A, A \supset B$

TABLE XIII

Rules for necessity

$(\square)$	$\dfrac{\vdash A}{\vdash \square A}$	$\square A, \square(A \supset B) \vdash \square B$	$\square A \vdash \square \square A$	$A \Rightarrow B \equiv \square(A \supset B)$

If we allow both $\Rightarrow$ and $\supset$ (material implication), the axioms simplify to something very close to S4. The rules for $\supset$ are given in Table XII. We then define

$$\square A = (\top \Rightarrow A)$$

The derived rules for $\square$ are given in Table XIII.

Conversely, given rules ($\square$) we can derive all we need about $\Rightarrow$, so with the aid of $\supset$, we have an equivalent formulation. This falls short of S4 only in the lack of the rule: $\square A \vdash A$. There is no harm in adding this.

Does this metatheorem justify modal logic? No, not by itself since it is only a formal result. But it at least shows that the rules are not as willfully arbitrary as might be thought in just seeing the axioms. And it has given us a good exercise in keeping clear about rules and derived rules.

Oxford University

BIBLIOGRAPHY

[1] Curry, H. B., *Foundations of Mathematical Logic*, McGraw-Hill, 1963.
[2] Scott, D., 'Background to Formalization', in *Truth, Syntax and Modality* (ed. by H. Leblanc), North-Holland, 1972, pp. 244–273.
[3] Scott, D., 'On Engendering an Illusion of Understanding', *J. of Philosophy* **68** (1971), 787–807.
[4] Scott, D., 'Completeness and Axiomatizability in Many-Valued Logic', *Tarski Symposium* (ed. by L. Henkin), Amer. Math. Soc. (in press).

BENGT HANSSON

A PROGRAM FOR PRAGMATICS

The best way to delimitate the field of pragmatics, at least from one side, is probably to try to fix the boundary between it and its neighbour, semantics. So I will begin this paper with an attempt to characterize semantics. After that I will consider the frontier at the other side, in particular the border to the general theory of speech acts. Finally I will give a few examples of philosophical problems, or rather types of philosophical problems, the structure of which I think will be more conspicuous in the light of the distinctions made in this paper.

Since I am interested in a rather precise definition of *pragmatics*, and in particular in one which contrasts with *semantics*, I will disregard those uses of the latter term which tend to embrace the whole field of philosophy of language or theory of meaning in a very general sense, but instead concentrate on definitions close to the one made famous by Charles Morris: semantics is the study of the relation between signs and their 'designata'.

Applied to proper names and nouns for tangible objects this definition seems clear enough: the word *Bill* designates Bill, the man, and the word *snow* designates snow, the meteorological phenomenon. We run into some trouble, however, when we come to abstract nouns and whole phrases: is the designatum of the word *greedy* the abstract concept of greedyness and is the designatum of the compound symbol *snow is white* the fact that snow is white? If so, we loose a good deal of the gain in concreteness that semantics was meant to provide by going from sounds to things.

The Tarski-inspired solution to this problem is to introduce conditions of truth and applicability: to know the designatum of a sentence is to know under which conditions it is true and to know the designatum of an abstract noun is to know when it is applicable. Instead of saying what the designatum *is*, ontologically, we only say what it means to know it. This of course immediately leads to semantic discoveries of the type '*snow is white* is true if and only if snow is white', but it also leads to an

S. Stenlund (ed.), Logical Theory and Semantic Analysis, 163–174. All Rights Reserved.
Copyright © 1974 by D. Reidel Publishing Company, Dordrecht-Holland.

important generalisation concerning the words corresponding to so-called logical constants: one can do semantics for words like *and* and *or*, not by pointing out something as their designata, but by describing how they operate on the truth conditions of the sentence-tokens they conjoin.

With other rules taking care of quantifiers we arrive at the full-blown model-theoretic semantics. By considering so-called models, i.e. systems of objects with extensionally interpreted constants and predicates, it provides, strictly speaking, only a semantics for logical constants, but it is easily supplemented with trivial semantic rules to cover ordinary descriptive discourses.

A major achievement was the introduction in the late 50's of model systems or possible worlds. Instead of looking at only one model at a time, one considers several simultaneously together with a relation of alternativeness or accessibility between them. This made it possible to let the truth value of a sentence in one model depend not only on the truth values of its subsentences in that model, but on their truth values in any accessible model. Such a semantics is suited for modal operators and some propositional attitudes.

There are of course many other parts of the language for which an adequate, generally accepted semantics is at most in sight – I will mention only sentences containing dispositional predicates, conditionals and non-declaratives – but there is no doubt that model-theoretic semantics has been a success, shedding much light on several important questions.

This is perhaps the reason why Richard Montague took it as his point of departure for his conception of pragmatics[1]. The general idea is to enrich our language with so-called index words, i.e. words like *I, now, here*, the meanings of which are determined by the situation in which they are uttered. If we think of each model or each possible world as containing information about who is the speaker, when something is said and where it is said, a sentence can be said to be true or false relative to such a model. The models are often called indices or points of reference in this connection. And with the crucial concept of true-at-an-index at hand we can do Montaguean pragmatics just as we did semantics.

I think it is a good idea to start a pragmatic program by studying sentences containing index words, but for reasons that will appear later I am not prepared to identify that study with pragmatics. But even as an indispensable prolegomena to pragmatics, the study of indexical expressions needs a little elaboration. I will mention three types of problems which have to be solved before we can say that we understand the behaviour of index words to a satisfactory degree.

It is clear that the introduction of *I* requires a speaker coordinate, that *you* requires a listener coordinate, that *now* requires a time coordinate, that *here* requires a space coordinate and so on for a few well-behaved indexicals. These coordinates are all easily represented in an index point. The first problem has to do with the fact that already such an innocent-looking indexical as *we* has two different uses: one including and one excluding the listener. (Many languages have different pronouns for these two occasions.) In *we've had a wonderful night, haven't we?* the listener is definitely included, while he is equally definitely excluded in *we lived in London then, you know*. Shall we say that *we* is ambiguous in the same way as e.g. *bill* is ambiguous? It is a very unintuitive solution and a very arbitrary one: it would be possible to split up *we* into as many pieces as we please by introducing new distinctions. We obviously need a new coordinate – an inclusive/exclusive *we*-determiner coordinate. Technically, it is a simple matter – we just introduce a 0 or a 1 at a new place in the index – but since its occurrence has to be determined by the context, we must find out precisely in which contexts it is to be a 0 and in which it is to be a 1. And this is not a simple formal matter, but a piece of empirical linguistic research.

We also need to know something about the logical relationships between sentences containing *I* and sentences containing *we*. *I saw a boat on the lake* should follow logically from *we saw a boat on the lake*, but *I saw seventeen boats on the lake* need not follow from *we saw seventeen boats on the lake* for some of us may have seen some of the boats and others the other ones, and *we will meet again* does not entail *I will meet again*. Some coordinate in the index must determine whether we have a collective or distributive use of *we*.

The second problem has to do with the great number of indexical expressions in our language. *I, you, here, now* and tensed verb forms are the standard examples, but there are many more: *home, away, right, left, mother, granny, likewise*, etc. Also most *the*-expressions are indexical – what *the man* refers to is determined by the context. All these types of indexicals require one or more new coordinates.

The common point of my two first problems is that we seem to end up with an overwhelming lot of coordinates in our indices if we want to include any substantial part of everyday language in our treatment. This does not suggest that Montague's approach is in any way wrong or less interesting, but only that there is little hope for making the theory of indexicals such a streamlined, nicely formalised theory as he seemed to esteem.

Obviously, we cannot find a limited number of features to put into an index and hope that they will represent the full context enough in detail. If an index is to contain sufficient information for the determination of truth values for all sentences, then it has to contain the whole context. This is perhaps a workable situation, but it clearly diminishes the explanatory power of the index point approach.

The third problem has to do with the interaction between intensional operators and indexicals. It seems as if e.g. *tomorrow* and *the next day* were just two variants of one and the same idea. But inside the scope of an intensional operator, such as *promise*, they behave differently: *the bishop promised to come tomorrow* means that he promised to come the day after this utterance was made, while *the bishop promised to come the next day* means that he promised to come the day after he made his promise. We must compare this with *the bishop promised to come next week* where we do not have a single word to substitute for *next week*. The point is once again that it is empirical linguistic research that is needed to deepen our insight into the theory of indexical expressions.

But let us assume that we have a sufficient familiarity with that theory – how does it relate to pragmatics? Robert Stalnaker has proposed [2] that Montague's step from sentences to truth values shall be split up in two – one from sentences to propositions and one from propositions to truth values, and that the study of the first step is to be regarded as pragmatics and the study of the second one as semantics. He gives the following example to illustrate the need for his distinction: someone says *he is a fool* and points in the direction of Daniels (who is not a fool) and O'Leary (an obvious fool). If it is not clear to you whom he is pointing at you are in doubt about the truth of the sentence uttered and you are so because you are in doubt about which proposition was asserted, while you are perfectly clear about the truth values of the propositions in each of the two possibilities. If, on the other hand, he clearly points at Daniels, but you do not know whether he is a fool, the source of your doubts is of a very different kind.

Stalnaker's point seems to be a good one, so we accept it from now on. This means that we split up the things in our former index points into two bundles, one called context and one called possible world. A sentence together with a context determines a proposition (the meaning of the sentence) and a proposition together with a possible world determines a truth value.

Within pragmatics we study how contexts help determine the meaning of individual sentence occurrences. But it is not Stalnaker's view that this activity is identical with pragmatics:

Pragmatics is the study of linguistic acts and the contexts in which they are performed. There are two major types of problems to be solved within pragmatics: first, to define interesting types of speech acts and speech products; second, to characterize the features of the speech context which help determine which proposition is expressed by a given sentence.[3]

Let us agree to call the study of indexical expressions pragmatics on the first level. If we think that this is a too narrow conception of pragmatics (as we in fact do) we want to extend it. But if we include the general theory of linguistic acts (as Stalnaker proposes) we end up with a very large and amorphous field. Of course, such fields need names too, but there are at least two good reasons not to choose 'pragmatics' for this one: first, names such as theory of speech acts or philosophy of language are already established; second, we are looking for a companion concept to 'semantics' and therefore for a reasonably sharply delimited concept – one which makes it illuminating to say e.g. 'let us separate the semantic and pragmatic aspects of the issue'.

If the study of speech acts is pragmatics on the third level, I will try to define pragmatics on the second level. It will differ only finely from the first level, but I think that a few interesting philosophical problems dwell in the intermediate region. In the idiom of speech acts I will restrict myself to the utterance of sentences for the purpose of expressing propositions. My general formula will be 'the study of how the proposition expressed is related to the sentence uttered', where, for the interesting cases, I want 'the proposition expressed' to be distinguished from 'the literal meaning of the sentence'.

Obvious cases of this phenomenon are when language is used metaphorically or ironically. Both *cowards die many times before their deaths* and *for Brutus is an honourable man* literally mean something else than the proposition they express. But this may also be true when language is used in a straightforwardly declarative way.

Let me explain what I mean by a square and obvious example: John always confuses the names of Bill's wife Susan and Bill's sister Sue. This is well-known to Bill, so when John says *I hope Sue's cold is getting better*, Bill understands that it is his wife who is referred to. In this communication situation the proposition expressed by John and the one conveyed to Bill are both that John hopes that Susan's cold is getting better, but neither is identical to the meaning of the individual sentence that was used to convey this proposition. If on the other hand John, for once in his life, got his things straight and really meant Sue, then the proposition expressed and the meaning of the sentence coincided, both being different from the proposition conveyed to Bill. In general we must distinguish between (a) the proposition expressed by the speaker, (b) the proposition conveyed to the receiver, and (c) the meaning of the sentence uttered. The distinction between (a) and (b) is probably of less philosophical importance than the one between these two and (c).

In this example John used the language incorrectly, but Bill's knowledge automatically corrected it. In other situations it is not a matter of correcting, but of complementing. If, in a normal situation, somebody says *before he left the headmaster gave a candy bar to each girl in the class* he is interpreted as having asserted that the boys did not get any.

At this point I would like to guard myself against a possible misinterpretation. I distinguish between the meaning of a sentence and the proposition expressed by it. But both these things must be kept apart from what we might call the information conveyed by the uttering of a sentence. This may embrace much more than the proposition expressed. To some extent this is perfectly trivial: the uttering of a sentence may convey the information that the speaker lisps, that he has a piercing voice, etc. – things that have nothing to do with the meaning of the sentence or the proposition expressed. But there is also a more subtle difference which has to do with what is vaguely called contextual implications. Something may well be implied without being expressed. Consider e.g. the sentence *there were ten or fifteen people around*, uttered by someone as a reply to a question about the size of the audience at a certain occasion. The fact that he used the expression *ten or fifteen* implies or suggests that he did not know the exact number. But this uncertainty was not anything he intended to communicate – he just wanted to give a rough estimate, not to tell anything about the uncertainty of his knowledge. The situation must be contrasted with the candy bar headmaster, where it was the speaker's intention to communicate the fact that the boys got no candy bar. I do not deny, of course, that *or*-expressions are sometimes used just for the purpose of communicating uncertainty – especially if there is heavy stress on the *or* like in *either John or Bill must have taken the wallet*. My point is only that some *or*-expressions are sometimes not so used, but that it even in these cases may be legitimate to infer the uncertainty.

Other cases of 'contextual implications' which are not under consideration here are those where the statement of something *a priori* expected is interpreted as implying that there were good reasons to assume the contrary. An entry like *captain sober today* in a log-book with no other entries about the captain does entitle you to infer that the captain is a tippler, but the log keeper did not *express* that in his entry, though he certainly wanted to imply or suggest it.

In philosophically more relevant examples it is often the case that the proposition expressed is clear enough, but that the meaning of the sentence is either vague or difficult to determine. This has to do with the fact that philosophical analysis to such a great extent is backward reasoning. In an ordinary situation of speech production we think of the speaker as having a proposition or at least a rough idea of a proposition in mind. There are several sentences which would express that idea, perhaps with different degrees of accuracy. If the speaker masters the language he chooses one of these sentences. There is, so to speak, a function, yielding a set of sentences for each proposition. When a listener decodes a message he must use the *inverse* function – given a sentence, he must find a proposition such that the given sentence is in the set assigned to that proposition. An individual sentence-token, given in its context, seldom presents serious problems. But when a philosopher proposes to analyse a sentence, he usually considers only the sentence-type, thereby trying to capture all its instances in one go. If the instances are homogeneous enough it may work well, but sometimes the following anomalous situation comes up: for each possible instance there is no proposition such that the speech production function assigns this instance as one of the normal expressions of it. Sentence-types of this sort can be found in e.g. linguistic discussions of intensional contexts. Let me only mention *a unicorn is an entity such that a man such that he seeks it loves a woman such that she seeks it*[4]. For each proposed meaning of this sentence we have to admit that anyone who really meant that, would normally have expressed himself otherwise. This is of course not to say that such sentences are meaningless, only that it is impossible to ascribe a definite meaning to them, based only on the configuration of words.

Let us now take an example from an authentic philosophical discussion. It is perhaps not terribly important, but it is easy to unveil. It has been maintained by some authors that there is a certain kind of permission, so-called free-choice permission, characterised by the fact that it conforms to the following distribution principle:

$$P(p \vee q) \rightarrow Pp \ \& \ Pq$$

The reason for this is of course that we sometimes say e.g. *you may use form A or form B*, meaning that we allow someone both to use form *A* and to use form *B*, leaving the choice to him. But it is of course also possible to have another instance of the same sentence where one only wants to delimit a set of possibilities and where the one permitted has to follow other rules in his choice of the right form. Only in this second case is *or* used disjunctively. Since a disjunctive reading of *or* is standard we may say that the last interpretation gives the literal meaning of the sentence, but we are equally justified in saying that the meaning is indeterminate. We are now able to reconstrue the ideas behind the formula above: $P(p \vee q)$ is a literal formalisation of *you may use form A or form B* in the sense that it is obtained by substituting standard formal counterparts for the different phrases in the linguistic expression – '*P*' for *you may*, '*P*' for *use form A*, '$\vee$' for *or* and '*q*' for *(use) form B*. In our terminology this means that $P(p \vee q)$ represents the literal meaning of the sentence (on one conception of this notion).

Now it is an empirical fact that we are justified to infer that we are allowed to use form *A* and also allowed to use form *B* almost in all cases when an instance of our sample sentence is uttered. This is of course formalised *Pp & Pq*. But this inference is *not* one from the literal meaning of the sentence, but one from the proposition expressed by it, as can be seen from the fact that it is not valid for a few special instances. We are thus in no way justified to say that *Pp* & *Pq* follows from *P*(*p* ∨ *q*), only that it follows from the proposition expressed by *you may use form A or form B*. What, then, is this proposition? In most contexts, I think, simply *Pp* & *Pq*.

Perhaps the root of the problem is the unsuspicious identification of *or*-expressions with disjunctive expressions that many text-books in logic are guilty of. The preceding example shows that there may well be *or*-expressions without any disjunctive state of affairs being involved. We can see this more clearly if we notice that *or* may be replaced by *and* without any substantial change in the proposition expressed. Would a defender of free-choice permission then claim that *P*(*p* ∨ *q*) and *P*(*p* & *q*) are equivalent? Another example of the same phenomenon is *boys or girls under twelve admitted free* as compared with *boys and girls under twelve admitted free*. Another case where *or* is not used for forming a disjunction is in *I do not know if I will be there or not*, for it does not mean that somebody is at a loss whether he will be in the disjunctive state of affairs of either being or not being there.

A related problem is Ross's 'paradox' in deontic logic. Most systems of deontic logic validate a rule which says that if an action is a logical consequence of another action, then an obligation to do the first action follows logically from an obligation to do the second one. Since, in particular, *p* ∨ *q* follows logically from *p* the following formula will be valid:

$$Op \to O(p \vee q)$$

But, Ross says, *you ought to post the letter or burn it* does not follow from *you ought to post the letter*. True in most contexts, but irrelevant! There is no reason to assume that the proposition expressed by *you ought to post the letter or burn it* is the proposition formalised as *O*(*p* ∨ *q*). Certainly there is a one-to-one correspondence between the parts of the formula and the parts of the linguistic expression, but that, at most, entitles us to conclude something about the literal meaning of the sentence. The proposition represented by *O*(*p* ∨ *q*) is something like that you ought to act in such a way that the disjunctive state of affairs consisting in either the letter being posted or the letter being burnt becomes true. This certainly holds, but it is not very informative, given *Op*. On the other hand, the proposition expressed by *you ought to post the letter or burn it* is, in a typical context, that you ought to act in one of two ways, the choice being up to you.

Ross's 'paradox' immediately leads over to the general problem of applying logical methods to philosophical questions. The language of formal logic is designed to represent propositions, not to reflect the structure of ordinary language. Of course it often happens that we can find a structural similarity between a formula and a sentence, but e.g. the usual way to formalise a universally quantified sentence as an implication shows that it is by no means necessary.

A logical analysis often goes like this: we start with a few ordinary language sentences, possibly given in their contexts. We do our best to understand what propositions they express and we represent these propositions in a formal language. The logical machinery then works for a while and it finally produces some logical consequences. We are anxious to check if these consequences are acceptable, so we translate them back into ordinary language. This is often done by a more or less mechanical replacement of formal symbols by ordinary language expressions according to some 'standard reading' of the symbols. Such a translation of $O(p \lor q)$ would yield *you ought to post the letter or burn it*. The problem with this kind of mechanically construed sentences is that they are, as it seems, instances without any context. When we try to find out what propositions they express we seem to have no other clue than the mere configurations of words. Were this really so Ross would be justified in his interpretation of $O(p \lor q)$. But this view is a mistake. Even mechanically construed 'standard readings' of formulas have a kind of context: they are endpoints in deductive chains of formulas, beginning with representations of ordinary language sentences. The general principles for the construction of the formal language and the way it represents propositions may also serve as a kind of context which helps determine a correct interpretation. In the case of Ross's 'paradox' this context excludes the reading according to which the agent is permitted to choose.

A similar line of reasoning may be applied to the problem of substitutivity in intensional contexts. This is a very complicated and difficult problem and I am convinced that it is so because several different philosophical issues have been tangled in a few examples. Of course I cannot hope to solve even the smallest of the problems involved in this paper, but I think that pragmatic considerations can help to illuminate the issues in at least two respects.

Let us take the following example as our starting-point: *John knows that* 9 *is greater than* 7 is true for a certain John. In view of the true identity *the number of major planets* = 9 we would perhaps expect *John knows that the number of major planets is greater than* 7 to be true, but our logical intuition tells us that this is not a consequence of the given premises. The first step towards a solution is the Quineian observation that the last sentence can be understood in two ways: either opaquely as asserting that John knows that there are more than seven major planets, or transparently as asserting that John knows about that number which in fact is the number of major planets (be this known to John or not) that it is greater than seven. No doubt, most instances of the sentence-type express the first of these propositions and only instances with special contexts express the second one. But the fact that we have got the sentence-instance above by substituting *the number of major planets* for 9 in *John knows that* 9 *is greater than* 7 is clearly such a special context. The very fact that we have obtained a sentence as a result of certain logical operations delimits the set of acceptable interpretations of that sentence and in the case above it provides good evidence that it has to be interpreted transparently, i.e. in such a way that the inference is valid.

The other point in this connection concerns the interpretation of identity statements. Above we did not hesitate to refer *the number of major planets* = 9 to that category, but we must also note that it is equivalent to *there are* 9 *major planets*, a sentence without any surface signs of being an identity statement. One way to interpret *the number of major planets* = 9 is to assume that it asserts the proposition that the two linguistic expressions *the number of major planets* and 9 refer to one and the same object. But this is not a proposition about the number nine, but one about the English language. If we want this interpretation to combine with the sentences about John we must interpret them in a corresponding way – as asserting e.g. that John knows that the linguistic expression *the number of major planets* denotes something which is greater than seven. But on this interpretation there is no reason to assume that substitutivity will hold.

On another interpretation *the number of major planets* = 9 is purely referential: it says that that object which is the number of major planets is identical to nine. On such an interpretation substitutivity will no doubt hold, but our identity statement does not say that there are nine major planets – it only asserts the analytical proposition that nine is identical to itself. The fact that there are nine major planets is not part of the proposition expressed, but is something which determines *which* proposition is expressed instead. Such an interpretation requires the reading of the John-sentences to be the transparent one, thereby making the inference valid.

As a final example where pragmatic considerations may solve a problem I would like to discuss a principle in the logic of preference, proposed by both Sören Halldén and G. H. von Wright[5], namely that p is preferred to q if and only if $p \& -q$ is preferred to $-p \& q$. They both argue along the following lines: when somebody says that he prefers p to q he always compares in his mind (p without q) with (q without p). But this is an argument from a sentence uttered to a proposition expressed, and, as we have seen, there is no necessary connection between the two. Halldén's and von Wright's observation is no doubt very valuable, but it is not an observation to the point that pPq (where P stands for the relation of preference) and $(p \& -q) P(-p \& q)$ mean the same thing, but only to the point that p *is preferred to* q is almost invariably used to express the proposition that p without q is preferred to q without p, a proposition that is rightly formalised as $(p \& -q) P(-p \& q)$ and not as pPq.

University of Lund

NOTES

[1] See e.g. 'Pragmatics' in *Contemporary Philosophy – La philosophie contemporaine* (ed. by R. Klibansky), Florence 1968, or 'Pragmatics and Intensional Logic', *Synthese* **22** (1970).
[2] 'Pragmatics', *Synthese* **22** (1971).
[3] 'Pragmatics'.
[4] 'Universal grammar', *Theoria* **36** (1970).
[5] In Halldén's *The Logic of 'Better'*, Lund-Copenhagen 1957 and in von Wright's two studies *The Logic of Preference*, Edinburgh 1963, and 'The Logic of Preference Reconsidered', *Theory and Decision* **3** (1972).

GÖRAN HERMERÉN

MODELS

I. INTRODUCTION

It would no doubt be a gross exaggeration to say that the term 'model' is always used in a clear and consistent fashion by scientists and philosophers.[1] However, there seems to be some agreement on the following minimum requirement: X is a model of Y, only if X and Y have the same or a similar structure.[2]

But this explanation is not very illuminating; it has to be supplemented by answers to questions like: What is meant by the expression 'the same or a similar structure'? How does one decide in a particular case whether X and Y have the same or a similar structure? What, incidentally, is the value of the variables X and Y? After what principles are elements and relations in X and Y selected, when the structures of X and Y are compared?

A closer examination of writings on models clearly shows that scientists use and talk about several different kinds of models, and it is not at all obvious that these models can be analyzed in the same way. A first step towards a clarification of the notion of model and of the functions of models in science should then be to describe and distinguish between various kinds of models, and that is what I intend to do in this paper.

The present paper is an outline of a part of a larger study on the relations between models, theories and reality. In order to be able to say anything illuminating about these relations, it is necessary to make certain distinctions. Obviously, the questions 'How are models related to theories?' and 'How are models related to what they are models of?' have to be answered in different ways, depending on what kind of models and theories one has in mind.

I shall here try to pave the way for a rational discussion of these questions by distinguishing in an admittedly sketchy way between some kinds of models. The exposition makes no claim of completeness whatsoever, and I shall not go into details about various kinds of replicas and

S. Stenlund (ed.), Logical Theory and Semantic Analysis, 175–191. All Rights Reserved.
Copyright © 1974 by D. Reidel Publishing Company, Dordrecht-Holland.

analogy machines; they are of a rather limited theoretical interest and are anyway rarely confused with the kinds of models I am going to discuss here. Instead I shall call attention to some less obvious distinctions which seem to be worth making and which sometimes (and quite recently) have been overlooked.[3]

II. SCALE MODELS

If X is a scale model of Y, then X and Y are both physical objects. Suppose Y is a ship and X is a scale model of Y. Then X and Y are very much alike, though X is much smaller than Y. Every part of the model corresponds to a similar part of the ship, and the proportions between the parts of the model correspond to the proportions between the parts of the ship. X is simply a more or less faithful replica of Y, if X is a scale model of Y.

The similarities between X and Y can in this case be more or less extensive, depending on the number of properties of Y that are represented by the model. Using the number and kinds of similarities as a point of departure, it is possible to distinguish between different types of scale models. If X and Y are made of the same material and work in the same way, X can be said to be a complete scale model of Y. In the example discussed above this means that both the ship and the model are equipped with working engines in different size. Obviously most scale models are not complete in this sense.

If one wants to demonstrate the structure of our planetary system, it may be very useful to work with scale models, especially from a pedagogical point of view. In this case the model will be much smaller than the thing modeled, in other cases it will be much bigger. In all cases the model and the thing modeled have the same structure. But scale models are not only used for pedagogical reasons in demonstrating something that exists. They are also used in constructing new objects like planes, cars and bridges, since it is easier and much less expensive to make experiments in wind tunnels and so forth with models than with complete and full size planes; we cannot afford to destroy a bridge every time we want to see if it is able to carry a certain weight.

I shall not discuss the relations between scale models and various types of analogues, like hydraulic models of economic supply and demand. I have described scale models here at the outset, because it is useful to introduce these models as contrasts to the ones to be discussed in the following sections.

III. MATHEMATICAL MODELS

The difference between scale models and mathematical models is obvious enough: if X is a mathematical model of Y, then X is not a replica or a more or less faithful copy of Y. However, this does not mean that the notion of a mathematical model is very clear.

Sometimes the term 'mathematical model' is used in such a wide sense that any model containing mathematical expressions is said to be a mathematical model. In that case many of the models to be discussed later on in this paper will be classified as mathematical models. But this usage will not be adopted here. I am going to use 'mathematical model' in a perhaps rather narrow sense: to refer to convenient (simplifying) mathematical expressions of empirical data. Thus, I shall say that X is a mathematical model of Y, if and only if X is a set of mathematical equations, Y is data about some empirical process or system, and X fits Y.

The notion of fitness in the last clause of this preliminary definition may need some clarification. Let X be a wave equation and let Y be a swinging pendulum. Then X fits Y in the sense that X describes (but does not explain) Y, provided that some or all of the nonlogical constants and variables of X have been given a particular empirical interpretation. The same equation might fit data about other processes (oscillating electric circuits, persons walking back and forth restlessly), but then the nonlogical constants and variables in the equation will have to be interpreted differently.

A simple example may help to explain this idea. By consulting statistical yearbooks we can get information about the number of births in a country over a certain period of time: at t_1 the number was n, at t_2 the number was n, etc. This can be described by a graph ψ (see next page) and the curve in the graph can be described by an equation which then fits the empirical data. This equation will also fit data about all other processes which can be illustrated by a similar graph.

Now it should be made quite clear that in this section I have used the term 'mathematical model' in a rather narrow sense, and that there has been a development within the social sciences from models which merely summarize and describe empirical data to models which can be used for explanation, prediction and control. The latter models are connected

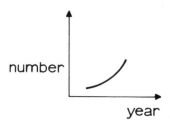

with theories in a way which I am going to discuss in the next section, and they have to satisfy a number of requirements which are not satisfied by merely descriptive models. The distinction between such descriptive models ('mathematical models' in my sense) and models involving theories about reality is in my view very important; and therefore I suggest that the latter are called 'theoretical models', though I know quite well that the term 'mathematical model' is sometimes used (particularly by social scientists) in such a wide sense that it includes also theoretical models and perhaps other kinds of models as well.

To sum up: terminological disputes should be bypassed as quickly as possible in order to get to the theoretically and philosophically interesting issues. Whatever terminology is preferred, I think it is obvious that if a model is merely a description of the available data about some process and does not involve a theory about this process, it does not provide any explanations. But many models in mathematical form are based on such theories. This is true of the next kind of models to be discussed here.

IV. THEORETICAL MODELS

The term 'theoretical model' is used in various ways. When I use this term, I am referring to models of the following kind: the billiard ball model of gases, Bohr's atom model and the Crick-Watson model of the DNA-molecule. If X is a theoretical model of Y, then X is not a physical object distinct from Y, as is the case if X is a replica or a scale model of Y. Instead, X is a set of hypotheses about Y, usually stated in mathematical form.[4]

Thus, when the billiard ball model is referred to in the kinetic theory of gases, one does not have in mind a scale model consisting of small elastic spheres in a box but a series of hypotheses about gases and their inner structure of the following kind: that gases consist of molecules, that these molecules do not exert any forces on each other except at impact, that they move in straight lines except in the moment of collision, and so forth. The laws of the movement of these molecules can be stated within the framework of classical Newtonian mechanics. (Needless to say, it is important to distinguish between these hypotheses and the diagrams or pictures, which sometimes are used to illustrate the model. I shall call these diagrams 'visual models'.)

These hypotheses involve certain simplifications; some complications are intentionally disregarded. By using these hypotheses as a point of departure, it is possible to deduce principles relating, for instance, the pressure, volume and temperature to each other (Boyle's law); and it is also possible to explain different experimental results in the sense that descriptions of them can be deduced from the hypotheses and certain initial conditions. The value of the model is depending on how well it explains known experimental findings, and what and how many laws can be deduced from it.

There is a vast literature on the complexity and difficulties inherent in notions of testing,[5] but this is not the place to discuss these problems. For my purposes it is quite sufficient to say that in this respect theoretical models are very much like theories: they are tested in roughly the same way, and the problems that arise in testing theories also arise in testing theoretical models, and vice versa. In this respect they differ from some of the models to be discussed below.

Indeed, the main reason for using 'model' rather than 'theory' here seems to be that in using the word 'model', one makes clear that one does not claim to give a definite and exhaustive (whatever that is) theory about, say, the inner structure of gases, but rather a preliminary approximation.

V. SET-THEORETICAL AND INTERPRETATIVE MODELS

Set-theoretical and interpretative models are conceptually related to each other, and to explain the difference between them I shall have to use the concept of a formal system.[6]

A simple example might help to clarify what I have in mind. Let us suppose that S is a formal system, and that two of the axioms in S are

(A.1) $x \circ y = y \circ x$
(A.2) $(x \circ y) \circ z = x \circ (y \circ z)$

These axioms might be interpreted in several ways, as is well known. They can be given arithmetical, logical and geometrical interpretations. In the first case 'x' and 'y' are variables for numbers, '$\circ$' is the mathematical operation of addition and '$=$' is interpreted as identity. According to the axioms this operation is commutative and associative. But 'x' and 'y' can also be interpreted as sentential variables, '$\circ$' as the conjunction, and '$=$' as material equivalence; and this interpretation again yields a true statement.

I shall now say X is a *set-theoretical model* of Y, if and only if there is a formal system S such that (i) X is a set of entities and operations, and (ii) Y is an axiom or a set of axioms in S, and (iii) X satisfies Y, i.e. turns Y into true statements.[7] The entities mentioned in this definition can be of several kinds (events, numbers, balls, linguistic expressions, and so forth) and it is therefore possible to distinguish between several kinds of set-theoretical models, depending on, for example, whether the entities are abstract or not. Furthermore, I propose to distinguish between (1) the set of entities along with operations and relations that satisfy a particular system of axioms, and (2) the set of names of these entities, operations or relations. When I talk about set-theoretical models, I have only (1) in mind.

However, by replacing the variables in the axioms according to certain specified rules with elements in the second type of set, i.e. with names of entities, operations and relations, it is possible to turn the axioms into true sentences. These sentences are interpretations of the axioms; and I shall say that X is an *interpretative model* of Y, if and only if X is such an interpretation of the axiom system Y. In this case the model consists of sentences and not of entities, relations and operations. Rules indicating what variables in the axioms may be replaced with what names I shall call rules of interpretation. By using different sets of rules of interpretation it is possible to obtain several different interpretative models of one and the same formal system.[8]

Social scientists often seem to feel very alienated or frustrated, when philosophers of science talk about models in the way I have done in this section. But I shall not in this context discuss if and to what extent the kinds of models they are familiar with (say, Easton's model of the political system) can be explicated by some of the concepts discussed here. This will have to be left for a separate investigation. Rather, I would like to touch very briefly on a different question: what is the use of these models? They can be used in several ways in the construction and testing of theories.

Suppose, for instance, that one wants to show that a system of axioms is consistent. A familiar strategy in such cases is to try to invent a model of this system. If X is a concrete set-theoretical model, i.e. consists of a finite set of objects like sticks and relations like being longer than, and if X satisfies the postulates in a formal system S, then we have established the *absolute* consistency of S. If, however, X satisfies the postulates in S, and X is an abstract set-theoretical model, i.e. consists of an infinite set of entities and relations from some other abstract postulate system S', then we have established the *relative* consistency of S; S is consistent, if S' is consistent.

The latter strategy has been applied successfully to solve the problem of the consistency of Non-Euclidean geometry; plane and solid Lobachevskian geometry – in which Euclid's famous parallel postulate does not hold – can thus be shown to be as consistent as plane and solid Euclidean geometry by a model devised by Henry Poincaré. Moreover, it is possible to set up an arithmetical model of Euclidean plane geometry and thus to show that Euclidean plane geometry is consistent, if the real number system is consistent. Accordingly, Lobachevskian place geometry is consistent, if the real number system is consistent.[9]

Finally, if the set of postulates in a formal system can be shown to be consistent, it can normally be given many true interpretations. For instance, a formalized Boolean algebra can be interpreted as a calculus of classes, propositions, and spatial areas as in the Venn diagram.

VI. FORMAL MODELS

The term 'formal model' is defined by Abraham Kaplan in the following way: "a model *of* a theory which presents the latter purely as a structure of uninterpreted symbols."[10] The attempt to create a formal model in the sense envisaged by Kaplan may be stimulated by discoveries of formal or material analogies between phenomena of different kinds, e.g. the spread of an epidemic and the spread of drug abuse.

Such analogies are far from unusual in science, and they can be illustrated by an example used by Carl G. Hempel.[11] According to Poiseulle's law the flow of a fluid in a pipe can be described by the formula

$$(1) \qquad V = c \cdot (p_1 - p_2)$$

which means that the volume V of fluid flowing through a fixed cross-section per second is proportional to the difference in pressure between the ends of the pipe $(p_1 - p_2)$.

This formula has the same form as Ohm's law, according to which a flow of an electric charge in a wire can be described as follows:

$$(2) \qquad I = k \cdot (v_1 - v_2)$$

which means that the quantity I of electric charge flowing through a fixed cross-section of the wire per second is proportional to the potential difference maintained between the ends of the wire. Since c is inversely proportional to the length of the pipe, and k is inversely proportional to the length of the wire, we have here a nice example of structural similarity between two scientific laws.

To put it somewhat more precisely: the analogy between Ohm's and Poiseulle's laws can be described as a syntactic isomorphism between two corresponding sets of laws. And this means, as Hempel points out, that the empirical terms "occurring in the first set of laws can be matched, one by one, with those of the second set in such a way that if in one of the laws of the first set each term is replaced by its counterpart, a law of the second set is obtained; and vice versa."[12]

A structural similarity of this kind suggests that it might be fruitful to try to find out if the two theories – or parts of them – in which these laws are included have the same or a similar formal structure, and if this structure can be presented in the form of an axiomatic system or an uninterpreted calculus. Such investigations have been carried out, some-times with spectacular success, for instance in the comparisons between optic and electro-magnetic theories. A specification of this formal struc-ture would then be a formal model in Kaplan's sense. And if the structure can be specified in the form of an uninterpreted calculus, then this cal-culus is a formal model of the theory in question.

The concept of a formal model defined in this way is obviously closely related to the concept of an interpretative model discussed in the previous section: if X is a formal model of Y, then Y is an interpretative model of X. This, of course, shows that one of these notions is dispensable, but I will not discuss here which one, if any, should be dropped. What I want to do is to clarify the relations between these notions.

A final point: if X is a theoretical model of Y, then Y is a class of events or processes and X is a set of hypotheses or assumptions about Y. But if X is a formal model of Y, then the range of significance of the variables is different: Y is a theory and X is an uninterpreted calculus. Accordingly, these notions are clearly quite distinct.

VII. BRAITHWAITE'S AND RUDNER'S CONCEPT OF A MODEL

In his book *Scientific Explanation* R. B. Braithwaite discusses the rela-tions between models and theories.[13] He there uses 'model' in a sense which seems to be different from any of those previously discussed, if I understand him correctly. His usage has been followed by Richard Rudner.[14] Models in this sense – which for want of better labels I intend to call B-R models – are related to (though different from) formal as well as set-theoretical and interpretative models. The relations between these four kinds of models can be described as follows.

Let X be a formal model of the two theories T and T', and let, following Rudner, T be a theory of personality and T' be a theory of pigment. The formal model of these two theories is a calculus, a formalized axiomatic system. T and T' have the same structure and they are interpretations of this axiomatic system. These interpretations are based on two non-identical rules of interpretations, which presuppose two different sets of entities, operations and relations which the theories are about. We can say that the two sets of entities that these theories are about are two set-theoretical models of one and the same calculus; and the different interpretations of this calculus can, according to the usage I have proposed, be said to be different interpretative models of the calculus.

So far I have indicated how formal, set-theoretical and interpretative models are related to each other. But how are B-R-models related to them? According to Rudner's usage we can in this case say that the theory T is a model of or for T' or vice versa. Whatever one chooses to say depends on several circumstances, above all what the investigation in question is about. If one wants to find out what factors influence personality and is familiar with the theory of pigment T', then it is possible to use T' as a model of or rather for T, i.e. for the construction of T, and this model may then have a certain heuristic value. If, however, one wants to study pigment and is familiar with T, it is in an analogous way possible to use T as a model for the construction of T'.

The relations between the four different kinds of models can be illustrated graphically (see Figure 1).

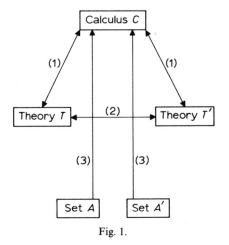

Fig. 1.

Here T and T' have been obtained from C with the help of two different sets of rules of interpretation R and R', and A and A' are the sets of entities and operations or relations which the theories are about and which satisfy the axioms in C.

In that case the following statements hold: (a) C is a formal model of both T and T', (b) T and T' are interpretative models of C, (c) A and A'

are two different set-theoretical models of C, and (d) T is a B-R-model of T' or the other way round, depending on which of the two theories that is epistemologically prior to the other. By closely examining the values of the variables X and Y in 'X is a model of Y', it can also readily be seen that the concept of theoretical model discussed in Section III cannot be identified with any of the other four kinds of models.

VIII. OUTLINE OF A SYSTEMATIC CLASSIFICATION OF MODELS

Some of the models which have been discussed in this paper can be compared to each other – and to other kinds of models – in the way indicated by Figure 2.

Value of Y ⟍ Value of X	Y = physical object	Y = event, process or system	Y = theory	Y = uninterpreted postulates
X = physical object	X is a scale model of Y			
X = diagram or picture		X is a visual model of Y		
X = system of hypotheses or a theory		X is a theoretical model of Y	X is a B-R- model of Y	
X = uninterpreted postulates			X is a formal model of Y	
X = set of entities and operations				X is a set- theoretical model of Y
X = set of names of entities and operations			.	X is an inter- pretative model of Y

Fig. 2.

This figure suggests a number of bases of division for a somewhat more systematic classification of models than is common in philosophy of science: (1) the values of the variable X, (2) the values of the variable Y, and (3) the relations between X and Y. For example, if the basis of division is only the value of the variable Y it is possible to distinguish between object models (Y is a physical object), static models (Y is a state of affairs), process models (Y is a process), system models (Y is a – physical, biological, or political – system of some kind), and so forth.

In addition to (1), (2) and (3) I would like to mention the functions of the model, i.e. the intended and actual use of models in science. This gives us a fourth possibility of classification. The first two bases of division are obvious enough from the diagram, and there is no need in the present context to spend more time on them. But this is not true of the two latter, to which I shall now turn. The first of them will be discussed in this section; the other will be saved to Section IX.

As far as the relations between X (the model) and Y (the thing modeled) are concerned, it is possible to distinguish between at least the following kinds of models:

(1) *Isomorphic models.* X is isomorphic to Y in the following sense: there is a one-one mapping from the elements of X to the elements of Y satisfying the condition that if a relation R holds between the elements a and b in X, then a corresponding relation R' holds between the corresponding elements a' and b' in Y.

(2) *Partially isomorphic models.* We can here distinguish between the following three cases: (i) some structures in X are isomorphic to some structures in Y, (ii) all structures in X are isomorphic to some structures in Y, and (iii) some structures in X are isomorphic to all structures in Y.

(3) *Homomorphic models.* The elements of Y have been divided into two or more equivalence classes. These equivalence classes have been ordered by one or more relations, and the structures obtained in this way are isomorphic to X in the sense explained above.

(4) *Partially homomorphic models.* It is here possible to distinguish between three different kinds of partially homomorphic models in roughly the same way as I did above in the discussion of three kinds of partially isomorphic models.

This enumeration makes no claim of completeness, and it should be an interesting exercise to see whether all the models discussed in the previous sections belong to some of these four categories. But since the space is limited, this exercise must be left to the reader. Instead I will discuss briefly the last basis of division mentioned above: the functions or uses of models.

IX. THE USES OF MODELS

Different models can have different functions, and one and the same model can also have different functions at the same time or in different contexts. A good model can probably be used in all or nearly all of the ways discussed in this section. Moreover, it should be stressed that it is difficult to draw a sharp line between some of the functions separated below.

After these preliminaries, I propose to distinguish between the following kinds of models, using the function of the model as a basis of division:

(1) *Data-organizing models.* Data are not relevant in themselves but only if they can be used as evidence for or against a hypothesis. Lacking precise hypotheses, a scholar can use a model when he is about to collect and organize data. Furthermore, the model can help him to survey large and complex sets of data.

(2) *Descriptive models.* The speed of the population growth can be described by the so-called logistic function, and this is a convenient and elegant way of summarizing known facts mathematically. The equations used can in their turn be illustrated by graphs or diagrams of various kinds.

(3) *Pedagogical models.* Models are sometimes used in the classroom to demonstrate the structure of the planetary system or the relations between the smallest parts of matter. Like the previous ones, these models can be said to describe whatever they are models of, but they are neither statements nor equations but physical objects or systems.

(4) *Explanatory and predictive models.* The function of many models is frequently not only descriptive: models are also used to explain or predict, say, processes of emigration or turn-overs in political systems. Moreover, such models may be used to regulate decision-making processes, the spread of epidemics, and so forth.

(5) *Heuristic models.* This is probably the function of models that is

most frequently stressed in textbooks in philosophy of science: the
models are used by scientists as a device to generate hypotheses and
theories. For instance, electronic models of the brain can suggest hypotheses, which then will have to be tested experimentally by neurolo-
gists and psychologists.

(6) *Test models.* A set-theoretical model can be used to test the consistency of a set of axioms, as I have already mentioned. Hypotheses
about the durability of certain materials can be tested experimentally by
scale models. The model is then tested systematically in wind tunnels and
so forth under various conditions to check whether the hypotheses in
question are correct.

(7) *Interpretative models.* The function of a model can also be to
interpret the postulates of a theory. Maxwell's equations, to take a fairly
well-known example, can be interpreted in several ways by different
set-theoretical models satisfying the equations. A formalized Boolean
algebra can, as I have already indicated, be interpreted in many ways.

Again, there is no need trying to aim at completeness. Models can
have other functions, and for some purposes it may be interesting to make
a still finer classification and distinguish between different kinds of, say,
explanatory and predictive models.

X. CONCLUDING REMARKS

What is the point of all these distinctions? The literature on models in
science is vast. Different authors use different terminology and ask different questions. It would be an interesting task to take a close look at models
in various disciplines – econometric models, stochastic models, learning
models, cybernetic models, mechanical models, electronical models, and
others – to see if and to what extent they can be analyzed by the conceptual
framework outlined here (which I believe they can). However, since the
space is limited this will again have to be left to the reader as an exercise.

Whatever terminology is used, the differences between the various
kinds of models should not be overlooked. The reason for this is simple.
Let us consider some of the more frequently discussed problems about
models: What are the criteria of adequacy of models? What is the relation
between models and theories? What is the relation between models and
reality? How are models constructed and tested? What is the function

of models? Clearly, the answer to these questions depends on what kind of model one has in mind. For example, there is no reason to believe that there is one set of criteria of adequacy that could or should be applied to all models. Thus, we do not have one set of questions concerning models but several sets, one for each kind of model.

To show this I shall now comment on only one of these five questions: what is the relation between models and theories? The answer to this question will not be the same for scale models, theoretical models, and set-theoretical models. In the first case the model is a copy of something that exists in reality or is under construction, but there is no obvious relation at all to a theory; no theory needs to be involved in the construction of a scale model. In the second case it seems very difficult to draw a sharp line between model and theory; if there is a difference, it concerns the claims of accuracy or the degree of acceptability. In the third case, finally, model and theory are clearly distinct and related to each other as follows: if X is a set-theoretical model of Y, then Y is the calculus of some theory and X is a set of entities, relations and operations satisfying the axioms in this calculus.

These distinctions can also shed interesting light on the thesis that the notion of a set-theoretical model is the fundamental one, and that all other kinds of models can be derived from or defined in terms of this notion. This thesis has been accepted, repeated and defended by many contemporary philosophers of science, including Abraham Kaplan and Patrick Suppes.[15] But it is still, I think, an open question if it is correct. Can all the kinds of models discussed here be defined in terms of set-theoretical models? And how about all the diverse things that are called models in the social sciences?

University of Umeå

NOTES

[1] This paper is based on notes made for a lecture I gave at the University of Uppsala in 1971. I want to thank the participants of the discussion for stimulating comments. I have also benefitted from discussions with Martin Edman, Hans Stenlund, and Uno Zachrisson at the university of Umeå.
[2] See e.g. Kaplan (1964), p. 263. The intuitive idea is that since the model and the thing modeled have the same or a similar structure, we can learn something about the latter by studying the former.

[3] See, for instance, the recent discussion between Peter Achinstein and T. R. Girill in 1971–1972; bibliographical details in the list of references.

[4] For a more detailed exposition of theoretical models see Achinstein (1965) and (1968). Cf also Törnebohm (1970).

[5] For a recent discussion of such problems see Lakatos and Musgrave (1970).

[6] The concept of a formal system is explained and illustrated in Kyburg (1968), Chapters 1 and 2.

[7] This conception of a model is essentially due to Tarski (1953): "A possible realization in which all valid sentences of a theory T are satisfied is called a model of T" (p. 11). See also Tarski (1956), p. 416.

[8] The distinction between interpretative and set-theoretical models may not be very important in practice. But it is useful to distinguish between the two sets (1) and (2) mentioned in the text, if one wants to understand clearly what is meant by saying that a set satisfies the axioms in a calculus.

[9] For details see Eves and Newsom (1965), Sections 4.3 and 6.3.

[10] Kaplan (1964), p. 268.

[11] Hempel (1965), p. 435.

[12] Hempel (1965), p. 436.

[13] Braithwaite (1953), Chapter 4.

[14] Rudner (1966), pp. 23–28.

[15] See Kaplan (1964), p. 267, and Suppes (1960) and (1967), Chapter 1.

BIBLIOGRAPHY

Achinstein, Peter, 'Models, Analogies, and Theories', *Philosophy of Science* **31** (1964), 328–350.

Achinstein, Peter, *Concepts of Science. A Philosophical Analysis*, John Hopkins Press, Baltimore, 1968.

Achinstein, Peter, 'Theoretical Models', *British Journal for the Philosophy of Science* **16** (1965), 102–120.

Achinstein, Peter, 'Models and Analogies: A Reply to Girill', *Philosophy of Science* **39** (1972), 235–240.

Arrow, K. J., 'Mathematical Models in the Social Sciences' (ed. by D. Lerner, and H. D. Lasswell), *The Policy Sciences*, Stanford 1951, pp. 129–154.

Black, Max, *Models and Metaphors*, Ithaca 1961.

Braithwaite, R. B., 'The Nature of Theoretical Concepts and the Role of Models in an Advanced Science', *Revue International de Philosophie*, 1954, fasc. 1–2.

Braithwaite, R. B., *Scientific Explanation*, Harper, New York. 1953.

Braithwaite, R. B.,'Models in the Empirical Sciences', *Logic, Methodology, and Philosophy of Science* (ed. by E. Nagel, P. Suppes, and A. Tarski), Stanford University Press, Stanford 1962.

Brodbeck, May, 'Models, Meaning, and Theories' (ed. by L. Gross), *Symposium on Sociological Theory*, New York 1959, pp. 373–403.

Carnap, R., *Foundations of Logic and Mathematics*, University of Chicago Press, Chicago, 1939. Sections 24 and 25 reprinted in *Philosophy of Science* (ed. by A. Danto and S. Morgnebesser), World, Cleveland, 1960, pp. 150–158.

Eves, Howard and Newson, Carroll V., *An Introduction to the Foundations and Fundamental Concepts of Mathematics* (rev. ed.), Holt, Rinehart and Winston, New York, 1965.

Freudenthal, H. (ed), *The Concept and the Role of the Model in Mathematics and Natural and Social Sciences*, Reidel, Dordrecht, 1961.

Girill, T. R., 'Formal Models and Achinstein's 'Analogies'', *Philosophy of Science* **38** (1971) 96–104.

Girill, T. R., 'Analogies and Models Revisited', *Philosophy of Science* **39** (1972), 214–244.

Hempel, Carl G., *Aspects of Scientific Explanation*, Free Press, New York, 1965.

Hesse, Mary, *Models and Analogies in Science*, New York & London 1963.

Hesse, Mary, 'Models in Physics', *British Journal for the Philosophy of Science* (1954), 198–214.

Kaplan, Abraham, *Conduct of Inquiry*, Chandler, San Francisco, 1964.

Kyburg, Henry, *Philosophy of Science*, MacMillan, New York, 1968.

Lakatos, Imre and Musgrave, Alan, *Criticism and the Growth of Knowledge*, Cambridge University Press, London, 1970.

Models and Analogies in Biology: Symposia of the Society for Experimental Biology **XIV**, Cambridge, England, 1960.

Nagel, Ernest, *The Structure of Science*, Harcourt, Brace, and World, New York, 1961.

Rudner, Richard, *Philosophy of the Social Sciences*, Prentice Hall, Englewood Cliffs, 1966.

Suppes, Patrick, 'A Comparison of the Meaning and Uses of Models in Mathematics and the Empirical Sciences', *Synthese* **12** (1960), 287–301.

Suppes, Patrick, *Set-Theoretical Structures in Science*, Stanford 1967.

Tarski, Alfred, 'A General Method in Proofs of Undecidability, (ed. by A. Tarski, A. Mostowski, and R. M. Robinson), *Undecidable Theories*, North-Holland Publishing Co., Amsterdam, 1953.

Tarski, Alfred, 'Contributions to the Theory of Models', *Proceedings Kon. Ned. Ak. Wet.*, 1954.

Tarski, Alfred, *Logic, Semantics and Metamathematics*, Oxford 1956.

Törnebohm, Håkan, 'The Growth of a Theoretical Model: A Simple Case Study', *Physics, Logic, and History*, Plenum Press, New York, 1970, pp. 79–86.

JENS ERIK FENSTAD

REMARKS ON LOGIC AND PROBABILITY

1. In this note we will comment briefly on two problem areas in the foundation of probability and randomness.

The first concerns how one constructs a formal or mathematical model of the intuitive or preformal notion of a random sequence, and how well such a model 'fits the facts', i.e. how well it corresponds to our preformal intuition.

The second problem centers on how to interpret the notion of probability. Here we assume that a formal analysis is given, viz. the usual axiomatics of probability theory. And we shall inquire under which circumstances this model can be applied, i.e. what is the range of applicability of the formal calculus of probability.

We will not present any new technical results in this note. Our aim is rather to convince the reader that some use of logic does give an insight into the epistemological aspects of probability and randomness.

In conclusion we make some remarks on 'logic and probability' versus inductive logic.

2. We assume that the reader has some familiarity with recent work on random sequences. A good reference is the book by Schnorr [4], but see also the recent note by Martin-Löf [3]. Our aim is to point to a few conclusions that can be drawn from this work.

First, we are convinced that recursion theory, i.e. the mathematical theory of algorithms, has been invaluable in setting up a formal or mathematical model of the intuitive notion of a random sequence.

But recursion theory is not a unique entity: There is e.g. a multitude of 'recursion theories' over the set of natural numbers, and several of these theories may separately lay some claim to 'naturalness'. To mention two examples: (1) There is a 'least' theory, viz. the ordinary theory of (partial) recursive functions. (2) Hyperarithmetical theory, which is connected with the idea of predicative definability (recursive Borelsets).

There is a general abstract notion of a *computation theory* over

S. Stenlund (ed.), Logical Theory and Semantic Analysis, 193–197. All Rights Reserved.
Copyright © 1974 by D. Reidel Publishing Company, Dordrecht-Holland.

the natural numbers (see e.g. [2]). And we claim that associated with each such computation theory there are 'good' notions of random sequence.

This, we believe, is as far as a formal analysis can go. The computation theory one may want to use to make precise the notion of random sequence, depends on the particular intuitive ideas one entertains. If one, as e.g. Schnorr [4], wants to stress "der intuitive Begriff des effektiv nachprüfbaren statistischen Zufallsgesetzes," then the 'natural' choice is ordinary recursion theory (or even, one may argue, some restricted part of it).

However, if the guiding idea is that a random sequence is a sequence where there is *no* law governing the behavior of the sequence, i.e. that there is *no* definable dependency between the elements of the sequence, then hyperarithmetical theory, as proposed by Martin-Löf [3], is *a* natural choice, – but by no means the only natural choice of underlying computation theory.

Granted that the proposed model of randomness is the 'correct' one, one is led to conclude that there is no unique notion of randomness, that randomness is not a 'physical' phenomenon: Your choice of *a* notion of randomness depends on the use you have in mind.

3.   The fundamental question of 'applied' probability theory is simply this: Under which circumstances can the notion of probability be applied. Or, put in slightly different words, what is the range of applicability of the formal calculus.

We do not pretend to have a satisfactory answer. What we want to discuss is the following problem: What are the possible *interpretations* of the notion of probability, i.e. we are interested in a representation theory for the probability concept. More precisely, we shall assume that a probability function is defined on a suitable formal language, and then describe a general representation of it in terms of probability measures defined on models (i.e. 'possible worlds') associated in a canonical way with the language.

As a first approximation let L be a first order language and let c be a probability function defined on the formulas of L. Let S be the set of models of L. It follows from the completeness theorem of first order logic that c induces a σ-additive probability measure λ on S. One may further show (for details see [1]) that c also induces on each model

$M \in S$ a probability measure μ_M such that for every formula p of L we have the following expression for $c(p)$:

(1) $\qquad c(p) = \int_S \mu_M(p[M]) \, d\lambda(M);$

where $p[M]$ is the set of sequences from M which satisfy the 'property' p in M. Under fairly general conditions we may conclude that for finite models M,

(2) $\qquad \mu_M(p[M]) = \text{fr}(p, M),$

where fr (p, M) denotes the frequency of the 'property' p in the model (or 'sample') M.

Formulas (1) and (2) show that any probability function c on the language L can (under suitable assumptions) be written as an average value of 'observed' frequencies in models M of L. And a model of L is a precise, technical counterpart of the vague, but heuristically useful idea of a 'possible world'. Note also that for monadic languages a finite model is nothing but an urn.

We should at this point remark that fixing on a formal language does give preciseness, but also rigidity. Other authors, as e.g. H. Jeffreys, may also start with a probability function defined on some unspecified language. After some introductory discussion of the elementary axiomatics of probability theory the formulas of the language may take on forms such as '$dx \, d\theta$'. Leaving the syntax indeterminate is nothing wrong. But it entails that one loses the precise notion of model associated with the language. And it seems to us that in discussing the range-of-applicability problem there is some merit in fixing the language, hence having a precise notion of model.

Absolute probabilities are of a limited value in discussing e.g. uniform distributions over infinite (discrete, non-compact) spaces. A next approximation consists in studying conditional probability functions $c(p \mid t)$ defined on L. Here p can be any formula of L, but for simplicity we assume that t is a condition of finiteness, i.e. a sentence t_n of L saying that there exist exactly n individuals.

We may again carry through an analysis similar to the one above, and under suitable assumptions, which are essentially equivalent to de Finetti's assumption of exchangeability, one may show that associated with the family $c(. \mid t_n)$ of conditional probabilities and a 'property' p of L, there is an absolute probability c^* on L such that if p_r^n is a formula of L which asserts that r out of n individuals have the 'property' p. Then

$$(3) \qquad c^*(p_r^n) = \binom{n}{r} \int_0^1 \xi^n (1 - \xi)^{n-r} \, d\Phi(\xi),$$

where Φ is a distribution function concentrated on the interval $[0, 1]$. One should note that whereas the λ of formula (1) is independent of p, the function Φ depends on p.

Formulas such as (1) and (3) represent a kind of natural limit to what one can obtain through a formal analysis. The λ of (1) and the Φ of (3) cannot be further specified unless extra assumptions (e.g. of symmetry or invariance) are added. But the representation theorems, nevertheless, give a general scheme for interpreting *any* notion of probability as long as it satisfies the formal rules of the calculus. But, we must add, only as long as we restrict ourselves to first order languages.

However, there are possible extensions of the above analysis to certain countable (admissible) languages, which would yield a similar analysis going beyond the Bernoulli-case considered above.

4. 'Logic and probability' usually means *inductive logic*, say, in the Carnapian sense. However, the use of recursion theory in Section 2 and of model theory in Section 3 is not in any sense tied up with theories of inductive logic. Indeed, our aim in this note has been to argue that there is a role for the formal apparatus of logic, which is independent of any theories of inductive logic, in the epistemological analysis of ideas of probability and randomness.

Recently, theories of inductive logic have been constructed which allow universal laws or hypotheses to have non-zero probability. This is interesting and refutes some of the formal arguments against the earlier systems of inductive logic. But we remain a bit sceptical that the 'growth of knowledge', which seems essentially to involve conceptual changes, can be adequately analyzed through some single global system of in-

ductive logic, or – for that sake – through some sort of Bayesian con-
ditionalization.

University of Oslo

BIBLIOGRAPHY

[1] Fenstad, Jens Erik, 'The Structure of Logical Probabilities', *Synthese* **18** (1968), 1–23.
[2] Fenstad, Jens Erik, 'On Axiomatizing Recursion Theory', in *Generalized Recursion Theory*, North-Holland, 1973.
[3] Martin-Löf, Per, 'On the Notion of Randomness', in *Intuitionism and Proof Theory*, North-Holland, 1970.
[4] Schnorr, Claus Peter, 'Zufälligkeit und Wahrscheinlichkeit', *Lecture Notes in Mathematics*, No. 218, Springer-Verlag, 1971.

SÖREN STENLUND

ANALYTIC AND SYNTHETIC ARITHMETICAL
STATEMENTS

1. In recent time the analytic-synthetic distinction has been maintained expecially by proponents of logical empiricism. The analytic truths have been described as truths which are tautological, empty of content and independent of facts. All logical and mathematical truths have been classified as analytic truths.

The opinion that logical and mathematical truths are tautological and empty of content was perhaps reasonable at the time of the discovery of formalization. When Principia Mathematica was forthcoming it seemed possible to obtain a complete, consistent and decidable formalization of all logical and mathematical truths. These hopes were however, ruined by the incompleteness and undecidability results. All mathematical truths can never be codified in some formal system and not even elementary logic admits of a mechanical decision procedure. The situation is even worse in set theory which was regarded as logic by Frege and Russell. The independence results show that the present evident properties of the notions of set and membership are not sufficient to decide all questions of truth and falsity in the set-theoretical universe.

It seems to me therefore that the analytic-synthetic distinction which we have inherited from Frege and logical empiricism is not very interesting. It is certainly very far from the ideas underlying the analytic-synthetic distinction of Kant, who brought the distinction into prominence.

In this paper I shall not discuss the doctrine of analytic and synthetic truths in general. Neither shall I attempt to deal with the recent discussion of this doctrine (by e.g. Quine and others). My purpose is only to suggest a precise meaning of the analytic-synthetic distinction within a limited theoretical framework, namely arithmetic. The idea behind my distinction is based on some of the most important remarks which Kant makes on the distinction. My distinction will be formally very precise which Kant's distinction is not. I shall therefore allow myself to interpret some of Kant's remarks in my own way. I want to emphasize that my purpose is not to give a consistent picture of Kant's all remarks on the analytic-synthetic distinction.

S. Stenlund (ed.), Logical Theory and Semantic Analysis, 199–211. *All Rights Reserved.*
Copyright © 1974 *by D. Reidel Publishing Company, Dordrecht-Holland.*

2. The analytic-synthetic classification I shall propose will be such that a true arithmetical sentence which is not analytic will be termed synthetic. I shall therefore begin to discuss analyticity. Kant's most explicit definition of analyticity was limited to subject-predicate judgments: "Analytic judgements say nothing in the predicate that was not already contained in the concept of the subject" (*Prolegomena*, §2).[1] The notion of analyticity that I shall propse will not be so limited and I shall therefore start from the following statements of Kant where there is no explicit reference to subject-predicate judgements.

(1)   ... analytic propositions, which may be produced merely by analysing our conceptions – ... (*Critique*, p. 213)[2]

(2)   If we are to form a synthetical judgement regarding a conception, we must go beyond it, to the intuition in which it is given. If we keep to what is contained in the conception, the judgement is merely analytical – it is merely an explanation of what we have cogitated in the conception. (*Critique*, p. 214)

(3)   Analytical judgements do not teach us any more about an object than what was contained in the conception we had of it; because they do not extend our cognition beyond our conception of an object, they merely elucidate the conception (*Critique*, p. 218)

The analytic-synthetic classification of Kant seems to be a logical or semantical classification. It is made with respect to the logical structure and the content of judgments (cf. *Prolegomena*, §2). The *a priori-a posteriori* classification on the other hand is epistemological, since it refers to our grounds for holding a judgement true. Frege seems to interpret Kant somewhat differently. According to him "these distinctions between a priori and a posteriori, synthetic and analytic, concern, as I see it, not the content of the judgement but the justification for making the judgement" (*Grundlagen*, §3).[3] Frege seems thus to contend that both distinctions are epistemological. This opinion of Frege seems to me to be in a certain sense justified. In many (if not most) of Kant's remarks about the nature of analytic and synthetic judgements he refers to knowledge. In the remark (3) for example, he explains the analytic-synthetic distinction in terms of *how* the judgement in question *can be known* or *is seen to be true*: It is analytic when it can be seen to be true by keeping to what is contained in the conception occurring in the judgement. Also, Marc-Wogau[4] has pointed out that the analytic-synthetic classification refers to statements which have the character of knowledge and is equivalent to the distinction between analytic and synthetic knowledge. The classification I shall propose below is based on the idea that the difference between analytic and synthetic truths is completely reflected on an epistemological level i.e. in the way in which statements are seen to be true. More precisely, I shall assume that the question wether a certain true mathematical proposition is analytic or synthetic can be answered by looking at the proof of it (or, at least some proof of it). The classification is based on a distinction between two different ways in which arithmetical statements are proved and not so much on a semantical analysis of arithmetical statements.

3.   According to Kant an analytic truth concerning a conception can be seen to be true only by keeping to what is contained in the conception. The crucial point here is to understand the phrase "... is contained in the conception." I shall adopt the following idea:

(6)   A statement is analytic if it is true by sole virtue of the definition of the concepts it contains.

This is a well-known idea. My interpretation of it will, however, be a bit different from what is usual. I shall use the word 'definition' in a specific sense to be explained below and I shall take the qualification 'by sole virtue of' more seriously than usual.

As pointed out by Marc-Wogau[5] the idea that analytic truth is truth by definition is an important line of thought in Kant's work. It is particularly obvious in Kant's discussion of the nature of mathematical truths. Combine, for example, the remark (2) with the following ones

(7)   ... that which I actually cogitate in my conception of a triangle, ... is nothing more than a mere definition (*Critique*, p. 213)

(8)   In mathematics, ..., we cannot have a conception prior to the definition; it is the definition which gives us the conception. (*Critique*, p. 216)

Since according to Kant an analytic judgement only makes explicit what we actually cogitate in a certain conception, these remarks show that Kant identifies analytic truth with truth by sole virtue of definitions.

4.   It is important for the notion of analyticity based upon (6) to give a precise meaning to word 'definition' and the phrase 'by sole virtue of'. I shall begin by discussing the notion of definition I shall be using.

According to the Frege-Russell tradition a definition is merely a convention of notational abbreviation. A definition introduces some specific expression, the definiendum as an arbitrary shorthand for some complex expression, the definiens. From this point of view, a definition plays no essential role within a theory; its only role is within the linguistic description of the theory. This view on definitions as linguistic conventions is perhaps the most natural one from a realistic point of view: To define is only to give notations to objects external to ourselves.

The notion of definition I shall use is different. I shall – for the purpose of this paper – adopt Kant's conceptualistic and constructive view of mathematical concepts: mathematics proceeds by construction of concepts in pure intuition. From this point of view the role of definitions is different. A definition does not just give a notation to an object or a concept; *it also describes the construction of the concept*. It codifies the way in which we form our conceptions and abstractions. Definitions within a theory are not linguistic conventions but codifications of the way in which the concepts of the theory are created. To take an example, the concept of being a natural number is defined in terms of 0 (zero) and $'$ (successor) by the following stipulations:

(i)   0 is a natural number
(ii)   If t is a natural number, then so is t'
(iii)   Nothing is a natural number unless it follows from (i) and (ii).

These stipulations do not just define the concept of being a natural number as an extension; it also indicates how the natural numbers are constructed. Namely, from 0 by iteration of the successor operation. The role of definitions in mathematics just explained seems to be the one Kant intends when he says:

... mathematical definitions are constructions of conceptions originally formed by the mind itself (*Critique*, p. 216)

and a few lines below he says

In a mathematical definition the conception is *formed*, ...

Another important point for my interpretation of analyticity as truth by definition is the following: There are certain concepts which are *not defined*. In arithmetic there are certain undefined arithmetical concepts such zero and successor, and we also need certain undefined logical notions to express mathematical truths. In Kant's terminology, these undefined notions are among our *a priori* concepts.

The notion of a real definition and an implicit definition is not a definition in the sense of the present paper, in general. For example it is sometimes said that the logical axioms of quantification theory implicitly define the logical operations. We say instead that the axioms give a formal characterization of the undefined, primitive logical operations of quantification theory, which we had and understood informally before the axioms were put down. The axioms do not *give* the meaning of the logical operations but are valid *by* the (informal) meaning of these operations. To take another example, the Peano axioms for the natural numbers do not define the natural numbers, but are seen to be valid by the meaning of the concepts they contain.

We shall work form the assumption of a difference between defining in the sense of formally characterizing an already intuitively understood notion and defining in the sense of constructing a (new) concept. It is the latter notion of definition we are referring to.

Using the notion of definition just explained I shall paraphrase the idea (7) as follows

(7')   A statement is analytic if it is true by sole virtue of the definition of the (defined) concepts involved.

How should then the phrase 'by sole virtue of' be understood? According to Kant an analytic judgement concerning a conception only makes explicit what we actually think in the conception. Its truth can be seen discursively, i.e. by keeping to what is contained in the conception. To see the truth of a synthetic statement on the other hand we have to go to intuition. Parallel to this distinction between the discursive and intuitive method I shall – following Poincaré[6] – introduce a distinction between *verification* and *proof*, to be made precise below. Verification but not proof is needed to see the truth of an analytic statement. A verification of a statement only brings out what is already contained in the definition of the concepts involved. We therefore expect a verification in contrast to a proof to be *mechanical*, which will be verified below. This means that it is mechanically decidable wether a certain arithmetical sentence is analytic or not. As I interpet Kant's remarks on the analytic-synthetic classification, this should be taken as one adequacy condition on any formal explication of analyticity.

5. We consider a language of first order predicate logic with the following *primitive* or *undefined symbols*

> 0 (zero), ′ (successor), ⊥ (absurdity),
> | (truth), ∀ (universal quantification)

and the following *defined symbols*
Predicate symbols:

> N(nat. number), =(equality)

Operation symbols:

> + (addition), · (multiplication),
> → (truth-functional implication), ¬ (truth-functional negation).

As notations for *individual variables* I shall use $x, y, z, \ldots$. The *numerical terms* are defined as usual and I shall use $r, s, t, u, \ldots$ as syntactical notations for numerical terms. The *formulas* are ⊥ and ⊤ and whenever t and s are terms, then Nt and $t = s$ are formulas. If A and B are formulas, then so are $A \rightarrow B$, ¬A and $\forall x A$. As syntactical notations for formulas I shall use $A, B, C, \ldots$. I shall also use the following metamathematical symbols

> $=_{\text{def}}$ (identity by definition)
> ⩾(reduction)
> ≡(definitional equality)

These symbols are binary relation symbols which hold either between numerical terms or between formulas. I shall use $\alpha, \beta, \gamma, \ldots$ as syntactical variables ranging over terms and formulas. The expressions $\alpha =_{\text{def}} \beta$, $\alpha \geqslant \beta$, $\alpha \equiv \beta$, are, however, well-formed only if α and β are both terms or both formulas. In the expression $\alpha =_{\text{def}} \beta$ we say that α is the definiendum and β is the definiens

The *definitions* or the *defining axioms* are the following

$$N0 \underset{\text{def}}{=} \top \qquad (0=0) \underset{\text{def}}{=} \top$$
$$Nt' \underset{\text{def}}{=} Nt \qquad (0=t') \underset{\text{def}}{=} \bot$$
$$(t'=0) \underset{\text{def}}{=} \bot$$
$$(t'=s') \underset{\text{def}}{=} (t=s)$$

$$t+0 \underset{\text{def}}{=} t \qquad t\cdot 0 \underset{\text{def}}{=} 0$$
$$t+s' \underset{\text{def}}{=} (t+s)' \qquad t\cdot s' \underset{\text{def}}{=} t\cdot s+t$$
$$\top \to \top = \top \qquad \neg\top \underset{\text{def}}{=} \bot$$
$$\bot \to \bot \underset{\text{def}}{=} \top \qquad \neg\bot \underset{\text{def}}{=} \top$$
$$\bot \to \top \underset{\text{def}}{=} \top$$
$$\top \to \bot \underset{\text{def}}{=} \bot$$

Definitional reduction: We say that a term or a formula α *reduces* to a term or a formula β, iff there are terms or formulas $\alpha_1, ..., \alpha_n$, $n \geqslant 1$, such that α_1 is α and α_n is β and α_{i+1} has been obtained from α_i by replacing a definiendum in α_i by its definiens.

A reduction is thus the process whereby one (successively) replaces the defined terms in a numerical term or formula by their definientia. A term or formula is said to be in *normal form* if it does not contain a definiendum. We can then state the following result:

THEOREM: *Each term and formula reduces in a finite number of steps to a unique normal form independently of how the reduction is carried out.*

We say that two terms or formulas α and β are *definitionally equal*, in symbols $\alpha \equiv \beta$, iff α and β have normal forms which differ only in the naming of their bound variables.

Together with the defining equations we have the following *conversion rule*

$$\frac{A, A \equiv B}{B}$$

Note that this is properly speaking no rule of proof (like the rules below) but a kind of structural or linguistic rule. It says only that definitional equality preserves truth.

To state the remaining axioms and rules, we need some notation. Let $p, p_1, p_2, ...$ be variables ranging over the formulas $\bot$ and $\top$ only, and let $P(p_1, ..., p_n)$ denote an arbitrary propositional formula built up from the variables $p_1, ..., p_n$ by means of the truth-functional operations $\rightarrow$ and $\neg$. The *axioms* and *rules of proof* are the following:

(i) $\top$

(ii) $\dfrac{P(p_1, ..., p_n), \quad \text{for all values of} \quad p_1, ..., p_n}{P(A_1, ..., A^n)}$

(iii) $\dfrac{A, \; A \rightarrow B}{B}$

(iv) $\dfrac{A(x)}{\forall x A(x)} \qquad \dfrac{\forall x A(x)}{A(t)}$

       (subject to usual restrictions)

(v) $\dfrac{A(0), \; A(x) \rightarrow A(x')}{A(t)}$

Using the defining equations, the conversion rule and the axioms and rules of proof (i), ..., (v), one can derive the axioms and rules in more usual formulations of first order arithmetic. For example, the usual properties of equality and the third and fourth Peano axioms.

6.   By this formulation of first order arithmetic, especially the separation of the definitions from the other axioms and rules, I want to emphasize the constructive aspects of arithmetic. The definitions reflect the way in which the defined concepts have been constructed. For example, the definition of the concept N of being a natural number reflects the idea that our conception of natural numbers is the idea of starting with an object 0 and successively generating numbers by means of the successor operation. Kant seems to have had an at least analogous idea in mind when he says: "Arithmetic forms its own concepts of numbers by successive addition of units in time." (*Prolegomena*, §10).

The defining equations can be said to give the (conceptual) meaning to the defined symbols. This suggests the following definition: Two terms or formulas α and β are *synonymous* iff $\alpha \equiv \beta$, i.e. iff they are definitionally equal. From the theorem it follows that the synonymity relation is decidable, which is also satisfactory. It seems to me that any formal relation of synonymity should be mechanically decidable, if it is to mean sameness of meaning in contrast to sameness of reference.

The idea behind the notion of verification discussed above was that the truth of a statement is seen only on the basis of the definitions of the terms it contains. This leads to the following definition:

> A *verification* of a formula A is a reduction $A_1 \geqslant A_2 \geqslant \cdots \geqslant A_n$, such that A_1 is A and A_n is $\top$.

We are then ready to define the main notion of this paper:

> A statement (expressed by a formula) A is *analytic*, iff A has a verification. (Equivalently: A is analytic iff A is synonymous with the truth-constant).

If we use 0, 1, 2, ... as abbreviations of 0, 0′, 0″, ... respectively, the following are examples of analytic arithmetical statements:

$$N7, \ 5+7=12, \ 1=1, \ \neg 0=1, \ 3=3 \rightarrow 3=3$$

The analytic arithmetical statements comprise all true equations between closed numerical terms, all formulas Nt where t is a closed numerical term and all true truth-functional formulas built up form these two kinds of atomic formulas.

No true formula containing quantification is analytic according to our definition. Not even the formula

$$(8) \qquad \forall x (x=x).$$

On the other hand, for each numeral n the formula

$$(9) \qquad n=n$$

is analytic. According to Kant $a=a$ is an example of an analytic statement used in geometry (*Prolegomena*, §2). At the risk of putting too much into Kant's words one might think that this difference between (8) and (9) is one way of understanding his remark about propositions such that $a=a$ that "... they serve only as links in the chain of method but not as principles" (*Prolegomena*, §2). The reason that true quantificational statements are synthetic is that their truth cannot be established merely by verification but rests essentially on principles of proof.

The most important principle of proof in arithmetic is the principle of mathematical induction which allows us to infer a universal statement that $A(x)$ holds for all x from the premisses $A(0)$ and $A(x) \rightarrow A(x')$. The induction rule can be said to summarize an infinite number of inferences of the form

$$A(0), \quad \frac{A(0), \ A(0) \to A(1)}{A(1)}, \quad \frac{A(1), \ A(1) \to A(2)}{A(2)}, \dots$$

in which each inference is justified by modus ponens and the preceding one. Each one of these inferences may be replacable by a purely mechanincal verification. But the insight that we can continue this list as infinitum when we have proof of $A(0)$ and of $A(x) \to A(x')$ cannot be replaced by a purely mechanical verification. It cannot be verified only on the basis of the definitions of the terms involved. Looking at Kant's explanation of the synthetic nature of many geometric principles, this feature of the induction rule seems to me to be the one which is relevant for the analytic-synthetic classification.

Having characterized the induction principle as a source of synthetic truths in arithmetic, it is not a big step to recognize that the rules for quantification are of the same nature. The inference of universal generalization

$$\frac{\begin{array}{c} \vdots (x) \\ A(x) \end{array}}{\forall x A(x)}$$

can be said to summarize an infinite number of inferences

$$\begin{array}{cccc} \vdots (0) & \vdots (1) & \vdots (2) & \\ A(0) & A(1) & A(2) & \dots \end{array}$$

which are identical except for containing different numbers in x: es place. The insight that we can continue this list ad infinitum and infer the universal statement $\forall x A(x)$ when we have a proof

$$(10) \qquad \begin{array}{c} \vdots (x) \\ A(x) \end{array}$$

which is uniform in x cannot be replaced by a purely mechanical verification. It is not based solely on the definitions of the terms involved. Understanding is needed to recognize that (10) is typical for all the infinitely many cases.

I think that this view is supported by some of Kant's examples of geometric principles and his discussion of their proofs. In such proofs we construct an arbitrary geometric figure of a certain kind and then deduce a certain property using this particular representative, and then infer the *universal* statement that all geometric figures of this kind has the property. It is, according to Kant, the understanding which justifies this inference. The geometric representative plays here the same role as the 'dummy symbol' x in the proof (10), from which we infer the universal statement $\forall x A(x)$.

It will perhaps come as a surprise that not even a statement such as

(11) $\forall x(x=x) \rightarrow \forall x(x=x)$

is analytic although it is an instance of the propositional tautology $A \rightarrow A$. One might think that (11) is justified solely by the meaning of $\rightarrow$ as given by its defining equations. The truth of (11) is, however, also based on the assumption that the formula $\forall x(x=x)$ will have a truth-value, i.e. that it equivalent either to $\top$ or to $\bot$. This in turn is something which does not follow by sole virtue of definitions. It is justified by reflection on the meaning of the (undefined) universal quantifier.

All instances of the truth-functional tautologies are therefore not analytic according to our notion of analyticity. If $P(p_1,...,p_n)$ is a propositional tautology in the variables $p_1,...,p_n$ and $A_1,...,A_n$ are closed arithmetical statements, then $P(A_1,...,A_n)$ is analytic iff $A_1,...,A_n$ are analytic or their negations are analytic. The analytic statements are also closed under modus ponens. This is true provided that the propositional logical operations have their truth-functional interpretation.

7.   It is interesting to compare our notion of analyticity with with Kant's two main characterizations of this notion. According to the first one the predicate is contained in concept of the subject in an analytic statement. Let us consider as an example the statement

N2

i.e. 2 is a natural number. The predicate is here the property of being either 0 or being obtained from 0 by iterating the successor operation. The consept of the subject is to be obtained from 0 by iterating the successor operation as exhibited by the symbol 0″. It seems reasonable here to say that the predicate is 'contained in' the concept of the subject and this is precisely what is verified in the reduction

$$N2 \geqslant N1 \geqslant N0 \geqslant \top$$

Another characteristic property of analytic statements is according to Kant that they rest wholly on the principle of contradiction (*Prolegomena*, §2). Let A be an analytic statement, then it is easy to see that there is a reduction

$$\neg A \geqslant \cdots \geqslant \bot$$

so we have $\neg A \equiv \bot$. If we take $\neg A$ as an assumption, we can derive the absurdity $\bot$ using *only* definitions and the conversion rule. So if we negate an analytic statement we can derive an absurdity without using any logical or arithmetical axiom or rule of inference. The principle of contradiction can therefore be said to be the altogether sufficient principle of analytic statements (even if it is not necessary).

As the reader has noticed numerical equations such as

(12) $7 + 5 = 12$

are analytic according to our definition although it is Kant's classical example of a synthetic judgement *a priori*. How is this difference to be explained? I think one finds the answer by looking at Kant's explanation of why (12) is synthetic. Kant seems to think of addition as a primitive undefined operation: "... the concept of the sum of 7 and 5 contains nothing futher than the unification of two numbers into a single..." (*Prolegomena*, §2). He seems to think of addition as the operation of putting together or of counting. This notion of addition is different from ours which is defined or constructed: The concept of $7 + 5$ being defined as $(7 + 4)'$ which in turn is defined as $(7 + 3)''$ and so on. Kant's notion of addition may be the more important one from a genetic or commonsense point of view, but I maintain that our notion of addition, defined by recursion is the basic one for pure arithmetic. If we took addition as a primitive undefined operation in our formal system and put down its properties such as associativity etc. as axioms, we would arrive at the same conclusion as Kant. But from a purely arithmetical point of view and a constructive view on arithmetical concepts, that would be wrong it seems to me.

8.   It is important to remember that the analytic-synthetic classification we have arrived at presupposes an idealistic view on arithmetic. In particular it presupposes that there are certain logical and mathematical notions which are more *basic* than others and are taken as primitive undefined notions. Each other mathematical concept is constructed as described by *the definition* of the concept.

I shall not try to discuss the reasonableness of this view. Neither shall I try to argue that the particular choice of primitives and definitions above is ultimate. My purpose has been not so much to answer the question: "Which arithmetical statements *are* analytic and which ones *are* synthetic?" It has been rather to discuss the ideas behind the analytic-synthetic classification. I have tried to suggest a precise meaning of the ground for the classification in terms of the distinction between verification and proof, referring to some of Kant's most important remarks on the classification.

It goes without saying that our analytic-synthetic classification is of no interest from a realistic point of view for which the choice of primitives is only a matter of taste and for which the choice among extensionally equivalent definitions is immaterial, being only different ways of expressing truths about an objective reality external to ourselves.

University of Uppsala

NOTES

¹ We refer to the translation of Kant's *Prolegomena* by Peter G. Lucas, Manchester University Press, Manchester, 1953.
² We refer to Kant's *Critique of Pure Reason* (transl. by J. M. D. Meiklejohn) in *Great Books of the Western World*, Vol. 42, Chicago 1952.
³ We refer here to the translation of Frege's *Die Grundlagen der Arithmetik* as: *Foundations of Arithmetic* by J. L. Austin, Basil Blackwell, Oxford, 1953.
⁴ See *Kant's Doctrine of the Analytical Judgment*, p. 100, in K. Marc-Wogau *Philosophical Essays*, Library of Theoria, No. XI, Lund 1967.
⁵ See Marc-Wogau, *ibid.*, p. 104.
⁶ See p. 4 of H. Poincaré *Science and Hypothesis*, The Walter Scott Publishing Company, LTD, New York, 1905.

INDEX OF NAMES

TABULA GRATULATORIA

Thorbjörn Alfredsson
Eivor Alfredsson
Jens Allwood
Jan Andersson

Bertil Belfrage
Jan Berg
Catarina Berg
Lars Bergström
Karel de Bouvère
Gunnar Brandell
Carl-Göran Burman

Jan-Åke Candefjord
Gustaf Cavallius
Brian Chellas
Merry Chellas
Niels Egmont Christensen
Anne-Lise Christensen

Germund Dahlquist
Thorild Dahlquist
Ann-Mari Henschen-Dahlquist
Sven Danielsson
Birgitta Danielsson
Louise Dubois

Matts Edin
Rolf Ejvegård
Lucia Ejvegård
Per Olof Ekelöf
Elisabeth Engdahl
Per Ericson
Ulf Eriksson
Inger Eriksson

Jens Erik Fenstad
Urban Forell
Ake Frändberg
Dagfinn Føllesdal
Vera Føllesdal

Claus Granath
Ingemund Gullvåg
Lars Gustafsson
Madeleine Gustafsson
Peter Gärdenfors

Ian Hacking
Dick A. R. Haglund
Sören Halldén
Bengt Hansson
Birgitta Hansson
Ingemar Hedenius

Astrid Hedenius
Robert Heeger
Birgitte Heeger
Ebba Hellbom
Göran Hermerén
Ingrid Hermerén
Risto Hilpinen
Leena Hilpinen
Jaakko Hintikka
Bengt Åke Hoff
Ragnar Holte

Anders Jeffner
Richard C. Jeffrey
Erlendur Jónsson

Hans Karlgren
Raili Kauppi
Aleksandar Kron

Dagmar Lagerberg
David Lewis
Stephanie R. Lewis
Lars Lindahl
Ingrid Lindahl
Sten Lindström
Ingrid Lindström
Per Lindström
Per Lindvall
Maria Lindvall

Andries MacLeod

Konrad Marc-Wogau
Ebba Marc-Wogau
Brian H. Mayoh
Knud Midgaard
Bengt Molander
Harald Morin
Manfred Moritz
Britta Moritz

Sten T. Neckö
Paul Needham
R. J. Nelson
Ilkka Niiniluoto
Göran Nilsson
Lennart Nordenfelt
Kerstin Nordenfelt
Rolf-Allan Norrmosse
Birgitta Norrmosse
Hans Nystedt

Jan Odelstad

Bo Petersson
Juhani Pietarinen
Dag Prawitz
Zalma Puterman
Helena Puterman
Ingmar Pörn

Bengt-Olof Qvarnström

Sixten Ringbom

Marianne Ringbom

Henrik Sahlqvist
Arto Salomaa
Kaarina Salomaa
Dana Scott
Michael Scriven
Krister Segerberg
Anita Segerberg
Lennart Sjöberg
Kit Sjöberg
Staffan Sjöberg
Margareta Sjöberg
Sverre Slögedal
Bo Sommarström
Inga Sommarström
Erik Stenius
Eva Stenius
Sören Stenlund
Rigmor Stenlund
Leif Stille

Björn Strand
Bertil Strömberg
Birger Sundberg
Nils Kristian Sundby
Bo Östen Svensson

Raimo Tuomela

Evert Vedung
Siv Vedung

Nils Wallin
Mariann Wallin
Erling Wande
Hjalmar Wennerberg
Berit Wennerberg
Georg Henrik von Wright

Claes Åberg
Lennart Åqvist
Kerstin Åqvist

Filosofiska Föreningen i Uppsala
Filosofiska Institutionen vid Lunds Universitet
Filosofisk Institut, Københavns Universitet
Filosofiska Institutionen vid Uppsala Universitet
Filosofiska Institutionen vid Åbo Akademi
Filosofi- och Psykologilärarnas Förening
Göteborgs Universitetsbibliotek
Institutionen för Filosofi vid Lärarhögskolan i Malmö
The Mattias Fremling Society

SYNTHESE LIBRARY

Monographs on Epistemology, Logic, Methodology,
Philosophy of Science, Sociology of Science and of Knowledge, and on the
Mathematical Methods of Social and Behavioral Sciences

Editors:

Donald Davidson (The Rockefeller University and Princeton University)

Jaakko Hintikka (Academy of Finland and Stanford University)

Gabriël Nuchelmans (University of Leyden)

Wesley C. Salmon (University of Arizona)

1. J. M. Bocheński, *A Precis of Mathematical Logic.* 1959, X + 100 pp.
2. P. L. Guiraud, *Problèmes et méthodes de la statistique linguistique.* 1960, VI + 146 pp.
3. Hans Freudenthal (ed.), *The Concept and the Role of the Model in Mathematics and Natural and Social Sciences. Proceedings of a Colloquium held at Utrecht, The Netherlands, January 1960.* 1961, VI + 194 pp.
4. Evert W. Beth, *Formal Methods. An Introduction to Symbolic Logic and the Study of Effective Operations in Arithmetic and Logic.* 1962, XIV + 170 pp.
5. B. H. Kazemier and D. Vuysje (eds.), *Logic and Language. Studies dedicated to Professor Rudolf Carnap on the Occasion of his Seventieth Birthday.* 1962, VI + 256 pp.
6. Marx W. Wartofsky (ed.), *Proceedings of the Boston Colloquium for the Philosophy of Science, 1961–1962,* Boston Studies in the Philosophy of Science (ed. by Robert S. Cohen and Marx W. Wartofsky), Volume I. 1963, VIII + 212 pp.
7. A. A. Zinov'ev, *Philosophical Problems of Many-Valued Logic.* 1963, XIV + 155 pp.
8. Georges Gurvitch, *The Spectrum of Social Time.* 1964, XXVI + 152 pp.
9. Paul Lorenzen, *Formal Logic.* 1965, VIII + 123 pp.
10. Robert S. Cohen and Marx W. Wartofsky (eds.), *In Honor of Philipp Frank,* Boston Studies in the Philosophy of Science (ed. by Robert S. Cohen and Marx W. Wartofsky), Volume II. 1965, XXXIV + 475 pp.
11. Evert W. Beth, *Mathematical Thought. An Introduction to the Philosophy of Mathematics.* 1965, XII + 208 pp.
12. Evert W. Beth and Jean Piaget, *Mathematical Epistemology and Psychology.* 1966, XXII + 326 pp.
13. Guido Küng, *Ontology and the Logistic Analysis of Language. An Enquiry into the Contemporary Views on Universals.* 1967, XI + 210 pp.
14. Robert S. Cohen and Marx W. Wartofsky (eds.), *Proceedings of the Boston Colloquium for the Philosophy of Science, 1964–1966, in Memory of Norwood Russell Hanson,* Boston Studies in the Philosophy of Science (ed. by Robert S. Cohen and Marx W. Wartofsky), Volume III. 1967, XLIX + 489 pp.
15. C. D. Broad, *Induction, Probability, and Causation. Selected Papers.* 1968, XI + 296 pp.
16. Günther Patzig, *Aristotle's Theory of the Syllogism. A Logical-Philosophical Study of Book A of the Prior Analytics.* 1968, XVII + 215 pp.

17. NICHOLAS RESCHER, *Topics in Philosophical Logic*. 1968, XIV + 347 pp.
18. ROBERT S. COHEN and MARX W. WARTOFSKY (eds.), *Proceedings of the Boston Colloquium for the Philosophy of Science, 1966–1968*, Boston Studies in the Philosophy of Science (ed. by Robert S. Cohen and Marx W. Wartofsky), Volume IV. 1969, VIII + 537 pp.
19. ROBERT S. COHEN and MARX W. WARTOFSKY (eds.), *Proceedings of the Boston Colloquium for the Philosophy of Science, 1966–1968*, Boston Studies in the Philosophy of Science (ed. by Robert S. Cohen and Marx W. Wartofsky), Volume V. 1969, VIII + 482 pp.
20. J. W. DAVIS, D. J. HOCKNEY, and W. K. WILSON (eds.), *Philosophical Logic*. 1969, VIII + 277 pp.
21. D. DAVIDSON and J. HINTIKKA (eds.), *Words and Objections: Essays on the Work of W. V. Quine*. 1969, VIII + 366 pp.
22. PATRICK SUPPES, *Studies in the Methodology and Foundations of Science. Selected Papers from 1911 to 1969*. 1969, XII + 473 pp.
23. JAAKKO HINTIKKA, *Models for Modalities. Selected Essays*. 1969, IX + 220 pp.
24. NICHOLAS RESCHER *et al.* (eds.). *Essay in Honor of Carl G. Hempel. A Tribute on the Occasion of his Sixty-Fifth Birthday*. 1969, VII + 272 pp.
25. P. V. TAVANEC (ed.), *Problems of the Logic of Scientific Knowledge*. 1969, XII + 429 pp.
26. MARSHALL SWAIN (ed.), *Induction, Acceptance, and Rational Belief*. 1970, VII + 232 pp.
27. ROBERT S. COHEN and RAYMOND J. SEEGER (eds.), *Ernst Mach; Physicist and Philosopher*, Boston Studies in the Philosophy of Science (ed. by Robert S. Cohen and Marx W. Wartofsky), Volume VI. 1970, VIII + 295 pp.
28. JAAKKO HINTIKKA and PATRICK SUPPES, *Information and Inference*. 1970, X + 336 pp.
29. KAREL LAMBERT, *Philosophical Problems in Logic. Some Recent Developments*. 1970, VII + 176 pp.
30. ROLF A. EBERLE, *Nominalistic Systems*. 1970, IX + 217 pp.
31. PAUL WEINGARTNER and GERHARD ZECHA (eds.), *Induction, Physics, and Ethics, Proceedings and Discussions of the 1968 Salzburg Colloquium in the Philosophy of Science*. 1970, X + 382 pp.
32. EVERT W. BETH, *Aspects of Modern Logic*. 1970, XI + 176 pp.
33. RISTO HILPINEN (ed.), *Deontic Logic: Introductory and Systematic Readings*. 1971, VII + 182 pp.
34. JEAN-LOUIS KRIVINE, *Introduction to Axiomatic Set Theory*. 1971, VII + 98 pp.
35. JOSEPH D. SNEED, *The Logical Structure of Mathematical Physics*. 1971, XV + 311 pp.
36. CARL R. KORDIG, *The Justification of Scientific Change*. 1971, XIV + 119 pp.
37. MILIČ ČAPEK, *Bergson and Modern Physics*, Boston Studies in the Philosophy of Science (ed. by Robert S. Cohen and Marx W. Wartofsky), Volume VII. 1971, XV + 414 pp.
38. NORWOOD RUSSELL HANSON, *What I do not Believe, and other Essays*, ed. by Stephen Toulmin and Harry Woolf. 1971, XII + 390 pp.
39. ROGER C. BUCK and ROBERT S. COHEN (eds.), *PSA 1970. In Memory of Rudolf Carnap*, Boston Studies in the Philosophy of Science (ed. by Robert S. Cohen and Marx W. Wartofsky), Volume VIII. 1971, LXVI + 615 pp. Also available as a paperback.
40. DONALD DAVIDSON and GILBERT HARMAN (eds.), *Semantics of Natural Language*. 1972, X + 769 pp. Also available as a paperback.
41. YEHOSUA BAR-HILLEL (ed.), *Pragmatics of Natural Languages*. 1971, VII + 231 pp.
42. SÖREN STENLUND, *Combinators, λ-Terms and Proof Theory*. 1972, 184 pp.
43. MARTIN STRAUSS, *Modern Physics and Its Philosophy. Selected Papers in the Logic, History, and Philosophy of Science*. 1972, X + 297 pp.

44. MARIO BUNGE, *Method, Model and Matter.* 1973, VII + 196 pp.
45. MARIO BUNGE, *Philosophy of Physics.* 1973, IX + 248 pp.
46. A. A. ZINOV'EV, *Foundations of the Logical Theory of Scientific Knowledge (Complex Logic)*, Boston Studies in the Philosophy of Science (ed. by Robert S. Cohen and Marx W. Wartofsky), Volume IX. Revised and enlarged English edition with an appendix, by G. A. Smirnov, E. A. Sidorenka, A. M. Fedina, and L. A. Bobrova. 1973, XXII + 301 pp. Also available as a paperback.
47. LADISLAV TONDL, *Scientific Procedures*, Boston Studies in the Philosophy of Science (ed. by Robert S. Cohen and Marx W. Wartofsky), Volume X. 1973, XII + 268 pp. Also available as a paperback.
48. NORWOOD RUSSELL HANSON, *Constellations and Conjectures*, ed. by Willard C. Humphreys, Jr. 1973, X + 282 pp.
49. K. J. J. HINTIKKA, J. M. E. MORAVCSIK, and P. SUPPES (eds.), *Approaches to Natural Language. Proceedings of the 1970 Stanford Workshop on Grammar and Semantics.* 1973, VIII + 526 pp. Also available as a paperback.
50. MARIO BUNGE (ed.), *Exact Philosophy – Problems, Tools, and Goals.* 1973, X + 214 pp.
51. RADU J. BOGDAN and ILKKA NIINILUOTO (eds.), *Logic, Language, and Probability.* A selection of papers contributed to Sections IV, VI, and XI of the Fourth International Congress for Logic, Methodology, and Philosophy of Science, Bucharest, September 1971. 1973, X + 323 pp.
52. GLENN PEARCE and PATRICK MAYNARD (eds.), *Conceptual Change.* 1973, XII + 282 pp.
53. ILKKA NIINILUOTO and RAIMO TUOMELA, *Theoretical Concepts and Hypothetico-Inductive Inference.* 1973, VII + 264 pp.
54. ROLAND FRAÏSSÉ, *Course of Mathematical Logic – Volume I: Relation and Logical Formula.* 1973, XVI + 186 pp. Also available as a paperback.
55. ADOLF GRÜNBAUM, *Philosophical Problems of Space and Time.* Second, enlarged edition, Boston Studies in the Philosophy of Science (ed. by Robert S. Cohen and Marx W. Wartofsky), Volume XII. 1973, XXIII + 884 pp. Also available as a paperback.
56. PATRICK SUPPES (ed.), *Space, Time, and Geometry.* 1973, XI + 424 pp.
57. HANS KELSEN, *Essays in Legal and Moral Philosophy*, selected and introduced by Ota Weinberger. 1973, XXVIII + 300 pp.
59. ROBERT S. COHEN and MARX W. WARTOFSKY (eds.), *Logical and Epistemological Studies in Contemporary Physics*, Boston Studies in the Philosophy of Science (ed. by Robert S. Cohen and Marx W. Wartofsky), Volume XIII. 1973, VIII + 462 pp. Also available as a paperback.
60. ROBERT S. COHEN and MARX W. WARTOFSKY (eds.), *Methodological and Historical Essays in the Natural and Social Sciences. Proceedings of the Boston Colloquium for the Philosophy of Science, 1969–1972*, Boston Studies in the Philosophy of Science (ed. by Robert S. Cohen and Marx W. Wartofsky), Volume XIV.

In Preparation

58. ROBERT S. COHEN and R. J. SEEGER (eds.), *Philosophical Foundations of the Sciences*, Boston Studies in the Philosophy of Science (ed. by Robert S. Cohen and Marx W. Wartofsky), Volume XI.
61. ROBERT S. COHEN and MARX W. WARTOFSKY (eds.), *Scientific, Historical, and Political Essays in Honor of Dirk J. Struik*, Boston Studies in the Philosophy of Science (ed. by Robert S. Cohen and Marx W. Wartofsky), Volume XV.
62. KAZIMIERZ AJDUKIEWICZ, *Pragmatic Logic*, transl. from the Polish by Olgierd Wojtasiewicz.

SYNTHESE HISTORICAL LIBRARY

Texts and Studies
in the History of Logic and Philosophy

Editors:

N. KRETZMANN (Cornell University)
G. NUCHELMANS (University of Leyden)
L. M. DE RIJK (University of Leyden)

1. M. T. BEONIO-BROCCHIERI FUMAGALLI, *The Logic of Abelard*. Translated from the Italian. 1969, IX + 101 pp.

2. GOTTFRIED WILHELM LEIBNITZ, *Philosophical Papers and Letters*. A selection translated and edited, with an introduction, by Leroy E. Loemker. 1969, XII + 736 pp.

3. ERNST MALLY, *Logische Schriften*, ed. by Karl Wolf and Paul Weingartner. 1971, X + 340 pp.

4. LEWIS WHITE BECK (ed.), *Proceedings of the Third International Kant Congress*. 1972, XI + 718 pp.

5. BERNARD BOLZANO, *Theory of Science*, ed. by Jan Berg. 1973, XV + 398 pp.

6. J. M. E. MORAVCSIK (ed.), *Patterns in Plato's Thought. Papers arising out of the 1971 West Coast Greek Philosophy Conference*. 1973, VIII + 212 pp.

7. NABIL SHEHABY, *The Propositional Logic of Avicenna: A Translation from al-Shifāʾ: al-Qiyās*, with Introduction, Commentary and Glossary. 1973, XIII + 296 pp.

8. DESMOND PAUL HENRY, *Commentary on De Grammatico: The Historical-Logical Dimensions of a Dialogue of St. Anselm's*. 1974, IX + 345 pp.

9. JOHN CORCORAN, *Ancient Logic and Its Modern Interpretations*. 1974, X + 208 pp.